The River Great Ouse

and its tributaries

including the Rivers Cam, Lark, Little Ouse and Wissey, the New Bedford River, the Relief Channel and the tidal Great Ouse to King's Lynn

CHRIS HOWES

Imray Laurie Norie & Wilson

The River Great Ouse

Summary of distances, locks and estimated times

Location	Miles	Locks	Hours
The Bedford Ouse Kempston to Brownshill	39	15	12
Tidal section Brownshill to Hermitage Lock	2·25	1	0·5
The Old West River Hermitage to Pope's Corner	11·5	1	6·25
The Ely Ouse Pope's Corner to Denver Sluice	20	1	5
Relief Channel Denver to tail sluice	11	0	3·5
Tidal Great Ouse Denver to King's Lynn	13	0	2*
New Bedford River Denver to Earith	20	0	4·25*
River Cam Pope's Corner to Jesus Lock	14·4	4	6·25
Reach Lode	2	1	0·3
Wicken Lode	1·5	0	0·3
Burwell Lode	2·5	0	1
River Lark Great Ouse to Jude's Ferry	10	1	3
River Little Ouse Great Ouse to Brandon	10·75	1	4
River Wissey Great Ouse to Whittington	13	0	3

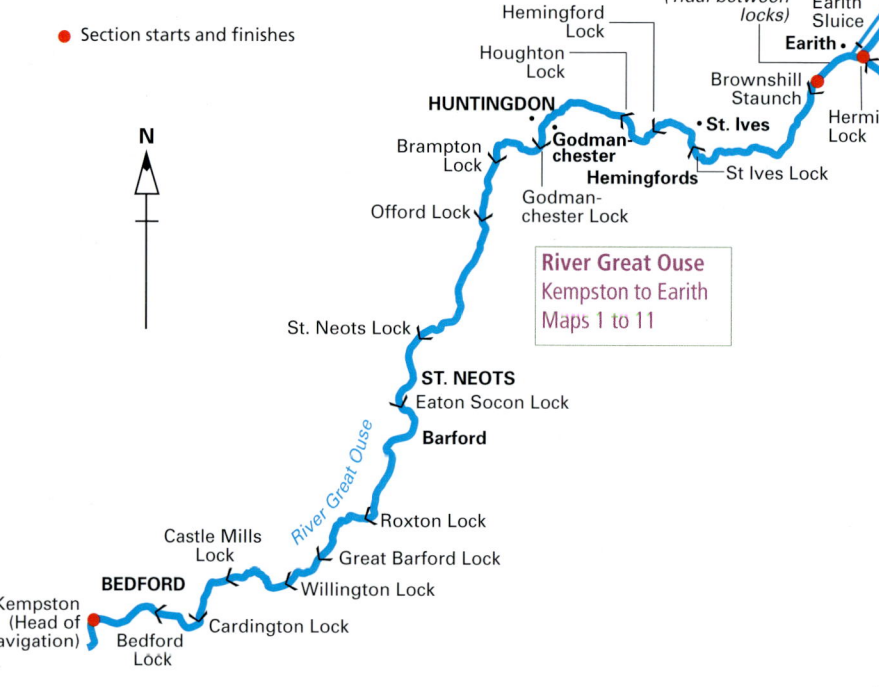

Published by
Imray, Laurie, Norie & Wilson Ltd
Wych House, St Ives,
Cambridgeshire PE27 5BT, England
www.imray.com
2023

All rights reserved· No part of this
publication may be reproduced, transmitted or used in
any form by any means –
graphic, electronic or mechanical, including
photocopying, recording, taping or
information storage and retrieval systems or otherwise –
without the prior permission of the publisher.

© Imray Laurie Norie & Wilson Ltd 2023
© Commentary – Chris Howes 2023
All photographs © Chris Howes unless credited

British Library Cataloguing in Publication Data
A catalogue record for this book is available from the
British Library.

ISBN 978 17867 9534 2 printed book

CAUTION
Every effort has been taken to ensure the accuracy of this
book. It contains selected information and thus is not
definitive and does not include all known information on
the subject in hand; this is particularly relevant to the
plans which should not be used for navigation. The
author and publisher believe that its selection is a useful
aid to prudent navigation but the safety of a vessel
depends ultimately on the judgement of the navigator
who should assess all information, published or
unpublished, available to him.

This work has been corrected to September 2023

Printed in Croatia by Denona

For important
corrections and updates
www.imray.com

Contents

Preface *6*

River Great Ouse navigation *9*

1 **River Great Ouse**
   The Bedford Ouse Kempston to Earith *31*

2 **River Great Ouse**
   The Ely Ouse Earith to Denver *101*

3 **Tidal crossing to The Middle Level navigations** *145*
   Denver Sluice to Salter's Lode

4 **The New Bedford (Hundred Foot) River** *153*
   Denver to Earith

5 **The River Great Ouse Relief Channel** *157*
   Denver Complex to Relief Channel Tail Sluice

6 **The tidal River Great Ouse** *165*
   Denver Sluice to King's Lynn

7 **The River Cam** *181*
   Pope's Corner to Jesus Lock, Cambridge & Cambridge Backs
   including the Cambridgeshire Lodes

8 **The River Lark** *223*

9 **The River Little Ouse** *235*

10 **The River Wissey** *247*

Appendix *257*

Index *262*

Preface

During the course of my life I've lived in two towns and one city on the River Great Ouse; Bedford, St Neots and Ely. Although I've also strayed to other parts of the country, somehow, and inexorably, I find myself drawn back to the Great Ouse.

In this guide I've tried to squeeze in as much 'boater-centric' information as possible. I hope that some of my passion for our great rivers of the east of England also comes through. I'm often found on these waters, with my narrowboat *Lily May*. If you see me, please say 'hello'. And if you find something that I've got wrong, that has changed since the guide was published, or you think I've omitted, please contact the publishers, Imray, and we will endeavour to include it in the next edition of the guide.

The river is an ever running theme which binds together the rich and varied history of the area. I've enjoyed reading up on Boudicca, the warrior Queen who challenged the mighty Romans, Eltheldreda who founded the great Cathedral at Ely, King Canute who regularly visited Ely, Hereward the Wake, known as the 'last Englishman' who stood up to the Norman Invaders, the beautiful university city of Cambridge, born out of Oxford's 'Town v Gown' riots in the early 13th century, Oliver Cromwell, John Bunyan, Cornelius Vermuyden and his Herculean drainage efforts, and many, many more heroes and villains. In a guide such as this, I can only scratch the surface of, or hint at, this history, but I hope that I've whetted your appetite to set out on your own journey of discovery.

In the preparation of this new edition of this guide I've revisited every part of the system that I've written about. My own boat may appear in several of my photos, but that's because she was always there with me!

Chris Howes
April 2021

Preface to seventh edition

This seventh edition is the second under my stewardship. I've been grateful for all the feedback I've received from users of the guide, and the friendly waves and 'hellos' from passing boaters. I've thoroughly enjoyed revisiting the guide for this edition. I've been away on the canals several times since writing the previous edition. More and more do I welcome my return to our lovely flowing waters!

The beauty of our rivers and wide range of nature are perhaps too closely a guarded secret amongst those of us who live on, or regularly boat, the waters of the Anglian Region. This guide is intended to both share that 'secret' and introduce and welcome new visitors to the region.

September 2023

The author

Chris Howes has spent most of his life on, and often unintentionally in, the water, messing about in boats. Some years ago he graduated from small self-propelled boats up to a larger motorised boat, when he and his wife bought a narrowboat built on the Middle Level. The boat and he are these days rarely parted! Chris is a past Chairman of Peterborough Branch IWA and regularly writes about, and photographs, waterways, and waterway issues.

Acknowledgements

I would like to thank the Environment Agency for their continuing support for boating, notably Paul Separovic, Nathan Arnold and 'Denver Dan' Pollard. We welcome a new EA Waterways Manager, Katherine Briscombe, with her enthusiasm to support boating. We miss several past EA members who have either retired or moved on to new challenges, including Irven Forbes, Ray Bowden, Mervyn Day, and Ben Di-Giulio. I'd like to thank the many boaters who have made suggestions and given me feedback, members of Peterborough Branch IWA, my wife Christine Colbert, Heather Boyce, Ivan Cane, Mike Daines, Sid Fisher, Kate and Keith Gibson, David Goode, Simon Judge, John Revell, Mike Rowse, Les Walton of Prickwillow Drainage Museum and the Great Ouse Boating Association (GOBA). I'm indebted to Robert Simper, whose book *Rivers to the Fens* remains a constant source of delight and information. I have walked in the considerable shadow of Andrew Hunter Blair, historian and author of previous guides.

I'd also like to express my gratitude to the team at Imray for giving me the opportunity to write on a subject dear to me, and for converting my enthusiastic ramblings into comprehensible content.

Imray books are updated at frequent intervals via free supplements available at
www.imray.com
Please email editor@imray.com with any specific comments or observations regarding the information in this guide.

On Facebook, several local groups provide helpful information and friendly boating related chat.
Search 'Spotted on the Great Ouse', 'The Great Ouse Boater' and 'Middle Level Boaters'.

Using the River Ouse Guide

Map pages

40 detailed maps of the river, tributaries and lodes, showing the main features of the navigation, local facilities, services and features of interest.

Descriptions of 'left bank' and 'right bank' follow the usual convention that they are described as such from a position looking **downstream**.

Note that if you are heading **upstream** the 'left bank' will, therefore, be on your right.

Map symbols			
	Navigation Authority (EA)		Footpath
	GOBA moorings		Long distance footpath
	Town or Borough Council		Drinking water
	Marina berths		Chemical disposal point
	Boat club		Toilet pumpout
	Visitor moorings (short stay)		Shower
	Single width lock		Refuse bin
	Double width lock		Fuel
	D shaped (triple width) lock		Shop
	Slipway		Public house
	Direction of stream		Café/restaurant
	Direction of navigation		Railway station
	Lock		Church
	Weir		Information
	Power cable		Post Office
	Footbridge	F&C	Fish and chips

8 RIVER GREAT OUSE

Navigation

The River Great Ouse from source to sea is 162 miles long. It is the fourth longest river in the United Kingdom, and is navigable by powered craft over half its length, from the village of Kempston, south west of Bedford, to The Wash, a distance of 84 miles. The name Ouse is from the Celtic *Udso-s*, and probably simply means 'water' or 'slow flowing river'.

What's so 'great' about this Ouse?

There are four rivers in England which are all called 'Ouse'.

The Sussex Ouse is a 42 mile long river which joins the sea at Newhaven.

The Little Ouse flows from the Norfolk/Suffolk border for 37 miles to join the Great Ouse near Littleport in Cambridgeshire.

The Yorkshire Ouse flows for 52 miles until it meets the River Trent at Trentfalls, where they both join the Humber estuary. The tidal section of the Yorkshire Ouse is a truly mighty river, as anyone who has seen the photos of Naburn Lock (below York) completely submerged below floods, or who has tried to steer from the Ouse on a falling tide into the lock at Selby, will testify.

The Great Ouse rises in Northamptonshire. Originally it found the sea below Wisbech, via the River Nene. It now joins the sea near King's Lynn after a comparatively sedate journey from its source.

So what makes this Ouse 'Great' - in comparison to its mighty 'big brother' in Yorkshire ? It was probably first called the 'Great Ouse' to differentiate it from the 'Little Ouse' which joins it below Ely. But round here, we believe that it is called 'Great' because it is simply one of the finest rivers in the country!

Imray guides to neighbouring waterways

Fenland Waterways *Chris Howes*
The River Nene *Roger Green*
Chart Y9 The Wash

The bewildered raindrop

The southern and western upland areas of Northamptonshire are the source of a number of southern England's major rivers. The Great Ouse rises in Wappenham and flows east to The Wash. The Upper Avon rises in Naseby and flows west into Warwickshire. The River Cherwell rises in Hellingdon and flows south to join the Thames in Oxford, and the River Nene rises on Arbury Hill and flows north east, also to The Wash.

Any drop of rain, falling within this comparatively small area of land, could be forgiven for not having the faintest idea whether it was going to end up in the Bristol Channel, the Thames Estuary, or The Wash.

If our confused rain drop has come down the Great Ouse, just as it reaches Denver, only 14 miles from the sea, it might be diverted into the Great Ouse Cut-Off Channel via the Diversion Sluice and pumped off in the opposite direction to Essex!

Sections of the Ouse

The approximately 162 mile long river Great Ouse can be divided into six sections:

1. **The non-navigable Great Ouse (73 miles)**
   Above Kempston – although accessible to small, generally self propelled boats, like canoes and skiffs, it is not navigable by powered craft.

2. **The Bedford Ouse (39 miles)**
   Between Head of Navigation at Kempston and Brownshill Staunch.

3. **The tidal Great Ouse (2¼ miles)**
   A short section of the river between Brownshill Staunch and Hermitage Lock the river is tidal.

4. **The Old West River (11½ miles)**
   Hermitage Lock to Pope's Corner (confluence of rivers Great Ouse and Cam). Typically it has little flow.

5. **The Ely Ouse (20 miles)**
   From Pope's Corner to Denver Sluice. Although once again a wide and comparatively deep river, the river is less prone to flooding than the Bedford Ouse because of the 'Cut Off Channel' which diverts excess water from the tributaries rivers Lark, Little Ouse and Wissey. Denver Sluice can also react quickly to deal with excess water in the river.

   The section downstream of the A10 bridge at Littleport, to Denver, is also known as **Ten Mile River** or **Ten Mile Bank**.

6. **Tidal Great Ouse (16 miles)**
   Below Denver Sluice until it joins the sea a couple of miles below the port of King's Lynn.

The tidal middle

The river Great Ouse must surely be unique in being the only river in the country that has a tidal middle section (Brownshill Staunch to Hermitage Lock) before returning to a sedate non-tidal state for another 30 miles. This is because the New Bedford River (the Hundred Foot River) is an open channel cut from the Great Ouse at Earith which joins the tidal Great Ouse immediately below Denver Sluice. Its function being to relieve waters from the Great Ouse. However as it is an open cut, although it takes water away on a falling tide, it also brings water in with the tide. The EA service moorings at Earith are rising flood moorings. During the summer season the rise and fall may only be 0·3m (1') but at spring tides it may increase to 0·75m (2'6").

Tributaries

Tributaries of the upper, non navigable, River Great Ouse
River Leck, River Tove, River Ouzel (or River Lovat)

Tributaries of the navigable, non tidal, River Great Ouse
River Ivel, River Kym, Alconbury Brook, Cottenham Lode, River Cam, Soham Lode, River Lark, River Little Ouse, River Wissey

Tributaries of the tidal River Great Ouse
New Bedford River (aka Hundred Foot River), Old Bedford River, Middle Level Main Drain, Great Ouse Cut Off Channel, Great Ouse Relief Channel, River Nar, Gaywood River, River Babingley, Rivers Purfleet and Millfleet

OS Maps

Landranger 132 North West Norfolk (including King's Lynn)
Landranger 143 Ely and Wisbech
Landranger 153 Bedford and Huntingdon (St Neots and Biggleswade)
Landranger 154 Cambridge and Newmarket

Navigation authorities

The Environment Agency is the navigation authority for all waters covered in this book except:

- the River Cam upstream of Bottisham Lock, which falls under the jurisdiction of the **Conservators of the River Cam**
- the tidal River Great Ouse downstream of Stowbridge, which falls under the jurisdiction of the **Kings Lynn Port Authority**

Environment Agency boat registration team

P.O. Box 544
Rotherham
S60 1BY

① 03708 506 506
boatreg@environment-agency.gov.uk

Middle Level Commissioners

85 Whittlesey Rd, March
PE15 0AH

① 01354 653232
www.middlelevel.gov.uk

Conservators of the River Cam

Clayhithe Office,
Clayhithe Road,
Waterbeach,
Cambridge
CB25 9JB

① 01223 863785
www.camconservancy.org

Boat Licensing and Registration

All vessels kept, used, or let for hire on the rivers Great Ouse, Cam, Lark, Little Ouse, Wissey, Old and New Bedford and the Relief Channel must be registered for use with the appropriate licencing authority. This includes vessels in marinas and privately owned moorings.

Depending on the type of craft you may need valid and up to date insurance and a boat safety certificate (BSS).

You can boat all the waters managed by the Environment Agency on an **EA registration** or **CRT Gold Licence**. Neither of these allow you onto either the Middle Level or the River Cam above Bottisham Lock.

The Navigation Authority for the River Cam above Bottisham Lock is the **Conservators of the River Cam**, and the authority for the Middle Level is the **Middle Level Commissioners**.

EA Visitor Registrations are available for short periods; 1 day, 7 days, and 31 days. The EA advise to allow two weeks for an application to be processed. Rates are based on boat length.

Since April 2021 you have been able to purchase a supplementary **Anglian Pass**. This is intended to provide seamless travel between neighbouring navigation authorities. As long as you first hold a valid registration for one of the three navigation authorities you can purchase a year long **Anglian Pass** which will give you access to all waters in the other two. The pass is available online:
www.visitanglianwaterways.org

In September 2020 the Middle Level Commissioners introduced a registration fee for their waters which lie between the rivers Great Ouse and Nene. Licences closely mirror the EA regulations, both in boat sizes and time periods, however neither an EA licence, nor a CRT Gold Licence, cover you for the Middle Level unless used in association with an Anglian Pass.

Any CRT (non-Gold) licence holder intending to visit Anglian Waters will need to first buy a short term EA licence, and then a short term licence for the Middle Level. Short term licences for the Cam are no longer available and a non-Gold CRT licence holder will have to buy a full year's licence for the River Cam.

This system is on the last year of its initial three year trial. There is a desire to keep this 'seamless' travel between authorities, so it is likely to continue little changed.

Legislation

The legislation which applies to all forms of river use is found in the following, and applies to all users:

The Anglian Water Authority Act 1977

The Recreational Waterways (General) Byelaws 1980

The Environment Act 1995

The Environment Agency (Inland Waterways) Order 2010

Copies can be obtained from the Environment Agency at WaterwaysAnglian@environment-agency.gov.uk

Speed limits

A number of speed limits apply across these navigations. Care must be taken at all times in the interests of safety to protect the water environment. Speed limits vary between 4mph on busier sections of the river, 7mph elsewhere, and 15mph on the tidal river.

Mindful of a general lack of speed measuring equipment fitted on many boats the EA installed three self timing sections, one at each end of the Old West River, and a third on the Ely Ouse between Ely and Littleport. These allow you to check whether you are complying with the speed limit, and give you a general idea what different speeds felt like.

There can be no excuses for speeding, with free apps available for smartphones, which accurately measure your speed. It should be emphasised the speed limit is a maximum, not a target or challenge. You should always slow down and absolutely minimise your wash when passing moored boats, oncoming traffic, and self-propelled boats including paddle boards, canoes, rowing boats and sailing boats.

Care and consideration must be shown when overtaking other vessels or turning, as well as near bridges and sharp bends. Vessels travelling upstream should always give way to those travelling downstream. This is because it is easier to stop when heading into the stream than when being carried along by it. It's rather like cycling - it's a lot easier to stop when pedalling up a hill, than when you're free-wheeling down one.

The old adage 'don't buy a boat if you're in a hurry' still applies.

Courtesy, patience, and consideration to other river users

Getting onto the Great Ouse, or its tributaries, in a boat in good weather is an enormous attraction to many. The captain of every powered vessel should already be aware that consideration must be made for other river users, irrespective of their size. With the increase in the availability of inflatable canoes, and a rise in the popularity of paddle boarding there are sections of the river, often near towns, where there are inexperienced river users not necessarily aware of river rules and etiquette. Often they don't realise that there is a right side of the river to be on. As always, slow down, and show courtesy, patience, and consideration.

There are some simple rules of the river:
- Keep to the speed limits
- Keep to the right when passing approaching craft
- Overtake on the left
- Never overtake near bends, bridges, approaching craft or moored craft
- Slow down and give way to small self-propelled craft
- Slow down when approaching other craft, bridges and narrows
- Try to avoid anglers' fishing lines
- Be alert and keep a sharp lookout

Open water swimmers

Open water swimming is another river based activity currently increasing in popularity. Some swimmers trail high visibility floats which attracts attention to their presence in their water. Without these floats it is remarkably easy not to spot a head bobbing up and down in the water. Recently I was travelling in my boat at a moderate speed when I heard someone shouting near me. They were warning me of a swimmer immediately in front of me whose presence in the water was obscured to me by my bows. I suspect that many swimmers don't realise that boats don't have brakes. I immediately put my boat hard a-stern, only to realise that the person hailing me was another swimmer, also without a high visibility aid, immediately behind me, and I was now in danger of reversing through her, propellor first!

Navigation keys and pump-out tokens

An Environment Agency navigation key, also known as an Abloy key, is required to operate locks, slipways, water-points and sanitary stations in the Anglian region. These can be bought at many marinas and are a 'must have'.

The controls for guillotine gates are generally in an Abloy key accessed cabinet. Many boaters leave their key in the lock while using a lock, expecting to return to re-lock the cabinet after they have left the lock. However one day another boat will arrive planning to use the lock after you, and a member of its crew will offer to raise (or lower) the gate behind you. It is all too easy to thank them, and steam off leaving your vital Abloy key still in the lock. It's often only when you can't unlock the cabinet at the next lock that you discover your mistake. Having done this several times myself, I now always remove the key from the lock once I've opened it, and only put it back in the lock when I want to close it again!

Windlass

As well as a navigation key you will need a windlass to operate locks. A standard 13/16 square (nominal 29mm) will do, but this only just fits over the end of the spindle of the winding mechanisms of some of the locks nearer Bedford. Some boaters opt instead for the the larger 13/8 square (nominal 34mm) windlass they bought to operate the locks on Middle Level. This gives a better purchase on these larger spindles.

Locks

Locks often feature an electrically operated guillotine gate at the upstream end, and V gates at the downstream end. Two locks are always staffed during opening times, Hermitage Lock and Denver Sluice. You can't just lock yourself through when the lock is unattended, and if you find one closed, you have to wait until it reopens.

St Ives and Houghton Locks often have volunteers to assist passage, and the volunteer programme is being expanded to Eaton Socon and Cardington Locks. Volunteers are also deployed at additional lock sites during busier periods such as in the run up to, and after, major river events such as the Bedford River festival.

Unless otherwise stated, you don't need to either refill (or re-empty) a lock as you leave. When departing a lock, gates can be left open (or up).

Several of the locks below Bedford are immediately next to weirs. This can produce turbulence at the landing stage below the lock. When travelling upstream hold your rope securely as you step onto the downstream landing stage, and be careful with your footing - if you don't want to go swimming after your escaped boat!

Any lock with a width less than 4·21m (13'10") is too narrow to accommodate two narrowboats side by side. However the published lock width refers to the opening width at the gates and a number of locks have side chambers which make the lock wide enough to accommodate up to three narrow boats side-by-side.

There are 6 of these locks, Eaton Socon Lock, Brampton Lock, Godmanchester Lock, Houghton Lock, Hemingford Lock and St Ives Lock, the side bays are known as 'pregnant bays' and the locks sometimes described as 'D locks'. The bays were added to increase capacity at pinch points on the system over the years to allow additional boats through on each lock cycle.

Guillotine gates

Guillotine gates are widely used in locks in the east of England, but may be a comparative novelty to visitors from the canals of central England. The important consideration is that a guillotine gate doesn't have slackers. When you press the 'open' button in the control box the gate will initially raise 6 inches. This lets water into the lock under the gate. The gate remains temporarily fixed in position for a timed period. Only once the lock has either filled, or nearly filled, and the time clock run down, will it allow you to fully open the guillotine. There are a few locks on the river Nene which electricity hasn't yet reached. The guillotine gates on these locks have large wheels which are operated manually, generally requiring 100 revolutions to lift or lower the gate. This can be quite hard work. Fortunately all the guillotine gates on the river Great Ouse and her tributaries are now operated by electricity.

Brownshill Staunch

Changing river conditions

Strong Stream Advice (SSA) and reversed locks

The upper reaches of the River Great Ouse above Earith are susceptible to rapidly rising water levels after heavy rain, due to the nature and rapid run-off in the catchment area. River users are advised to play attention to weather forecasts, particularly out of season. If you observe any of the following changes - a difference in water conditions, rising water levels, an increase in flow and current (perhaps most apparent at bridges), or a change in water colour -

St Neots reversed lock

the Environment Agency will almost certainly be operating sluices to regulate water levels.

Water levels naturally fluctuate and cannot be guaranteed. Care should be taken when the flow increases particularly passing under bridges or navigating obstacles in the stream.

Strong Stream Advice is provided by the EA in the form of text message, email, or telephone for the two areas Bedford to St Ives, and St Ives to Earith. This alerts you to rising waters, and resultant river closures.

Almost all the waters of the Great Ouse are diverted at Earith, either onto the Ouse Washes (via the Old Bedford River and River Delf) or to the tidal Great Ouse below Denver Sluice (via the New Bedford River). Similarly the head waters of the Rivers Lark, Little Ouse and Wissey are diverted into the Great Ouse Cut-off Channel, and enter the tidal Great Ouse above King's Lynn via the Great Ouse Relief Channel. The Old West River, between Hermitage Lock and Pope's Corner and the Ely Ouse from Pope's Corner to Denver are not so susceptible to flooding, and so are not covered by SSA.

In winter the Great Ouse rises quickly after rain, and subscribing to the free EA SSA service is strongly recommended. During periods of SSA the river is closed to navigation.

A technique known as 'reversed locks' is sometimes employed during periods of excessive flow and high water levels.

This involves chaining back the V gates (pointing doors) and part-lifting the vertical (guillotine) gate to allow an increase in flow. If a lock is reversed, on no account ever try and navigate through it. You should not approach a reversed lock, but moor up safely a distance away, contact the Environment Agency to let them know where you are, and wait for conditions to return to normal. In these circumstances it is permitted to remain on lock moorings until the warning is cancelled, but if you can find a good mooring away from the lock, this is greatly preferred.

Warning signs are displayed both upstream and downstream of locks and red warning lights (visible from a distance) are deployed on the top of the guillotine gate frame to indicate a lock is reversed.

A total of ten locks may be reversed on the Great Ouse:

Bedford, Cardington, Eaton Socon, St Neots, Offord, Brampton, Godmanchester, Hemingford, St Ives and Brownshill.

Weather and wind

There are few rivers in the country which can enjoy more hours of annual sunshine than the Great Ouse. Sadly we can't quite guarantee good weather every day of the year.

Many of us check to see when rain is expected, and plan our boating around it. However it is always a good idea to check, and take notice of, the forecast wind strength. As wind strength increases it becomes increasingly difficult to control a vessel, be it steel, wood or fibreglass. If the wind speed gets over 20mph it is a good idea to either moor up and wait until it blows over, or not go out in the first place. Anyone boating single handed will know that everything is that little bit harder without willing crew, and would be well advised to avoid boating at a lower limit, say 15mph.

15mph is Force 4 (moderate breeze) on the Beaufort Scale, and 20mph Force 5 (fresh breeze).

The further down the Great Ouse you find yourself, the more you are affected by wind speed. The Earith section (Brownhill Staunch to Hermitage Lock) is quite exposed, and below Pope's Corner the river widens, the countryside flattens out, there are fewer trees acting as windbreaks, so you are far more exposed to wind.

Moorings and facilities

Moorings

There are EA and public (Council) provided moorings on the non-tidal Great Ouse River including the Bedford and Ely Ouse Rivers. There are currently three EA moorings on the Relief Channel, and the new floating landing stage on the tidal River Ouse at Denver, constructed in 2020, will also double as a safe haven and temporary holding berth.

There are EA and public (council) provided moorings on the tributaries of the Great Ouse River including the Old West River, River Wissey, Little Ouse River, River Lark, River Cam and Cam Lodes.

Similarly GOBA offers a total of 25 mooring sites to their members, 16 on the Ouse, and 9 on its tributaries. Both EA and GOBA moorings are generally 48hr only (no return within 48hrs). Moorings are clearly sign posted and restrictions stated. See section plans and tables for details of moorings.

EA and council moorings are against a hard quay edge (hard moorings) and have fixed rings or bollards to tie to, GOBA moorings are mainly stretches of bank where it is permissable to drive mooring pins into the ground.

EA Moorings on the Ely Ouse

A number of EA moorings on the Ely Ouse have been closed for safety reasons. These include Queen Adelaide and two of their three moorings at Denver. It is not clear when repairs are scheduled. The refurbished Station Road moorings in Littleport have re-opened. If you're planning on meeting anyone at a specific mooring, it is advisable to check in advance on the EA's website.

During winter months check with the EA for temporary lock closures (for repairs and maintenance) before planning any journey.

East Cambs District Council have agreed that during adverse weather conditions - when they issue a Severe Weather Emergency Protocol - mooring time restrictions in Ely will be suspended.

Basic mooring guidelines
- Do not leave it too late in the day
- Moor facing upstream if possible
- Do not allow mooring lines and stakes to form unforeseen hazards
- Always leave moorings clean and tidy
- Where space is limited please moor abreast
- Moor close to other boats, avoiding large gaps between boats which restricts numbers
- Do not play loud music. Respect your neighbours.

GOBA (Great Ouse Boating Association)

GOBA is a 60 year-old organisation which provides mooring sites and represents the interests of boaters on the river Great Ouse and its tributaries. Annual membership is £28 (+ initial £2 joining fee) which at an average cost of £1/mooring site, offers excellent value for money for anyone intending to spend time cruising these waters. It is well worth joining GOBA. For more information visit www.goba.org.uk

The Boater's Handbook

In association with the Environment Agency and British Marine, the Canal and River Trust has launched a new edition of The Boater's Handbook. It is an incredibly useful resource for any boater, from novices to old hands alike. The Handbook is written for boat owners and hirers and contains lots of 'getting started' tips as well as important information about how to boat safely. It is intended to refresh memories and to be kept on board your boat as a handy reference guide.

The Trust wants all boaters to be aware of the key safety messages:

- **Avoid slips and trips!**
  Watch out for ropes, bollards, holes and other hazards, use grab rails and wear non-slip shoes. Don't try to jump from the boat onto the bank and wear a lifejacket if you can't swim.

- **Don't get crushed!**
  Keep your body out the way of a moving boat: don't fend off with your arms, legs or boat pole, and don't have limbs dangling over the side or your head out the hatch. Keep off the roof when you're underway.

- **Watch out for fire and fumes!**
  If you smell exhaust, gas, or petrol fumes raise the alert right away. Switch off appliances when you're not using them and keep ventilators open and free of obstructions. Remember that carbon monoxide poisoning is extremely dangerous: early signs include headaches, tiredness, sickness and dizziness, and anyone affected should get medical help right away.

- **Don't rock the boat!**
  Think carefully before climbing onto the cabin roof as the boat could become top heavy and roll over, and don't all stand together on the same side if it risks tipping the boat over.

- **Remember your lifejacket!**
  The water is often colder and deeper than you think.

A downloadable copy of the Handbook, and a video setting out key information, can be found on the Canal & River Trust web site, or a copy ordered by contacting CRT customer services

☏ 0303 040 4040
customer.services@canalrivertrust.org.uk

Mooring etiquette

In summer months there can be a considerable demand for moorings, particularly at weekends. Please moor in a considerate manner which allows other boats to also moor. Tie up close to an already moored boat, not in the middle of a gap between boats. Both GOBA and EA require you to do this if you are to use their moorings. Be prepared to double up with another boat.

Please be considerate of your environment and other boaters. Don't barbeque on the grass or mooring's surface. Please don't run your engine late at night, do not play loud music.

EA pump-out tokens

The EA self pump out facilities at Denver (near the A G Wright Sluice), Ely and Earith have been fitted with token operated payment mechanisms, however at the time of writing these are not connected and pump-outs are not charged. Tokens will be available from marinas and chandleries when the payment mechanisms are activated.

A number of marinas also provide pump-out services.

Returning to your boat after dusk

Many of the GOBA moorings are in remote countryside settings. You will need mooring pins, and a boarding plank can be extremely useful. I've several times rested up for the night on a GOBA mooring, set off for the pub in twilight for a meal, and found that it had turned to night when I returned. As you may well be walking along an unfamiliar rough riverside path without street lights, please don't forget to take torches with you for every member of your party.

Access for wider boats

The Great Ouse will accommodate boats up to 10' 6" (3·3 m) as far as Cardington Lock. To visit Bedford you shouldn't exceed 10'. For larger boats, particularly those with a keel, a careful eye should be kept on depth.

Cambridge is similarly accessible as far as Jesus Green Lock by boats up to 14' (4·3m).

Although Upware lock can fit boats up to 14' (4·3m) consideration should be given on the Cambridgeshire Lodes to the size and depth of the waterway, problems of passing other boats you may meet, and turning. It is advisable to walk any proposed route rather than just assuming that larger boats will get down it - and back again!

The River Lark is accessible to wider craft as far as Isleham Lock. The River Little Ouse appears narrower and shallower and I certainly wouldn't travel much past the aqueduct over the Cut-Off Channel in a larger boat.

The River Wissey is comparatively restricted at its confluence with the Great Ouse, but widens out after Wissington Beet factory.

Bridge heights

Published bridge headrooms are averages not minimums and actual headroom may be significantly less than the published height. Headroom is affected by river levels, and tides on the tidal sections. The Environment Agency provide a table of bridge heights at www.gov.uk/guidance/river-great-ouse-bridge-heights-locks-and-facilities

Transport connections

Both the river Great Ouse and its tributaries are well served by railway stations. For anyone taking an extended cruise there are ample opportunities for family and friends to visit by rail. On both the Great Ouse, and its tributaries, you are never more than 10 miles from either a railway station, or in St Ives, the guided bus.

On the **Great Ouse** there are railway stations at **Bedford**, **St Neots**, **Huntingdon**, **Ely**, **Littleport**, and **King's Lynn**, and at **St Ives** the guided bus connects with **Cambridge**.

On the **Relief Channel** there are stations at **Downham Market** and **Watlington**.

On the **tributaries of the Great Ouse** there are railway stations at **Waterbeach**, **Cambridge North** and **Cambridge (River Cam)**, **Lakenheath** and **Brandon (Little Ouse)**.

For further information on River Great Ouse navigation, the EA have produced a leaflet, *EA Waterway Users Information*, available to download at

www.visitanglianwaterways.org

The Inland Waterways Association

The Inland Waterways Association (IWA) was born from necessity back in 1945, when two forward-thinking canal enthusiasts, Tom Rolt and Robert Aickman, realised there was a need to protect the waterways of Britain, which were being abandoned and filled in at an alarming rate in favour of new road and railway networks. At a meeting in August 1945, at Tardebigge, near Bromsgrove on the Worcester & Birmingham Canal, plans for IWA were agreed between the two men and the Association was officially set up in February 1946. In November of that year, the first ever Bulletin was issued informing members that the Stratford Canal, Kennet & Avon and Suffolk Stour were the targets of the first IWA campaigns.

On the Stratford Canal, Rolt successfully challenged Great Western Railway (GWR), the then owners of the Stratford Canal, at Tunnel Lane, Lifford Bridge at Kings Norton. GWR had replaced a former drawbridge with a new bridge that was too low to allow boat passage along the canal, despite a statutory right of navigation existing. A question in Parliament and a notice of intention to navigate, forced GWR to lift the bridge to allow Rolt, in his narrowboat Cressy to pass.

The successes of these early actions gave IWA the confidence needed to start campaigning far and wide, further buoyed by the rise of leisure boating, which swelled membership numbers during the 1950s, '60s and beyond.

Today, IWA speaks for all users of the inland waterways network, which includes 6,500 miles of rivers and canals across England and Wales as well as the Scottish Canals. IWA works tirelessly to help protect and restore these waterways through its lobbying and campaigning activity, whether on a government level, with changes to legislation or the introduction of new transport initiatives, or on a more local level with council-led planning issues or decisions from navigation authorities. Local campaigning is undertaken by IWA's network of branches across the country.

Through its Waterway Recovery Group, IWA works with canal restoration trusts around the country, providing a volunteer workforce, expert engineering and planning advice and information on how to raise the necessary funds. Over 500 miles of canal have been restored and put back to water in the course of IWA's history, with many more currently undergoing restoration.

In this region the IWA is represented by the Great Ouse Branch. This friendly and active branch meets regularly, and welcomes new members. To learn more about the IWA's illustrious history, current campaigns, or to find out some of the many benefits of membership, visit www.waterways.org.uk. The site will also give you up to date contact details for your local branches.

Walking

There can be little better equipment with which to enjoy the varied countryside that the Great Ouse flows through, than a stout pair of boots and a map. In addition to ramblers, many boaters like to walk sections, often choosing to walk from one lock to another.

We have endeavoured to describe the location of paths serving each river section, and include them in our maps.

www.huntingdonshire.gov.uk/leisure/parks-nature-reserves-and-green-spaces/ouse-valley-way/

Great Ouse Valley Trust

The Great Ouse Valley Trust was launched in 2018 to promote, protect and enhance the special landscape of the river valley within Cambridgeshire.

This is a precious, tranquil countryside of national importance, not only for its rich biodiversity, history and scenic beauty, but also because it gives real identity to this part of East Anglia.

The Trust is a coalition of partners from local parish and town councils as well as national organisations including the National Trust, CPRE, RSPB, BHS and local groups including boating enthusiasts. They are seeking designation as an Area of Outstanding Natural Beauty from Natural England and have recently launched a supporter group.

The Trust works through its partners with many projects in landscape enhancement with programmes of willow and poplar planting and restoration, new hedges and wildflower meadows.

They are working with Cambridgeshire County Council to improve the route of the Ouse Valley Way long distance footpath and to ensure its proper maintenance and way marking. The path's length through Cambridgeshire is around 26 miles making it the ideal setting for the annual Ouse Valley Marathon staged in September.

The river and its surroundings offer a unique experience and an opportunity to enjoy nature at its best. The Trust is committed to ensure this is available to everyone whether you access it by foot, bike, horse or boat and whether your passion is history, nature, fishing, running or just the simple enjoyment of a peaceful world away far from the pressures of modern life and fast cars.

You can find out more about the Trust on their website, or follow them on Facebook.

www.greatousevalleytrust.org.uk

Heron on Duck Mill Weir, Bedford

Wildlife Trust for Bedfordshire, Cambridgeshire and Northamptonshire

A local wildlife charity supported by over 1000 volunteers and over 36,000 members that protects and cares for wildlife and wild places across Bedfordshire, Cambridgeshire and Northamptonshire. The trust manages most of their reserves in the Nene Valley with a key focus on 'Living Landscapes' that connect these smaller sites together in a bigger, more joined up area helping wildlife to move freely through the countryside without barriers.

www.wildlifebcn.org

Canoeing

Once the first Covid-19 lockdown of 2020 had been relaxed, many more canoeists and paddle boarders took to the river Great Ouse and her tributaries than I have ever before seen. These are great waters and there are few better ways to experience them than by 'simply messing about in boats'. However you should always remember:

- To wear a buoyancy aid.
- That all boats must either be registered with the Environment Agency, or through British Canoeing.
- You should keep to the right hand side of the river (the exact opposite of driving on the road).
- To make sure you are visible to other river users.
- That powered vessels can't quickly change direction, don't have brakes and can't stop quickly.

The River Great Ouse and her tributaries sadly don't have a network of canoe portage points to help you get in and out of your vessel at locks.

Great crested grebes

Locks are extremely dangerous places to be in, and although you are allowed to take a canoe through a lock, I personally discourage it. If you do go through a lock, always hold onto something secure, and be wary of the likelihood of sideways movement of larger vessels also in the lock caused by the turbulence of water being let in. Don't put yourself in position where you could be squashed between a boat weighing several tons, and the side of the lock!

Canoeists sometimes ask me if they can come through a lock with me. I invariably reply that I'm happy to tow their boat through, but only if they're not in it. As a canoeist myself I recognise the difficulties of getting on and off the water when there aren't any portage points. I frequently suggest that they use the conveniently low stern of my narrowboat to get in and out of their boat. Over the years I've earned many thanks, and even the odd ice cream, this way.

www.britishcanoeing.org.uk
www.gopaddling.info/rivers/river-great-ouse/

Useful contacts and links

Inland Waterways Association
☏ 01494 783453

River and Canal Rescue
☏ 01785 785680

River and Canal emergency
☏ 08000 718021

RSPB (East of England)
☏ 01603 660066
Out of hours
☏ 0300 121 0475

British Marine Life Rescue
☏ 01825 765546

Navigation

Conservators of the River Cam
☏ 01223 863785

EA Customer Contact Centre
☏ 03708 506506 (Mon - Fri 8-6)

EA incident hotline
☏ 0800 80 70 60 (24hrs)

EA flood line
☏ 0345 988 1188

EA River Great Ouse Operational Manager
☏ 01733 464327

EA River Inspector
Bedford Ouse
Kempston to Godmanchester Lock
☏ 07768 171256
Downstream from Huntingdon
☏ 07717 423512

EA River Inspector
Ely Ouse, Tidal Ouse and all tributaries
☏ 07889 111829

King's Lynn Borough Council (moorings)
☏ 01553 774 297

King's Lynn Harbourmaster
☏ 01553 773411

Middle Level Commissioners
☏ 01354 653232

Middle Level Officer
☏ 07725 1344170

Wash Pilot
Darryl Hill, ☏ 07909 880071
washguide@gmail.com

Locks

Denver Lock	☏ 01366 382340
Denver Complex	☏ 01366 382013
Hermitage Lock	☏ 01487 841548
Salter's Lode Lock	☏ 01366 382292

Mobile boat engineers

Pat Tierney	☏ 07895 094755
Boat Serv	☏ 07736 770 777
Alex Lloyd	☏ 07887 802 746
Jays Marine Services	☏ 07776 130 921
Stuart Mould	☏ 07472 630713
T J Stoneham	☏ 07740 199304
Cliff Wall	☏ 07786 837651

Diamond Mechanical Services
Breakdown and rescue
☏ 07841090922

Karl Day Marine Services
Engineer and engine supplies
☏ 01480 461414 / 07785 934545

Fenland Spirit Services
Engineer and engine supplies
☏ 07753 836 499

St Ives Engine Services Ltd
Service, repairs, fuel cleaning
☏ 01480 462111

WTech Leisure Services
Engineer and engine supplies
☏ 01780 752606

Marinas and boatyards on the Great Ouse

Bridge Boatyard
Ely CB7 4DY
Overnight/longterm moorings, boat hire, repairs, diesel, gas and coal
☎ 01353 663726

Buckden Marine
Buckden PE19 5BH
Long term moorings, self service diesel and pump-out.
☎ 01480 812660

Crosshall Marine
St Neots, PE19 7GE
Long term and overnight moorings, repairs and boat sales
☎ 01480 472763

Denver Moorings
EA long term moorings on the east bank at Denver
☎ 01366 382013

Ely Marine Ltd
Ely CB7 4AU
Long term moorings, diesel and petrol, sales, repairs
☎ 01353 664622

Fish and Duck Marina
Pope's Corner
CB6 3HR
Long term moorings, sales, small boat hire, diesel, chandlery
☎ 01353 649580

Hartford Marine
PE28 2AA
Overnight/ long term moorings. All services including petrol and diesel, chandlery.
☎ 01480 454677

Hermitage Marina
Earith, PE28 3PR
Overnight/long term moorings.
☎ 01353 664 622

Huntingdon Boat Haven
PE29 2AF
Long term moorings, some services.
☎ 01480 411977

Jones Boatyard
St Ives, PE27 5ET
Long term/overnight moorings (boats >40'). All services, boat sales, chandlery.
☎ 01480 494040

Kelpie Marine
Tempsford MK44 3DS
Long term moorings and overnight if availability, boat sales.
☎ 01234 870249

Lazy Days Boat Hire
Huntingdon Boat Haven,
Godmanchester PE29 2AF
☎ 07951 785305

Littleport Boat Haven
CB6 1QG
Long term moorings, slipway for hire, boat sales and hire, boat cleaning
☎ 01353 863763

Priory Marina
Bedford MK41 9DJ
Long term moorings and service.
All facilities including diesel and petrol.
☎ 01234 351931

Purvis Marine
Riverside Car Park, Hartford Road,
Huntingdon PE29 3RP
Boat hire and repair.
☎ 01480 453628

Rivermill Marina
Eaton Socon, St Neots, PE19 8GW
Long term moorings.
☎ 01480 473456

Riverside Marine Services,
Needingworth, PE27 4TW
Long term moorings, sales, chandlery, repairs.
☎ 01480 468666

Marinas and boatyards on the Great Ouse (cont.)

St Neots Marina
PE19 2BW
Long term moorings, diesel, pump-out.
☎ 01480 472411

Stretham Ferry Marina
Stretham CB6 3LU
Long term moorings.
☎ 01353 648383

The Boat Yard
1 Annesdale, Ely
CB7 4BN
Repairs and new builds
☎ 01353 668551

Twenty Pence Marina
Wilburton CB6 3PX
Long term moorings.
☎ 01954 251118

Westview Marina
Earith PE28 3PN
Long term/overnight moorings, sales, chandlery, repairs.
☎ 01487 840089

Wyton Moorings
Wyton PE28 2AA
Long term and overnight moorings, repairs.
☎ 01480 455898

Marinas and boatyards on the Tributaries

River Cam

Upware Marina
CB7 5ZR
Long term moorings, services, repairs, sales

Tiptree Marina
CB7 5YJ
Long term moorings,
☎ 01223 440065

Shrubbs Wharf Marina
CB25 9HF
Long term moorings
☎ 01223 811812

River Lark

Riverside Island, Isleham
CB7 5SL
Long term moorings
☎ 01638 780663

Fenland Boat Moorings
CB25 9LN - CB7 5RG
Long term moorings
☎ 07939003681

River Little Ouse

Little Ouse Moorings
Brandon Creek PE38 0PR
Long term moorings ☎ 07713 465791

---

what3words is a system of geocoding that identifies any location, urban or rural, to within about 3m. The system's algorithm encodes geographic co-ordinates into a unique three dictionary word combination. For example, Denver Sluice can be identified by distracts.panther.artist.

The system is designed to work on devices with limited data storage and no internet connection and is ideal for emergency directions in the countryside, where postcodes cover too large an area to pinpoint a location accurately. The use of words, rather than a grid reference series of numbers, reduces the likelihood of transcription errors.

www.what3words.com

Public slipways

Note: public slipways may require an EA Abloy key. Many marinas also have slipways.

River Great Ouse

St Neots
Next to rowing club, Priory Lane, PE19 2PZ

Godmanchester
The Causeway, PE29 2HA
Small portable craft, limited vehicular access

Huntingdon
Next to rowing club
PE29 3RP

St Ives
Town Moorings, PE27 5FD

Earith
Behind Earith Village Hall

Ely
Waterside, CB7 4AU

Denver Sluice, PE38 0AZ
☎ 01366 382013

Tributaries of the Great Ouse

River Cam/Burwell Lode
Upware CB7 5ZR (Five Miles from Anywhere Pub)

River Wissey
Hilgay
Small portable craft, limited vehicular access

River Little Ouse, Brandon
Brandon Lock via Castle Recreation Fields

River Lark
Isleham (Isleham Lock Backwater)

Many boatyards have their own private slipways which you should expect to pay to use.

Water points

River Great Ouse

Bedford Sovereign Key
Great Barford near The Anchor PH
St Neots Town Moorings
St Ives The Waits Quay
Earith outside Westview Marina
Huntingdon, near old town bridge
Ely at services
Littleport opposite Swan PH
Ten Mile Bank at Modney Rd Bridge
Denver near AG Wright Sluice

Relief Channel

All three floating moorings include water points

River Cam

Just through **Reach Lode Lock** (near Fives Miles from Anywhere PH)
End of **Stourbridge Common**, Cambridge
Jesus Green Lido, Cambridge

River Lark
Prickwillow

River Little Ouse
Hilgay

Gas and diesel sales

Priory Marina, Bedford
Petrol, diesel, gas
☏ 01234 351931

Buckden Marina
Petrol, diesel, gas
☏ 01480 812660

Hartford Marina
☏ 01480 454677

Riverside Marine Services
Pike and Eel, Needingworth
☏ 01480 468666/ 07703 258414

Jones Boatyard, St Ives
☏ 01480 494040

Westview Marina, Earith
☏ 01487 840089.

Twenty Pence Marina
Gas, no diesel, no hire boats
☏ 01954 251118

Fish and Duck Marina
☏ 01353 649580

Bridge Boat Yard, Ely
Diesel
☏ 01353 663726

Ely Marine Ltd
☏ 01353 664622

Little Ouse Moorings
☏ 07713 465791

Pump-outs and elsan disposal

River Great Ouse

Priory Marina, Bedford
☏ 01234 351931

Buckden Marina
Elsan emptying
☏ 01480 812660

Hartford Marina
Pump out
☏ 01480 454677

Jones Boatyard, St Ives
Elsan emptying
☏ 01480 494040

Riverside Marine Services, Pike and Eel, Needingworth,
☏ 01480 468666

Navigation Authority services

River Great Ouse

Earith services
Outside Westview Marina
Waterpoint, pump-out, no elsan emptying

Ely Public Quay
Waterpoint, rubbish disposal, pump out and elsan emptying

Denver
Pump-out and elsan disposal
(near A.G. Wright Sluice), waterpoint, rubbish disposal

River Cam

Cambridge
Outside Jesus Green Lido
Waterpoint and pump-out

Family friendly boating pubs with moorings

These waters are well served by a variety of riverside pubs which offer food. These are popular destinations, particularly with day cruisers.

River Great Ouse
The Anchor at Great Barford
The River Mill, Eaton Socon
Brampton Mill
Houghton Mill
Old Ferry Boat, Holywell
The Pike and Eel, Needingworth
The Cutter, Ely
Riverside Bar & Kitchen, Ely
Urban Fresh, Ely
The Swan, Littleport
The Ship Inn, Brandon Creek
The Heron, Stowbridge (Relief Channel)

River Cam
Fort St George, Cambridge
The Plough, Fen Ditton
The Bridge, Clayhithe
Five Miles from Anywhere, No Hurry, Upware

River Lark
Jude's Ferry pub, Jude's Ferry.

The towns of Bedford, St Neots, Huntingdon, St Ives, Downham Market and King's Lynn, and the cities of Cambridge and Ely, also all offer numerous other gastronomic opportunities.

Many of these pubs get busy during peak times, so advance booking to dine is recommended.

A rich aeronautical history

During WWII East Anglia earned the nickname the 'airfield of Great Britain', because of the high number of airfields in the region. An important legacy remains.
The Shuttleworth Collection at Old Warden (8½ miles from Bedford) is one of the most important collections of old aircraft in the world. Its earliest plane, still working, dates from 1909, a mere 6 years after the Wright brothers' first flight! It also features a collection of vintage and veteran automobiles.
In July it holds a popular airshow.
For opening times visit
www.shuttleworth.org

The Imperial War Museum, Duxford (10 miles from Cambridge) is Britain's largest aviation museum and includes 200 aircraft, military vehicles, artillery and minor naval vessels in seven main exhibition buildings. It includes a prototype Concorde which landed in 1977, shortly before the construction of the M11 motorway cut off the end of the runway, preventing Concorde ever taking off again. The museum periodically holds events, including the Battle of Britain Air Show Weekend every September.
For opening times and further information visit
www.iwm.org.uk

Bedford and Milton Keynes Waterways Trust

Geographically Bedford and Milton Keynes lie less than 20 miles apart, but any would-be boat traveller between the two has to take a 185 mile, 82 lock, 11 day trip down the River Great Ouse, across the Middle Level, up the River Nene, along the Northampton arm of the Grand Union Canal, and back South down the Grand Union.

This is despite the Great Ouse passing underneath the Grand Union canal at Cosgrove. When the canal was first constructed boats locked down to the Great Ouse, and then back up again. In 1811 the 'Iron Trunk Aqueduct' was constructed 40ft above the river to carry the Grand Junction Canal (as it was then called) across it.

This idea of making a navigable connection between the Great Ouse and the canal was first proposed in 1812, when the engineer John Rennie proposed a 15-mile canal from Fenny Stratford on the Grand Junction to Bedford, at an estimated cost of £180,807. In 1892 a Bill was prepared to extend navigation to the Grand Junction Canal at Cosgrove via 20 miles of canal and 25 locks. The Grand Union Canal crosses the river Great Ouse on the Iron Trunk Aqueduct, however the river meanders so dramatically, it was considered best to cut a new channel rather than canalising the existing river.

Brackley and Bedford are 40 miles apart, but the river travels an estimated 95 miles between them. The Bill proposed in 1892 was defeated after opposition from the railway companies, Bedford Corporation and Bedfordshire County Council. It was however revived in 1995 by the Bedford & Milton Keynes Waterways Trust.

Since 1995 the Bedford and Milton Keynes Waterways Trust has been campaigning to link the two waterways together. Their route, the core of a linear water park, envisages utilising the flooded former brick pits of Stewartby and Brogborough lakes. The 300ft high Brogborough hill is a major obstacle, and various proposed resolutions have included a tunnel, a Falkirk style wheel, or the innovative 'Brogborough Whirl', a spiral boat lift with two caisons which pass each other half way.

The Bedford and Milton Keynes Waterways Trust run a popular trip boat in Bedford, the *John Bunyan*, and have launched a second trip boat the *Electra*, at the Milton Keynes terminus of the proposed link, Campbell's Wharf.

The Iron Trunk Aqueduct crossing the Great Ouse at Cosgrove

1

THE RIVER GREAT OUSE KEMPSTON TO EARITH
The Bedford Ouse

Described travelling **downstream**

Narrowboat *Bleasdale* approaching the Head of Navigation

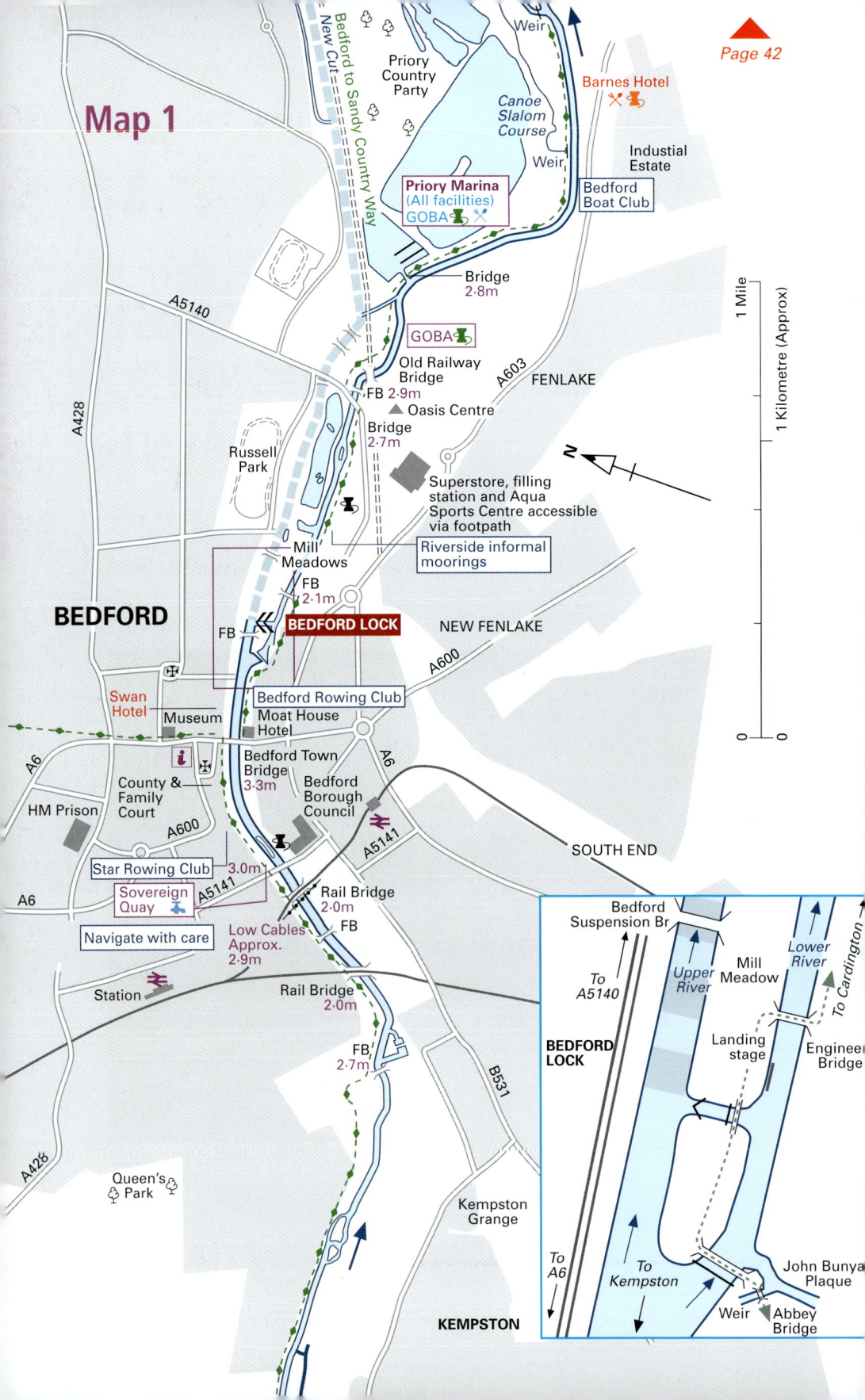

Map 1

Kempston to Bedford

Distance 2¼ miles
Time Less than 1 hour

River Great Ouse Kempston to Earith

Map 1 Kempston to Bedford

Lowest bridge Rail bridge 2·0m
Bedford Lock L 29·7m, W 3·3m, D1·1m, Head 3.0m (10'8")

Location	Lock width	Moorings and facilities								Victualling		
		Short stay	48hr	Long stay	Water point	Chemical disposal point	Pumpout	Refuse	Diesel	Shops	Pub	Café/restaurant
Sovereign Quay					🚰							
Borough Hall			☕							🧺	🍺	🍴
Riverside Park			☕							🧺	🍺	🍴
Bedford Lock	▯											
GOBA Fenlake Meadows (good for superstore)			☕							🧺		
Priory Marina			☕	☕	🚰	⬇	⛽	🗑	👤	🧺	🍺	🍴
Barnes Hotel		☕									🍺	🍴

RIVER GREAT OUSE

Navigation notes

The head of navigation is currently a low bridge across the river near the site of **Kempston Mill**, but is more realistically the landing stage a little way down river, just above which is the recommended turning point.

The river can be quite fast flowing here, particularly where it periodically narrows. There are often fallen trees and considerably more care and greater concentration are required than for the more languid lower sections. The area is popular with fishermen.

Heading downstream, houses gradually appear on the left bank, heralding the imminent arrival in **Bedford**. There are **two low railway bridges** to squeeze under, and modern flats on the right occupy the former site of **Bedford Britannia Ironworks**. To your left, out of sight, is the Charles Wells Brewery, which, for many years filled the air across Bedford with the smell of hops.

Passing under the **modern road bridge** which replaced a fine Victorian cast iron bridge (Prebend Street) you enter **Bedford**, and are immediately greeted on the right by **Borough Hall**, civic buildings opened in 1970 and considered a leading British example of the 'brutalist' style of architecture.

Initially obscured by the island, to the left is **Sovereign Quay**, which once provided visitor moorings. These have been moved to the right side of the river, in front of Borough Hall, but Sovereign Quay retains a boater's water point. Turn in in front of **Star Rowing Club**.

The new **Britannia Bridge** is a pedestrian bridge linking Bedford College to the town centre. To your left are the Grade II listed red brick **County and Family Courts**.

Bedford railway bridge heading downstream

Kempston Head of Navigation

Bedford railway bridge looking upstream

Bedford Bridge

We pass under **Bedford Bridge**, where the A6 once crossed the river. The present bridge dates to 1811, but there have been bridges on the site since at least 1224 when one was constructed from the rubble of the castle. J. M. W. Turner produced several paintings of the current bridge when it was still new.

Downstream of the bridge **Bedford Rowing Club** is on the right, and on the left the **Swan Hotel** with balustraded river frontage, past that is the Castle Mound, (built after 1100 by Henry I, and destroyed on the orders of Henry III in 1224), Higgins art gallery and museum.

Continuing downstream, the Victorian embankment was laid out in 1891. On the right is **Duck Mill Weir** with a white water canoe slalom course below, named after Etienne Stott, local boy and a gold medalist at the London Olympics in 2012.

Just beyond a footbridge, as you turn into the lock, you may catch a glimpse downstream of **Bedford Suspension Bridge**. This cost £32,000 when it was constructed in 1881. Just downstream is the **Butterfly Bridge**, another pedestrian bridge, opened in 1998 and which cost £370,000. It is interesting to speculate which bridge, in real terms, was the more costly.

Bedford Rowing Club

Butterfly Bridge

Bedford

Bedford Lock is at right angles to the river, and doesn't provide bollards for mooring upstream to open the top gate if it's shut, but a proposed lock refurbishment plans to improve moorings for locking. The lock itself is only 10'8" wide and won't accommodate two narrow boats side by side. Displayed in the lock is a silver coloured wheel. This was previously used to manually lift the guillotine gate prior to its electrification. This is a really pretty lock where you are guaranteed plenty of *gongoozlers* (onlookers). To your left is a Victorian Bandstand (where this author 'stole' his first kiss, long ago.)

You may come across the *John Bunyan*, the wide-beam trip-boat operated by the Bedford and Milton Keynes Waterways Trust. Wave and wish them luck, because when they are successful, one day boating from Bedford to Milton Keynes will be a 20 mile trip, not the current 185 mile, 82 lock, minimum 11 day journey.

We pass down onto the lower river, under probably the **lowest bridge you will encounter anywhere on the Great Ouse**. The headroom is not signed on the

Moorings and facilities

Town moorings opposite Sovereign Quay near Borough Hall (often still called by its former name, County Hall).

Water point at **Sovereign Quay** near Star Rowing Club.

Moorings at Riverside Park above the town bridge on the right bank, next to Bedford College and Borough Hall.

Further moorings on the lower river below the lock.

GOBA Fenlake Meadow moorings on right bank near the Oasis Centre pyramid. Popular for visiting superstore.

Priory Marina MK41 9DJ
Long and short term moorings and service.
All facilities including diesel and petrol.
☎ 01234 351931
GOBA arrangement in Priory Marina (one night free when you pay for a second night).

Other water users
There are two adult rowing clubs in Bedford, three schools rowing clubs and a canoe club. The waters are therefore at least as busy as in Cambridge. When moored you should be prepared to be disturbed by small boats and display vigilance and consideration when navigating. Remember 'power gives way to sail' - or in this instance 'to paddlers'.

Bedford Lock

Bedford is a pretty, historic, county market town. It boasts some notable Georgian architecture, but its general Victorian character is defined by its fine embankment, laid out in the 1890s.
There is much to see, do, and enjoy in Bedford, and it repays mooring for a couple of days.

Supermarkets include Iceland, Lidl, Marks & Spencer, Morrisons, Tesco, Sainsbury's, and Waitrose. There is also a Tesco Express and a Sainsbury's Local in the Town centre.
Of the major supermarkets, none are within comfortable walking distance of the moorings outside Borough Hall or on the lower river (when laden with shopping).
Out of town, Tesco in Cardington Road can be accessed from nearby **GOBA moorings**.

Town centre pubs serving food include The Embankment Hotel, The White Horse, The Pilgrim's Progress (Wetherspoon), The Slug and Lettuce, The Ship, The Castle, The Kings Arms, The Fox and Hounds and The Toby Carvery.

As you leave Bedford
Beefeater Priory Marina MK41 9RQ
☏ 01234 352883
The **Barnes Hotel** on the right bank half a mile after entrance to Priory Marina.
MK44 3SA
☏ 01234 270044

Bedford Oasis Centre swimming pool, Cardington Road
www.oasispool.bedford.gov.uk
and **Robinson Pool**
www.robinsonpool.bedford.gov.uk

The Higgins Bedford art gallery and museum is located in the historic buildings of Castle Brewery on Castle Street
www.thehigginsbedford.org.uk

South Bank Arts Centre houses Bedford College's gallery and theatre.
www.southbankarts.com

Markets
Bedford Charter Market
Wednesdays and Saturdays,
Harpur Square and St Paul's Square
Bedford Farmers Market
Second and fourth Thursday of the month in Harpur Square
'Handmade in Bedford' Market
Second Saturday of the month (March to December) in Harpur Square
Friday Market in Harpur Square,

Tourist Information Centre
St Paul's Church, St Paul's Square MK40 1SQ
☏ 01234 340163

Launderettes
Castle Road Launderette
129 Castle Rd MK40 3RF
1 mile from Town Bridge
Sparkle Clean Wash Laundrette
57 Tavistock St MK40 2RF

Public Transport
Bedford is on the main electrified railway line to London, nicknamed the 'Bed-Pan line'.
Buses run to Oxford and to Cambridge.

Boat trips
The *John Bunyan* is a 50 passenger trip boat which offers regular weekly cruises and private hire.
☏ 01946 690301
www.johnbunyanboat.org

Entrance to Priory Marina

bridge. This is because the river can rise or fall very quickly after rainfall upstream. It is a characteristic of some Great Ouse bridges not to sign a height, for this reason, but others do have height boards.

The river here is wide and slow flowing. There is an inlet to the left, at the back of the third of **Bedford's rowing clubs,** this one used by the local schools. The

Bedford Oasis centre pyramid

neighbouring weir featured, for many years, rollers for moving punts and heavy clinker built skiffs from one level of the river to the other. A water turbine for generating electricity has been installed in their place.

After a **road bridge** and a **pedestrian bridge** we pass under a **former railway bridge** which once carried the Bedford to Cambridge line, and which now forms part of the Ouse Valley Way and the Bedford to Sandy Country Way. The **large silvered pyramid** is home to Bedford Oasis Beach swimming pool (a 'fun' pool). The **GOBA moorings** on the right bank are convenient for the large Tesco Extra. Almost opposite is the entrance to **Priory Marina.**

After a long wide straight we slow to pass the moored boats of **Bedford Boat Club.** Next on the right bank, is the **Barnes Hotel and restaurant,** with very limited customer moorings. The Barnes

Barnes Hotel

offers attendees at functions the use of their day boat. Often the occupants are fuelled by champagne, and may be inexperienced boaters, and not particularly concentrating on navigation. Should you come across her, slowing down for, and giving the boat a wide berth, is recommended.

Walking and exploring

A path crosses the river on the Kempston footbridge which is currently the Head of Navigation, and joins the **Ouse Valley Way (OVW)**. After a short detour this joins the left bank of the river and accompanies it into **Bedford**.

The Ouse Valley Way footpath switches from the north bank to the south bank (righthand side travelling downstream) at the A5141 Prebend Street road bridge and continues riverside through an urban park, past a college under under **Bedford Town Bridge**.

After **Bedford Rowing Club** the path continues on the right bank near the river through parkland. You pass under a road, and the path immediately crosses the river on a former railway bridge. This part of the **Bedford to Sandy Country Way**, a National Cycle Route.

Local history

Bedford was a major river based trading centre in 18th century, but trade declined and by 1900 trade stopped and the locks were closed and allowed to fall into disrepair.

The River Ouse Locks Committee were granted responsibility in 1906 for Bedford to Great Barford.

The Ouse Drainage Board was formed in 1918, but had no powers to deal with navigation issues. The Great Ouse Catchment Board took over the navigation rights in 1930.

Ownership moved through the Great Ouse River Board (1952), the Great Ouse River Authority (1965), Anglian Water Authority (1973), National Rivers Authority (1989) and the Environment Agency (1996).

Ethnic diversity and multiculturalism

For over 100 years, Bedfordshire was the centre of the UK's brick-making industry. At its height, nearby Marston Vale was home to the world's biggest kiln and 167 chimneys, producing 500 million bricks per year. Brick making was hard, dirty work, and labour intensive. The brickworks attracted labour from around the world, some arriving as immigrants after WWII whilst others were former prisoners of war who had chosen to remain and make this country their home.

Former POWs also set up in other fields, notably restaurants and ice cream sales. Bedford gained the reputation of being one of the most ethnically diverse towns in the country. Today she remains one of the most diverse authorities in the east of England, with up to 100 different ethnic groups living within its boundaries. All of which makes for an enviably wide choice of cuisines when going out for a meal or take-away!

Navigation was finally restored in 1978, and is celebrated in the biennial **Bedford River festival** (see p.41) which has grown to be the second largest free outdoor event in the United Kingdom (after the Notting Hill Carnival).

John Bunyan (1628 - 1688) was imprisoned for 12 years in Bedford Gaol where he wrote *The Pilgrim's Progress from This World, to That Which Is to Come* (generally abbreviated to *Pilgrim's Progress*). This allegorical tale sold 100,00 copies during Bunyan's lifetime and has been translated into over 200 languages and to this day has never been out of print!

Other famous former residents include **Sir William Harpur** (1496 - 1574), in 1566 he and his wife Dame Alice gave an endowment to support certain charities including education. The resulting schools remain a large part of Bedford life. The notable prison reformer **John Howard** (1726 - 1780) also lived here.

Bedford County and Family Courts were constructed in 1881 by Alfred Waterhouse in the Gothic revival style. They are perhaps most famous for the trial of James Hanratty.

During WII East Anglia was home to many air bases, both British and American. The famous band leader, Glenn Miller, serving in the USAF, was stationed near Bedford, and gave his last public concert in Bedford Corn Exchange before he disappeared over the English Chanel in December 1944. There is a museum to him in Clapham, 4 miles north of Bedford.

Bedford Lock was restored and re-opened in 1956, but initially the opening height of the guillotine was restricted to prevent motor boats from reaching the upper river. This was to preserve this part of the river for rowing.

Monkey Island
Is 'Monkey Island', just below Bedford Rowing Club, a pleonasm? ('pleonasm' means two words used together which repeat each other, eg 'black darkness' or 'burning fire' - from the Greek pleon, meaning 'more; too much'). The name of the island derives, not from monkeys, but from the monks of one of the local abbeys - Elstow, or Bushmead, who owned the fishing rights. The word 'eyot' (also ait) means a small island in a river. So 'monkey' is a combination of 'monk' and 'eyot', and adding the word 'island' after it is a pleonasm - monk's island island. So good they named it twice!

Bedford River Festival

The festival began in 1978 to celebrate the re-opening of navigation to the town. Taking place in July every two years (on 'even' years) it has grown to be the 2nd largest outdoor event in the Country, surpassed in numbers only by the Notting Hill Carnival. Temporary mooring is permitted along the south side of the embankment. Booking in advance is necessary, but I've put Bedford River Festival on my 'not to be missed' list.

In 2020 the festival's biennial pattern was interrupted by the Covid-19 pandemic, but a festival was held in 2022 and it is planned to resume the two yearly pattern with the next festival in 2024.

Rowing regattas

Star New Year Head
Around 2nd Sunday in January

Bedford Eights and Fours Head
Around 2nd Sunday in February

Bedford Spring Fours and Small Boats Head
Generally around 1st Sunday in April

Bedford Regatta
Around 2nd Saturday in May

Star Regatta
Generally 2nd Saturday in June

Bedford Autumn Head
Generally around 2nd Sunday in October

Map 2

Page 46

Mill Farm
FB
Weir
WILLINGTON LOCK

10.0m

Gadsey Brook

Sewage Works

WILLINGTON

Danish Camp,
Day boat hire, coffee shop

10.0m

Cabins

10.0m

NOTE
There are no moorings between the old lock above Great Barford and the Sewage Works Bridge, Goldington.

Bedford to Sandy Country Way

Howbury Hall

A428

Road Bridge 6.2m

A421

Castle Dairy Farm
Weir
Bedford Castle Mill Airfield
CASTLE MILL LOCK
Risinghoe Castle (Motte)
Weir

River Great Ouse

Ouse Valley Way

1 Mile (Approx)
1 Kilometre (Approx)

Elm Farm Industrial Estate

A428

N

Sewage Works Bridge 2.6m

GOLDINGTON

Page 32

GOBA Goldington

New Cut

Navigation Channel

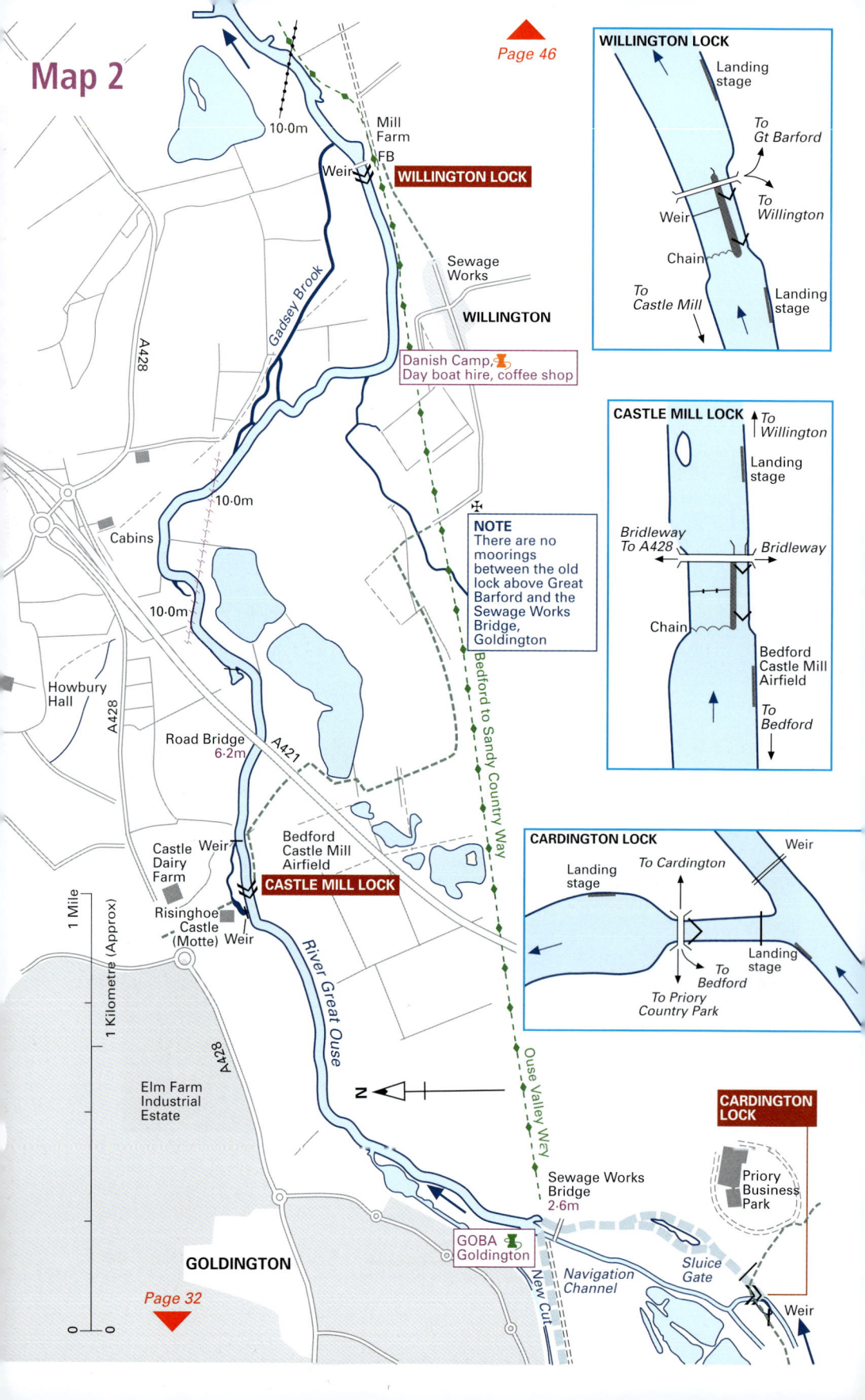

Sluice Gate

Priory Business Park

CARDINGTON LOCK

Weir

WILLINGTON LOCK

Landing stage
To Gt Barford
Weir
To Willington
Chain
To Castle Mill
Landing stage

CASTLE MILL LOCK

To Willington
Landing stage
Bridleway To A428 — Bridleway
Chain
Bedford Castle Mill Airfield
To Bedford

CARDINGTON LOCK

Landing stage
To Cardington
Weir
To Bedford
To Priory Country Park
Landing stage

Map 2

Cardington Lock to Willington Lock

Distance 4 miles
Time 1½ hours

River Great Ouse Kempston to Earith

Map 2 Cardington Lock to Willington Lock

Lowest bridge 2·6m
Cardington Lock L 28·5m, W 3·15m (10'4") D 1·5m Head: 2·75m
For boats over 3·15m (10'4") wide, Cardington Lock is the upstream limit of navigation
Castle Mill Lock L 29.5m, W 4·0m (13'1") D 1·2m, Head 4·3m
Willington Lock L 29·5m, W 4·0m (13'1") D 1·3m, Head 4·05m

Location	Lock width	Moorings and facilities								Victualling		
		Short stay	48hr	Long stay	Water point	Chemical disposal point	Pumpout	Refuse	Fuel	Shops	Pub	Café/restaurant
Cardington Lock	⬭											
GOBA Goldington			🏆							🧺		
Castle Mill Lock	⬭											
Danish Camp		📍										✕
Willington Lock	⬭											

RIVER GREAT OUSE 43

Navigation notes

After the Barnes Hotel, the next lock is **Cardington**. In summer local teenagers sometimes bathe off the downstream landing stage. I've always found them friendly, but it doesn't hurt to keep valuable items out of their sight. The top gate is an electrically operated 'guillotine' gate. This is the last time you will have the luxury of assistance from electricity at a lock until you reach Eaton Socon as the next four locks have V type manual gates top and bottom.

Half a mile beyond the lock, just downstream of the old railway bridge at Goldington, there is a short stretch of **GOBA moorings** on your left, which is probably your last chance to moor until you almost reach Great Barford.

On your left the **Elm Farm industrial estates** along Caxton Road mark the end of Bedford.

Castle Mill Lock

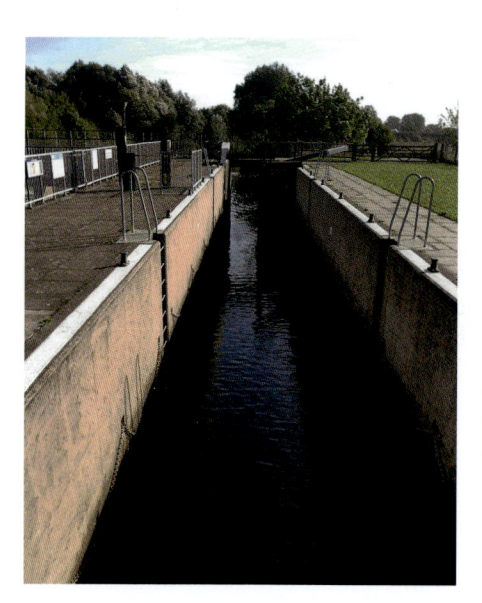

Castle Mill Lock moorings

Castle Mill Lock is the next lock. Personally I consider this probably the second worst lock to navigate (single handed and in the rain), in the entire English canal and river system - it is one of the most difficult and daunting locks in the country! (The dubious distinction of the worst, I reserve for Bath Deep Lock). Try to avoid single handed locking. This lock is very deep. Even when full, you need to climb down a ladder to reach your boat. The lock fills from the side (rather than the top gates) and it is difficult to tie your boat up securely. Let water in slowly! It is next to a weir, so when approaching the downstream landing stage care should be taken when stepping off the boat, and hold your rope securely!

Shortly after leaving Castle Mill Lock you will pass under the **Bedford bypass**. Anyone who remembers the previous strangulation of Bedford when all traffic had to pass through the town centre, including articulated lorries struggling to get around John Bunyan's statue on St Peter's Green, will know what a lifeline the opening of the bypass in 2009 provided to this county market town.

The land to the north starts to rise and there is a small collection of cabins on the left bank, behind which the OS map marks 'earthworks'.

Moorings and facilities

GOBA Goldington moorings left bank below old railway bridge.

Danish camp visitor centre
Bike and boat hire
Café/restaurant
www.danishcamp.co.uk

The Crown in Willington is a traditional village pub which serves food to eat in or takeaway
17 Station Road, MK44 3QH
☏ 01234 831024

Frosts Garden Centre on Sandy Road, **Willington** has café/restaurant
www.frostsgardencentres.co.uk

Under the **overhead electricity lines and a footbridge**, the river turns a corner on the edge of **Willington**. On the south bank lies **Danish Camp** *(see* Local history *below)*. Its visitor centre is based on a Norwegian style log cabin and includes a bar and restaurant. Their landing stages are fairly full with a trip boat (*The Artful Dodger*), and day hire boats, so cruisers wishing to visit the restaurant are advised to phone in advance ☏ **01234 838709**. The normal advisory caution around day hire boats is recommended.

Walking

As soon as you have crossed the river the **OVW** continues along the north bank of the river. It rejoins the **Bedford to Sandy Country Way** just past a sewerage works and abandons the course of the river, only picking it up 2 miles later at **Danish Camp**.

Local history

Cardington, is the home to two giant hangars, the largest enclosed spaces of their type in the country. They were constructed between WWI and WWII as airship 'sheds' and housed first the R31 and R32, and later the more famous R101 which tragically crashed in October 1930. Although airship production stopped after that disaster, one of the sheds has recently been used for the development of a new hybrid airship, and the other has been used to construct sets for a rich collection of films including *Chitty Chitty Bang Bang*, several *Dark Knight*, *Batman*, and *Star Wars* films, *Fantastic Beasts and Where to Find Them*, *Pinocchio*, and the most recent *Peter Pan* with Hugh Jackman.

Danish Camp lies on the south bank on the approach to Willington Lock. Danes or Vikings, using the river Ouse to attack Bedford around AD920, probably created a moated camp near here. It is truly remarkable to try and imagine Vikings dragging their longships up the river, and around or over obstacles in those pre-lock days. The Ouse was of course tidal at least as far as Ely, so they had less distance to travel then they would now. Prior to the Norman invasion (1066) Viking incursions were comparatively common - Peterborough Cathedral had been sacked in AD864. Nonetheless it would be another 800 years before the river was made 'navigable' to Bedford in 1689.

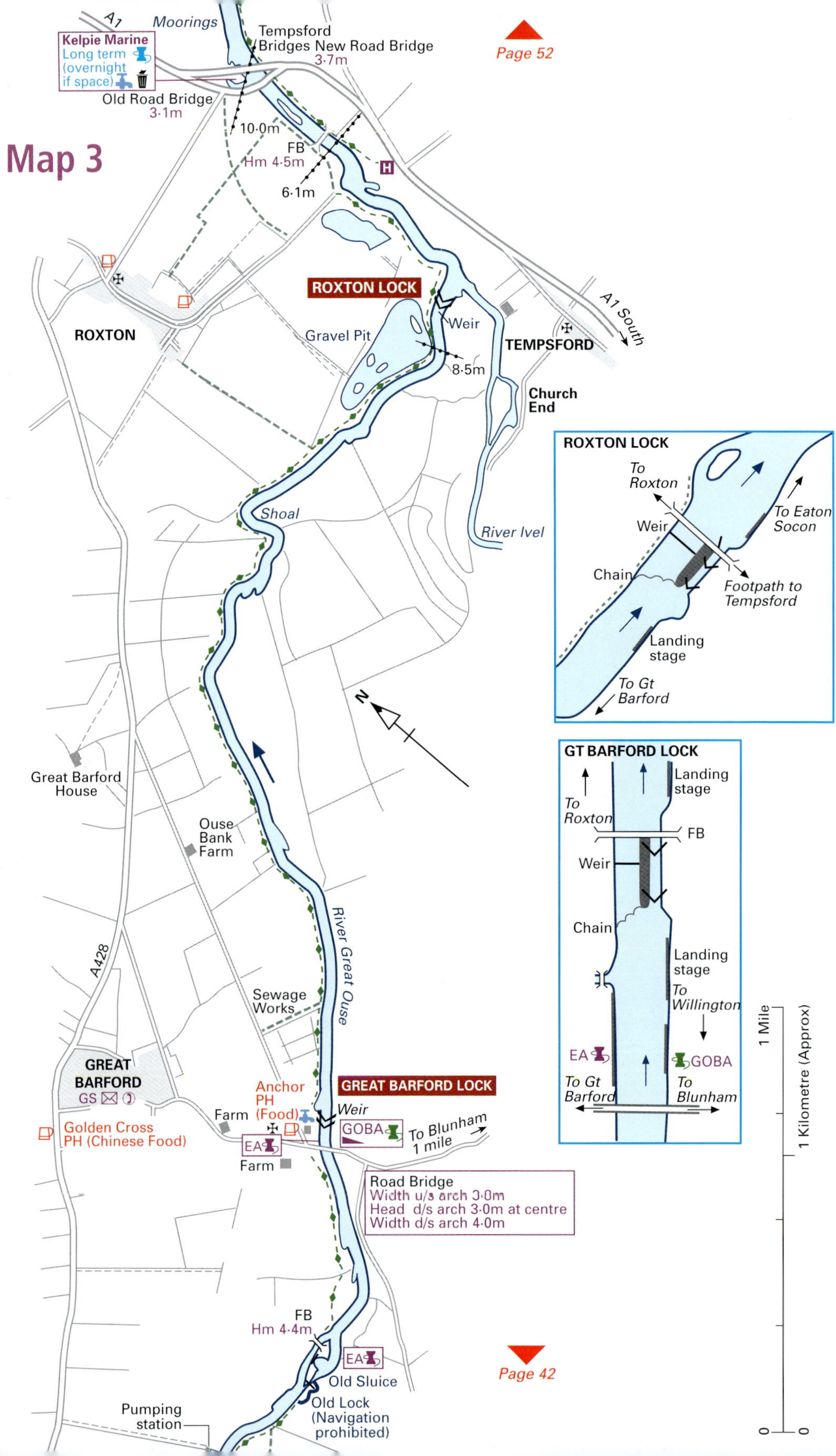

Map 3
A1
Moorings
Kelpie Marine
Long term
(overnight
if space)
Tempsford
Bridges New Road Bridge
3·7m
Old Road Bridge
3·1m
10·0m
FB
Hm 4·5m
6·1m
Page 52
ROXTON LOCK
Weir
Gravel Pit
8·5m
ROXTON
TEMPSFORD
A1 South
Church
End
Shoal
River Ivel
ROXTON LOCK
To
Roxton
Weir
Chain
To Eaton
Socon
Footpath to
Tempsford
Landing
stage
To Gt
Barford
N
GT BARFORD LOCK
Landing
stage
To
Roxton
FB
Weir
Chain
Landing
stage
To
Willington
EA
GOBA
To Gt
Barford
To
Blunham
Great Barford
House
Ouse
Bank
Farm
River Great Ouse
A428
Sewage
Works
GREAT
BARFORD
GS
Anchor
PH
(Food)
GREAT BARFORD LOCK
Weir
Farm
Golden Cross
PH (Chinese Food)
EA
GOBA
To Blunham
1 mile
Farm
Road Bridge
Width u/s arch 3·0m
Head d/s arch 3·0m at centre
Width d/s arch 4·0m
FB
Hm 4·4m
EA
Old Sluice
Old Lock
(Navigation
prohibited)
Pumping
station
Page 42
1 Mile
1 Kilometre (Approx)
0
0

Map 3

Great Barford Bridge to Tempsford Bridge

Distance 3 miles
Time 1½ hours

Map 3 Great Barford Bridge to Tempsford Bridge

Lowest bridge 3m Tempsford Old Road Bridge
Great Barford Lock L 26m, W 4·0m (13'1") D 1·2m Head 4·55m
Roxton Lock L 29·5m, W 4·0m (13'1") D 1·2m Head 2·75m

Location	Lock width	Moorings and facilities								Victualling		
		Short stay/visitor	48hr	Long stay	Water point	Chemical disposal point	Pumpout	Refuse	Fuel	Shops	Pub	Café/restaurant
EA old lock cut			🍺									
EA outside The Anchor PH Great Barford			🍺		🚰						🍺	✖
GOBA opposite Anchor PH Great Barford			🍺								🍺	✖
Great Barford Lock	◯											
Kelpie Marine			🍺	🍺	🚰			🗑				
Roxton Lock	◯											

RIVER GREAT OUSE

Navigation notes

About a third of a mile beyond **Willington Lock** there is an abandoned lock on the right bank, with **secluded EA moorings** at the entrance to a side channel ¼ mile further downstream - keep left and pass under a footbridge before arriving in **Great Barford**.

The attractive village of **Great Barford**, with its picture postcard riverside pub and church, offers the best access to the river Great Ouse between the towns of Bedford and St Neots and the river is enormously busy here. It is a Mecca for open water swimmers, canoeists, paddle-boarders, and in hot weather kids wanting a cooling splash. In summer the river is in use almost from dawn, right up to dusk.

The river is crossed by an early 15th-century, **seventeen arch bridge**. Several families of house martins have nested in its rough stonework, and they form quite a spectacle, swooping and darting to and from their nests when feeding their hungry young.

There are **moorings and a recently refurbished water point on the left bank outside the Anchor PH**, and **GOBA**

Abandoned lock above Great Barford Bridge

EA old lock moorings

Waterpoint on riverside green in front of The Anchor public house

The Anchor at Great Barford with All Saints church in the background

48 RIVER GREAT OUSE

Moorings and facilities

EA moorings by the old lock cut, right bank ½ mile before Great Barford Bridge (remote and looks idyllic).

EA moorings left bank **outside The Anchor PH, Great Barford.**

GOBA moorings right bank between lock and bridge, **Great Barford,** opposite The Anchor PH.

The Anchor at **Great Barford**, MK44 3LF
Hugely popular village pub serving food. Moorings outside and on opposite bank, but often fully taken in summer.
☏ 01234 870364

The Golden Cross at **Great Barford**, MK44 3JD ¾ mile from river
☏ 01234 87172

moorings on the opposite bank. The lock is popular with walkers and a crowd of *gongoozlers* is common in good weather. I've been known to split them into two rival teams, and challenged them to compete pushing open the heavy lock gates for me!

Below Great Barford the river banks become quite overgrown. The days of the 'lengthsman' who maintained a reach of the river (between locks) are long gone, and in some places only the middle third of the river is navigable because of fallen trees. This offers favoured habitat for heron and kingfishers and they can

Great Barford Bridge

RIVER GREAT OUSE

often be spotted. The heron flaps languorously away from the approaching boat, whereas the kingfisher darts past in a flash of electric blue.

Roxton Lock at **Tempsford** is the last of the four locks which feature manually operated V gates at the upstream end, rather than electrically operated 'guillotine' gates. One assumes that because of their remoteness it would have been prohibitively expensive to bring electricity for a 'guillotine' gate to these lock, but as each of the locks is parallel to a weir one wonders if in modern times they couldn't now generate their own electricity from the water going over the weir.

As you leave **Roxton Lock,** you are rudely reminded of the hustle and bustle of modern life as the A1 approaches from the east. Immediately below the lock the **River Ivel** (see opposite) joins. We pass the old Anchor PH, a once great coaching inn on the Great North road. Its moorings appear permanently occupied by residential boats, and it no longer operates as a pub but as a private club.

The north-bound A1 carriageway crosses the river on a handsome Grade II listed bridge dated 1820. This is mostly dressed sandstone quarried at Sandy, but detailed with Bramley (Leeds) fall stone. Shortly after the south-bound carriageway crosses on a modern concrete bridge. The two dramatically contrasting bridges sandwich between them **Kelpie Marine boat yard.**

Kelpie Marine, looking downstream through the arches of the 1820 Tempsford Bridge

Walking

Shortly after **Danish Camp** the **Bedford to Sandy Country Way** departs to the South, and the **OVW** continues next to the river to **Great Barford**. After Great Barford the OVW closely follows the north bank of the river (left hand travelling downstream) until **Tempsford**. Just short of the A1 the path turns abruptly west, and abandons the river until **Eaton Socon Lock**.

Local history

Great Barford was the Head of Navigation up to the mid seventeenth century and it boasted several wharves and many pubs. The 17 arch stone bridge was constructed in the fifteenth century. In 1777 it was repaired and widened using bricks.

Tempsford Bridge.
During a long period of imprisonment in Bedford Gaol (1661 to 1673) the Puritan preacher John Bunyan wrote the famous allegorical novel Pilgrim's Progress. This describes a metaphorical journey from the 'City of Destruction' (this world), to the 'Celestial City' (Heaven). The narrator travels through many perilous places including the Hill of Difficulty, the Valley of the Shadow of Death, the Village of Morality, the River of Death, Difficulty Hill and the Slough of Despond, a boggy mire-like swamp full of pilgrims' doubts, fears, temptations, lusts, shames, guilts, and sins. For those who like to match the metaphorical places with real life locations, it is now generally accepted that the 'The Souls' Slough' on the Great North Road near Tempsford was the real life model for Bunyan's Slough of Despond. As you pass under the road at Tempsford, I urge

> **Tempsford Museum**
>
> Tempsford museum is an absolute gem, and well worth visiting. Approaching its 10th anniversary, and situated in the village hall, it is a fantastic record of local life which includes as varied events as a battle in 917 against the Danes, and the WWII headquarters of the SOE (Special Operation Executive).
>
> Check opening times before visiting, nearest moorings are Great Barford, a three mile walk away.
>
> **Tempsford Hall** was very important in WWII, hosting the Special Operations Executive (SOE) as an agent reception and pre-flight preparation centre. The SOE included some of the very bravest agents who conducted clandestine reconnaissance, espionage, and sabotage, assisting resistance movements in occupied territories, risking torture and execution.

you to 'keep your chin up', banish despondent thoughts and look forward to that celestial town of hope ahead of you - St Neots!

19th and 20th century bridges carry the A1 over the river Great Ouse north west of Tempsford. This poses the question 'how did they cross the river before the bridges were built?'. The name 'Tempsford' provides the simple answer. The river was crossed by a ford right up to the end of the eighteenth century.

Any ford that was shallow enough to permit carriages to pass through, would not have been deep enough to facilitate the passage of commercial river traffic laden with grain and other cargos. When there were boats waiting to pass, a 'flash weir' was built up downstream, holding the water back so the level of the river rose. This was generally done at night.

RIVER GREAT OUSE

The earliest known representation of the first bridge carrying the Great North road across the river at Tempsford
Courtesy of Tempsford Parish Council

When there was enough water the boats would pass through, and then the temporary dam was removed, allowing the waters to fall again. During this damming the road would have been closed. **Tempsford Staunch** was constructed in 1674 and only finally removed in the 1970s. No evidence of the staunch remains today, but it may have disappeared under the concrete bridge carrying the south bound A1.

It is hard to imagine that a road which nowadays sees daily vehicle movements in the hundreds of thousands was regularly closed to allow boat traffic. One wonders whether the famous highwayman, Dick Turpin, who frequently used this section of the Great North road, would even recognise it.

The River Ivel

The River Ivel runs for 21 miles from its source at springs near **Baldock**, through **Biggleswade** to its confluence with the River Great Ouse at **Tempsford**. The river has a long navigation history. In the mid 1700s construction was initiated to make it navigable from Tempsford and it consequently had a prosperous and useful life well into the 1850s as a commercial artery. However, the coming of the Great Northern Railway caused its gradual decline. Today, it is the resort of canoeists and anglers and the Kingfisher Way initiative provides well-documented information about the attractive 21 mile walk along its banks.

It is currently navigable by small powered craft to **Church End, Tempsford**, and is potentially navigable to **Blunham**.

The River Ivel near its confluence with the Great Ouse

Walking

A path follows the River Ivel from its junction with the Great Ouse all the way to Biggleswade. Occasionally it leaves the river, but almost immediately returns.

Local history

The river was made navigable following an Act of 1757. Locks were constructed at Tempsford, Blunham, South Mills and Sandy. Biggleswade was supplied with coal, and the navigation was extended to Shefford in 1823 with a further locks at Biggleswade, Holme, Stanford and Clifton. Navigation on the canalised river was abandoned in 1876 when a dam was built across it at Sandy. The remains of Holme Lock remain, close to Jordans Mill, an historic attraction.

The derelict Holme sluice and lock near Biggleswade

RIVER GREAT OUSE 53

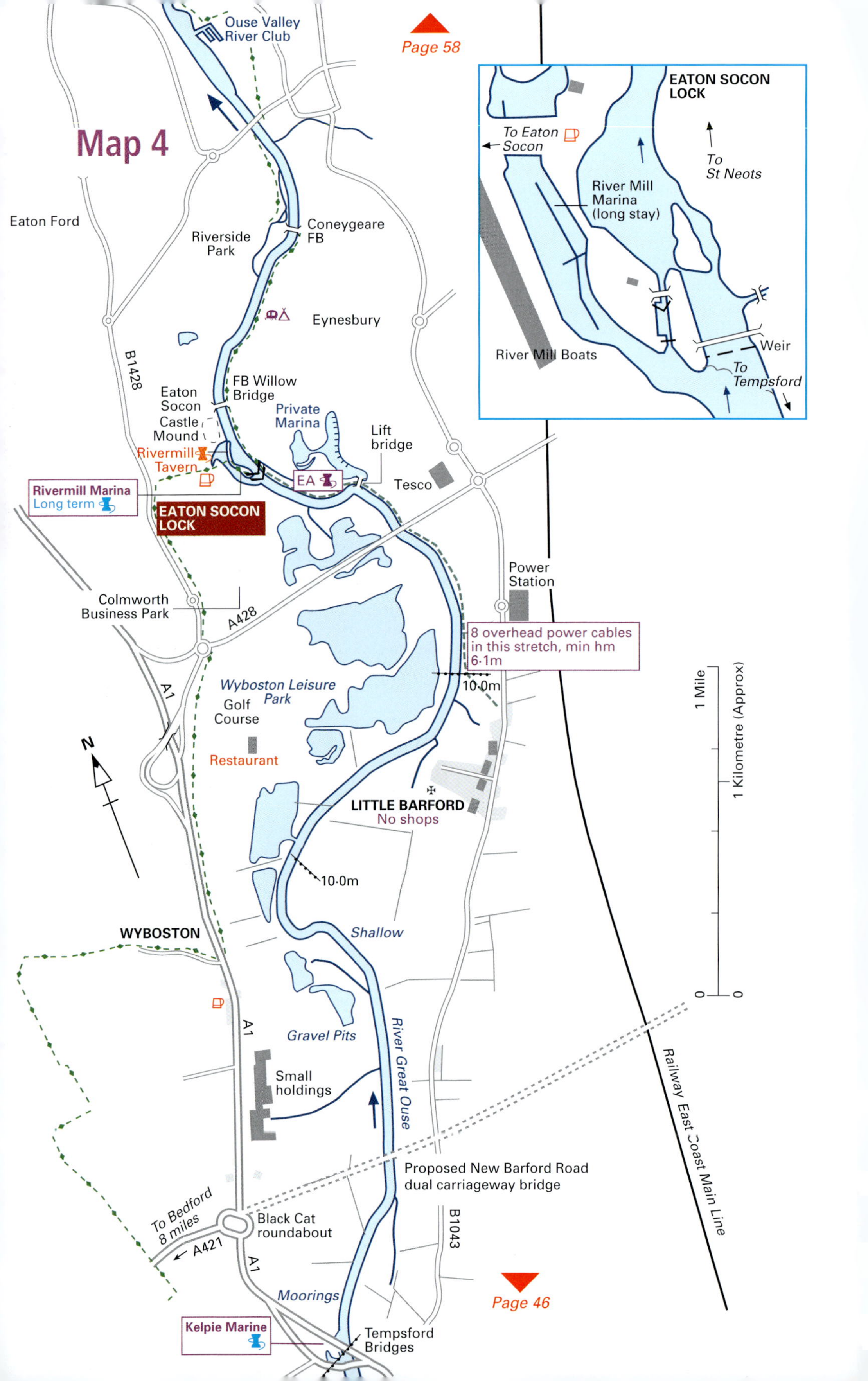

Map 4
Ouse Valley River Club
Page 58
EATON SOCON LOCK
To Eaton Socon
To St Neots
River Mill Marina (long stay)
River Mill Boats
Weir
To Tempsford
Eaton Ford
Riverside Park
Coneygeare FB
Eynesbury
B1428
FB Willow Bridge
Eaton Socon Castle Mound
Private Marina
Lift bridge
Rivermill Tavern
EA
Tesco
Rivermill Marina
Long term
EATON SOCON LOCK
Power Station
Colmworth Business Park
A428
8 overhead power cables in this stretch, min hm 6·1m
10·0m
Wyboston Leisure Park
Golf Course
A1
Restaurant
N
LITTLE BARFORD
No shops
10·0m
1 Mile
1 Kilometre (Approx)
0
0
Shallow
WYBOSTON
A1
Gravel Pits
River Great Ouse
Small holdings
Railway East Coast Main Line
Proposed New Barford Road dual carriageway bridge
To Bedford 8 miles
A421
Black Cat roundabout
B1043
A1
Moorings
Page 46
Kelpie Marine
Tempsford Bridges

Map 4

Tempsford Bridge to Eaton Socon Lock

Distance 4½ miles
Time 1¾ hours

Map 4 Tempsford Bridge to Eaton Socon Lock

Lowest bridge 3·1m Tempsford Old Road Bridge
Eaton Socon Lock (D shaped): L 31·5m, W at mouth 3·3m (10'9") D 1·6m H 2·7m

Location	Lock width	Moorings and facilities								Victualling		
		Short stay	48hr	Long stay	Water point	Chemical disposal point	Pumpout	Refuse	Fuel	Shops	Pub	Café/restaurant
EA Eaton Socon			🪧							🛒		
Eaton Socon Lock	⦀											
River Mill Tavern			🪧								🍺	🍴
River Mill Marina					🪧	Facilities for longterm moorings only						

RIVER GREAT OUSE 55

Navigation notes

After **Kelpie Marine** the river widens again, and as the roar of the A1 disappears you are treated to views across open countryside. After the river passes under electricity pylons, the neatly manicured lawns of **Wyboston Leisure Park golf course** to the west replace the meadows. The golf course eventually gives way to flooded gravel pits which are host to a variety of water based fun activities.

St Neots Rowing Club

Little Barford power station lies to the east, this was formerly the site of two coal fired power stations which were demolished in 1989. You may spot the remains of the structures which took water from the river to cool the towers, and returned the (now warmer) water back to the river. These warmer waters prevented the river from freezing during cold winters and the Cambridge University rowing crews used to visit the Great Ouse to practise, when the river Cam was frozen. There are rumours that a crocodile, bought as a pet, but which outgrew its welcome, was released into these temperate waters in the 1960s and survived for several years!

Eaton Socon Lock with a 'pregnant' or 'side' bay

56 RIVER GREAT OUSE

Moorings and facilities

EA Eaton Socon moorings above Eaton Socon Lock.

River Mill Marina, Eaton Socon, St Neots, PE19 8GW
Long term moorings.
☎ 01480 219612

The current power station on the site is a combined cycle gas turbine with a capacity sufficient to meet the electricity demands of over half a million households.

Beyond the power station, the appearance of commercial buildings announces your approach to **St Neots**, and the **A428 St Neots bypass** crosses the river.

New houses appear on the right bank, part of **Eynesbury**. Behind the houses is a large Tesco Extra. A lift bridge leads into an extensive, private mooring only marina. The nearest public moorings are the **EA moorings, also on the east bank**, above Eaton Socon Lock. From here it is a ¾ mile walk to Tesco.

Eaton Socon Lock is set at an angle off the river. To access the upstream lock moorings you pass the weir and the lock - so requiring you to reverse backwards from the moorings to enter the lock.

Immediately below the lock is the popular **River Mill** pub and restaurant. There are limited pub moorings, though the downstream lock moorings are probably more extensive than solely necessary for the lock. The pub welcomes boaters.

The River Mill at **Eaton Socon**, PE19 8GW, is a popular food pub with outside eating area.
☎ 01480 139 612

In **Eaton Socon** there are a number of pubs and former coaching inns, including The Miller's Arms, The Crown, The White Horse, The Old Sun, The Wagon and Horses, and The George and Dragon.

Eaton Socon has a range of shops including Tesco Express (¼ mile from River Mill PH) and a post office in the village.
Colmworth Business Park is approximately ¾ mile from the lock, near the A428 roundabout, and includes Aldi, KFC, Lidl, Screwfix and B&Q. On the other (east) side of the river there is a large Tesco Extra, about a ¾ mile walk from the lock moorings.

Walking

Between **Tempsford** and **Eaton Socon** lock there is no official riverside path.

The **Ouse Valley Way** rejoins the river at **Eaton Socon Lock** and follows it along its right bank (right hand travelling downstream) through a campsite, before crossing back across the river on a long pedestrian bridge.

Local history

Little Barford was once on the river's edge. There was a ferry, but crossing could be quite dangerous. In 1297 four people drowned while trying to cross, and a few years later the ferry man drowned. The construction of bridges at Great Barford and St Neots led to the ferry trade falling off, the village next to the river declined, and now only the church remains there.

Map 5

LITTLE PAXTON

Paxton Pits *No mooring*

Page 66

Gravel Pit

Shallow about 1.0m 6.1m

To Huntingdon

Sewage Works

Bridge 2.9m

6.1m

10.0m

ST NEOTS LOCK

Sluice

Island Common

ST NEOTS 'PAPER MILL' LOCK

To Little Paxton

Lock gates

To St Neots

Turn left to lock

Navigable for small cruisers for about 1 mile

River Kym

A1

Crosshall Marine Overnight/longterm

Priory Hill Park

N

St Neots Station

Golf Course

Lammas Meadow

B1041

B1043

To Cambridge 17 miles

A The Bridge House

B1048

Ouse Valley River Club

Rowing club & council offices

B1428

Priory Centre

ST NEOTS

Regatta Meadow

Informal public moorings

St Neots Bridge 2.8m

Hen Brook

St Neots Marina Longterm

EATON FORD

EYNESBURY

East Coast Main Line Railway

Riverside Park

Coneygeare FB

Ernulf School

Cricket Ground

Willow Br

Ouse Valley Way

B1043

B1046

Castle Mound

Rivermill Tavern

Sluices

Marina (private)

EATON SOCON

Rivermill Marina Long term Shops

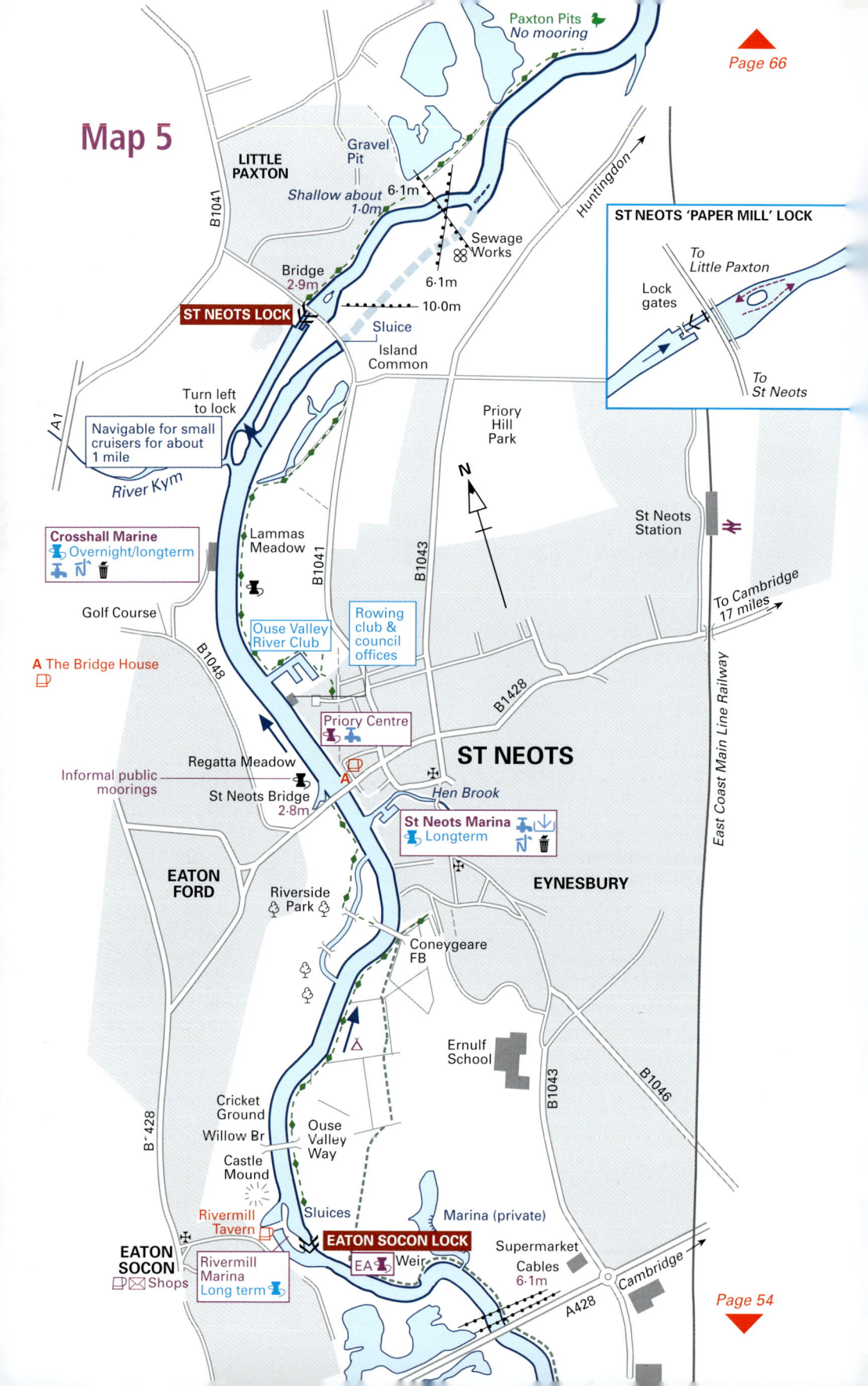

EATON SOCON LOCK EA

Weir

Supermarket

Cables 6.1m

B 428

A428

Cambridge

Page 54

Map 5

Eaton Socon Lock to St Neots Lock

Distance 3 miles
Time 1 hour 10 min

Map 5 Eaton Socon Lock to St Neots Lock

Lowest bridge St Neots Bridge 2·8m

Eaton Socon Lock (D shaped)
L 31·5m, W at mouth 3·3m (10'9") D 1·6m, H 2·7m

St Neots Lock L 32·9m, W 3·3m (10'9") D 1·05m Head 3·2m

Location	Lock width	Moorings and facilities								Victualling		
		Short stay	48hr	Long stay	Water point	Chemical disposal point	Pumpout	Refuse	Fuel	Shops	Pub	Café/restaurant
Eaton Socon Lock	000											
St Neots Marina				🏺	🚰	⬇	⛽	🗑				
EA Priory Centre			🏺		🚰					🧺	🍺	🍴
Regatta Meadow			🏺							🧺	🍺	🍴
St Neots Common			🏺									
Crosshall Marine (facilities for customers only)			🏺	🏺	🚰	⬇		🗑				
St Neots Lock	00											

Navigation notes

Downstream of the River Mill pub at Eaton Socon, on the left bank, are the earthwork remains of the former Eaton Socon Castle, a Norman construction.

The **Willow Bridge** crosses the river shortly downstream of the castle mound. Constructed in 2011, the bridge allows the school children of the Eaton Socon, a western district of St Neots, easier access to the town's two secondary schools, both of which lie on the east side of the river.

Beyond the Willow Bridge there is a popular **campsite** on the right bank. You are likely to encounter either fishermen, or children playing in the water.

You then come to **St Neots Riverside Park** on the left bank. This includes a skate board park, largely built by its users, this is one of the best and largest facilities of its kind in the country.

Next you will pass under the **Coneygeare footbridge**. In 2010 the current steel structure replaced a wooden bridge which had claimed the distinction of being the 'largest wooden single span bridge in the country', until it fell victim to that curse of wood - it rotted away.

A pub called The Coneygeare stood beside the playing field area from the 1970s but it was closed and demolished in 2002. The name 'Coneygeare' is long standing and derives from the French for a place to keep and breed rabbits (the French having introduced rabbits to the country after the Norman Conquest).

Below Coneygeare, moored boats on the right bank announce your arrival at **St Neots Marina** (formerly known as Brearley's). **Hen Brook** joins the river at what was once commonly known as Houseboat Corner *(see* Local History below*)*. The source of my 'crocodile in the river' story also tells another unproven tale of a 1960s group of burglars who robbed houses bordering Hen Brook and used a punt as their get-away vehicle. Perhaps an unfortunate encounter with the crocodile put an end to their nefarious activities.

St Neots

Downstream of the marina, there are **moorings on the west bank** immediately above St Neots Bridge, however some moorers may be uncomfortable with the proximity of the many visitors to that part of the Riverside Park and the nearby car park, which sometimes attracts night time 'boy racers'.

EA pontoon moorings looking upstream from the Priory Centre towards St Neots Bridge

St Neots is a thriving market town - the largest town in Cambridgeshire. With good moorings it rewards staying a day or two.

St Neots has a full range of **shops**, including several supermarkets. **Waitrose** is close to the **Priory Centre Moorings**. There is a **Co-op** less than one mile way (but up a steep hill) and a Lidl less than ½ mile away. St Neots' major supermarket, Tesco Extra, is over 1½ miles away and perhaps better accessed by foot from Eaton Socon.

St Neots boasts a range of **restaurants and take-aways**. Central pubs serving food include The Weeping Ash, The Bridge House, The Barley Mow, The Coach House, Brook & Barter, The Hyde Park.

Slightly further out are The Eaton Oak (Eaton Ford) and The Anchor in Little Paxton

Markets
General market every Thursday, Market Square Farmers' market second and fourth Saturday of every month in the Market Square.

Swimming pool at One Leisure St Neots, PE19 2SA
☎ 01480 388111

Launderette
Kleanco dry cleaners and laundry (service wash) 28a Hardwick Rd, Eynesbury, PE19 2UE
¾ mile

Tourist Information Centre in St Neots Museum, The Old Court, 8 New Street, St Neots, Cambs, PE19 1AE
☎ 01480 388788

Public transport
St Neots is on the main East Coast railway line. Buses: X5 Milton Keynes to Cambridge.

Moorings and facilities

Short mooring immediately **above the town bridge**, on the left hand bank.

EA pontoon moorings outside the imposing Priory Centre. There is a public water point on the pontoon. Space is not reserved for using this waterpoint.

Regatta Meadow moorings, opposite Priory Centre on the left bank.

St Neots Common or Lammas Meadow, on the right bank.

St Neots Marina, PE19 2BW
Long term moorings, pump-out.
☎ 01480 472411

Crosshall Marine St Neots, PE19 7GE
Overnight and residential moorings, repairs and boat sales.
☎ 01480 472763

Other river users
St Neots has a rowing club, canoe club, and dragon boat club, so all the usual consideration to small, unpowered vessels should be given.

St Neots Priory Centre moorings (with waterpoint) from Regatta Meadow on the opposite bank

RIVER GREAT OUSE 61

Immediately downstream of the **St Neots Bridge** there are **EA pontoon moorings outside the Priory Centre** (with water point). Sadly space isn't reserved for boats wishing to fill up, so you need to take the opportunity to access the water point, if it becomes available.

There are alternative moorings on the opposite side on **Regatta Meadow**. These moorings are suspended when there is racing on the river. These are more peaceful than the moorings upstream of the bridge on the same side of the river. Both are convenient for the town. Further moorings can be found downstream of **Ouse Valley River Club** on the right bank, on **St Neots Common**. Parts of Island Common and Lammas Meadow are SSSI.

St Neots Lock at Little Paxton, often called the Paper Mill lock

Onwards downstream of Crosshall Marine on the left bank, access to **St Neots Lock** is down the next sidechannel on the left, approximately 100m after the end of the boats moored at **Crosshall Marine**. There is a directional sign, but in summer months it can be obscured by reeds. You turn in front of some modern flats, built on the site of a former paper mill. Locals still refer to the lock as the 'Paper Mill lock'.

The **down stream lock moorings** are the other side of the busy B1041 road. Encountering a road may be something of a culture shock after many miles of rural cruising, and you should remember to take care crossing it. The lock is comparatively unusual on the Great Ouse in that the guillotine gate is at the downstream end, in the manner of the locks on the River Nene.

There is an island immediately below the lock with a poorly signed one way system. Downstream traffic should pass to the right (east) of the island, but this isn't often adhered to. Boats with deeper draughts may be better advised going straight on.

After the island, you will pass a row of boats moored at the back of houses. Most of these feature rising flood moorings, indicative of the volatility of the river after winter rain. About ½ mile below the lock the waters that had gone over the weir rejoin on the right hand side, and the river widens again.

Below St Neots Lock, as a second channel joins from the east, signs on the west bank announce 'Paxton Pits - No Mooring'. Visitors to the nature reserve shouldn't be discouraged, there are **GOBA moorings downstream** for visitors at Great Paxton.

Walking

The **OVW** travels down the left bank through **Riverside Park**, before once again returning to the right bank across St Neots town bridge. After a short section through town, it finds the river again on **St Neots' Common** (Lammas meadow) and follows the common, briefly leaving the river, until it joins Mill Lane, a minor road which leads to St Neots Lock. The **Ouse Valley Way** continues on the left bank, most of the time next to the river, past **Paxton Pits** and all the way to **Offord Lock**.

Regattas

St Neots Small Boats Head of River (rowing)
1st Sunday in October

St Neots Regatta (rowing)
Two day event generally last weekend in July

St Neots Dragon Boat Festival
Usually held 3rd weekend in August

These events are great fun, and worth watching. However navigating through them can be difficult, and is best avoided. If you do, always take instructions from marshals, and be prepared to wait patiently for races to finish before you proceed. Please remember that crews may have spent weeks training for the event they are finally taking part in, and don't want all that practice wasted because of one boat owners desire to avoid only a few minutes waiting.

IWA Festival of Water, held in St Neots in 2018

Local history

St Neots takes its name from a Cornish saint. Neot was a 9th century saint and friend of King Alfred. In 920AD the people of the Cambridgeshire town (then called Eynesbury) stole the relics of Saint Neot from a village of the same name in Cornwall, in an unorthodox attempt to boost tourism and increase the popularity of their priory. The name clearly came with the bones!

The first **St Neots Bridge** was built in 1580, possibly with stone from the Benedictine priory. The old bridge was demolished in 1964 and replaced with the current concrete structure. For many years St Neots Bridge formed the border between the neighbouring counties of Bedfordshire and Huntingdonshire. In old photographs the old bridge looks a glorious construction, but unusually was constructed only at one end in stone. It would be indiscreet to report which of the rival councils opted for the cheaper brick option.

In 1648 the **Battle of St Neots** took place. Although little more than a skirmish towards the end of the English Civil War (1642-1651), the victors (Parliament) declared a Public Holiday in celebration.

In the late 17th Century an exquisite jewelled Anglo Saxon object was found in Somerset, with the image of a man believed to be St Neot, and the words *'Alfred had me made'* incised in its gold mount. **The Alfred Jewel**, as it is called, takes pride of place in Oxford's Ashmolean Museum, and it is reproduced in coloured cobbles in St Neots' market square.

A famous resident was James Toller, the 'Eynesbury Giant', who lived between 1798 and 1818 and grew to be 8'6" tall! When he died, James was buried inside the local church, rather than in the graveyard, to prevent his body being stolen. In view of the local track record for stealing bones, this may have been a wise precaution!

St Neots became an important coaching centre situated on the Great North Road. It has the second largest market square in the country (only beaten by Nottingham) and in the 18th and 19th century coaching inns grew up around it, including the Cross Keys Hotel, Old Falcon Hotel and New Inn.

Just upstream of the St Neots Bridge is **Gill's Houseboat corner**. In 1887 Charles Gill had the wooden bridge over Hen Brook built, and converted an Ouse barge into a houseboat, Iris, where he lived. He built further houseboats which he rented out as holiday accommodation. Charles retired in 1922

Alfred Jewel mosaic official opening in 1999

and sold the business. In 1947 it was sold on again to Alan and Jean Brearley who developed St Neots Marina. It is still in the same family.

In 1895 **St Neots Spa** was opened at **Little Paxton**. It was intended to attract Londoners to visit by train. Its claims to benefit health were largely based on the alleged cure of a dog with sores bathing in water from a spring near the paper mill. The bottled water from this spring was promoted under the name 'Neotia'. The ambition was to create an East Anglian equivalent of Tunbridge Wells. The enterprise was not successful and by the end of the century there were already complaints that the site had become an eyesore.

At the beginning of the 20th century there were two bathing places in the river, one near the Coneygeare, and the other at Island Common.

St Neots unexpectedly found itself the centre of international media attention in 1935 when the world's first quads were born here. All 4 attended a celebratory event in 2015 at St Neots Museum.

There's only ever been one British Prime Minister assassinated in office. In 1812 Spencer Perceval was fatally shot in the lobby of the House of Commons by St Neots resident John Bellingham. Myra Chowins, a local historian, once observed to me: 'folks round here are hard to upset, but if you do, the results can be serious. St Neots killed a Prime Minister, and Huntingdon a King!' (referring to former Huntingdon resident Oliver Cromwell and the beheading of Charles I).

RIVER GREAT OUSE 65

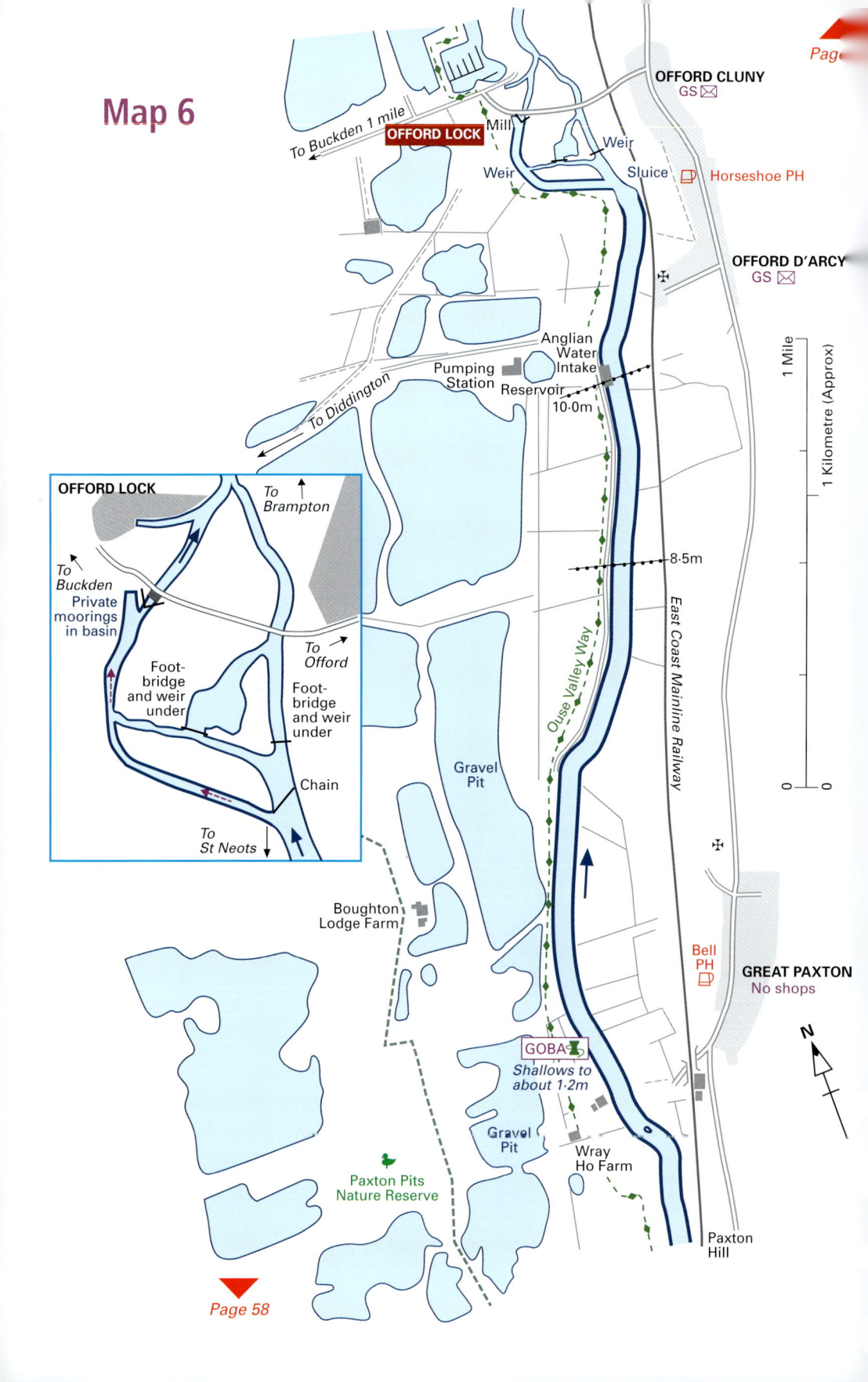

Map 6

To Buckden 1 mile →

OFFORD LOCK

Mill
Weir
Weir
Sluice

OFFORD CLUNY GS ✉

Horseshoe PH

OFFORD D'ARCY GS ✉

Pumping Station
Reservoir
Anglian Water Intake
10.0m

← To Diddington

8.5m

Ouse Valley Way

East Coast Mainline Railway

1 Mile
1 Kilometre (Approx)

OFFORD LOCK (inset)

To Brampton ↗
← To Buckden
Private moorings in basin
Foot-bridge and weir under
To Offord →
Foot-bridge and weir under
Chain
↓ To St Neots

Gravel Pit

Boughton Lodge Farm

Bell PH

GREAT PAXTON
No shops

GOBA
Shallows to about 1.2m

Gravel Pit

Wray Ho Farm

Paxton Pits Nature Reserve

Paxton Hill

N ↗

▼ Page 58

Map 6

Great Paxton to Offord Lock

Distance 2 miles
Time 50 min

Map 6 Great Paxton to Offord Lock

Lowest bridge 2·5m Offord Lock Bridge
Offord Lock L 30·5m, W 3·4m (11'1") D 1·05m, Head 2·7m

Location	Lock width	Moorings and facilities								Victualling		
		Short stay	48hr	Long stay	Water point	Chemical disposal point	Pumpout	Refuse	Fuel	Shops	Pub	Café/restaurant
GOBA Great Paxton			🍺									
Offord Lock	⌇										🍺	🍴

RIVER GREAT OUSE 67

Navigation notes

Approaching **Great Paxton** the **East Coast mainline railway** converges with the right bank. It will shadow the river all the way to Huntingdon, but generally is far enough away for the noise not to intrude.

A mile or so on, after a line of boats moored on the left bank, you come to the **GOBA moorings** from which **Paxton Pits** nature reserve is signposted.

On the right bank you pass two mysterious signs, all writing sun-bleached away. These look like 'lost' bus stops, but presumably warned of something passing under the river at this point. It is known that a major electricity cable, supplying St Neots, crosses the river somewhere around here so it would be a wise precaution to avoid anchoring between the posts.

The imposing concrete water management structure on the left bank is **Anglian Water's intake and pumping station** which supplies water to Graham Water reservoir 4 miles away.

Anglian Water pumping station

St Peter's Church Offord D'Arcy

Nearly 2 miles beyond the GOBA moorings, the slender spire of **St Peter's Church, Offord D'Arcy**, appears to the east. The railway passes so close to the church that one wonders if the vicar has to temporarily halt his sermon every time a high speed train roars past!

On the approach to **Offord Lock** the river divides. The navigation channel is to the west (left). To the west of the lock is the former site of **Buckden flour mill**. Old mill buildings and complementary new buildings constructed in similar style now provide homes in a picturesque setting. Immediately to the left of the lock the former dock provides moorings for residents.

Access to the lock's V gate is through the front garden of the neighbouring house - don't worry, this is normal practice, but do make sure you leave their gate closed.

Downstream lock moorings, like at St Neots Lock, are the other side of a road, so care is once again advised when crossing.

1 mile from the lock moorings is the village of **Buckden**.

Moorings and facilities

GOBA 'Paxton Pits' (Gt Paxton) moorings

The Bell PH on the High Street, **Great Paxton**
☎ 01480 700 107
The Horseshoe is in Offord D'Arcy PE19 5RH
☎ 01480 810293

Buckden has **three pubs**, all on the High Street
The George Hotel
☎ 01480 812300
The Lion
☎ 01480 810313
The Vine
☎ 01480 810367

Shops in **Buckden** include
Days Butchers, Buckden Supermarket, Buckden Pharmacy

Places to visit
Buckden Towers
www.buckden-towers.org.uk

Paxton Pits Nature Reserve is a rich mosaic of wildlife habitats covering 78 hectares of beautiful lakes, riverside, meadow, reedbed, scrub and woodland.

The Reserve is also home to the Wildlife Trust for Bedfordshire, Cambridgeshire and Northamptonshire's Environmental Education Centre. which runs events for children and families.

www.paxton-pits.org.uk

Local history

The 'Cluny' in **Offord Cluny** derives from Cluny Abbey in Burgundy who owned the manor between the 11th and 15th centuries. It is not so clear where the 'D'Arcy' in **Offord D'Arcy** originates from. It first appears in records in 1279.

Buckden Towers include the remains of 12th-century fortified palace that once belonged to the Bishops of Lincoln. **Buckden** provided a convenient place to break the journey between London and Lincoln during the construction of Lincoln Cathedral. It is now a religious retreat and the grounds are open to visitors.

RIVER GREAT OUSE 69

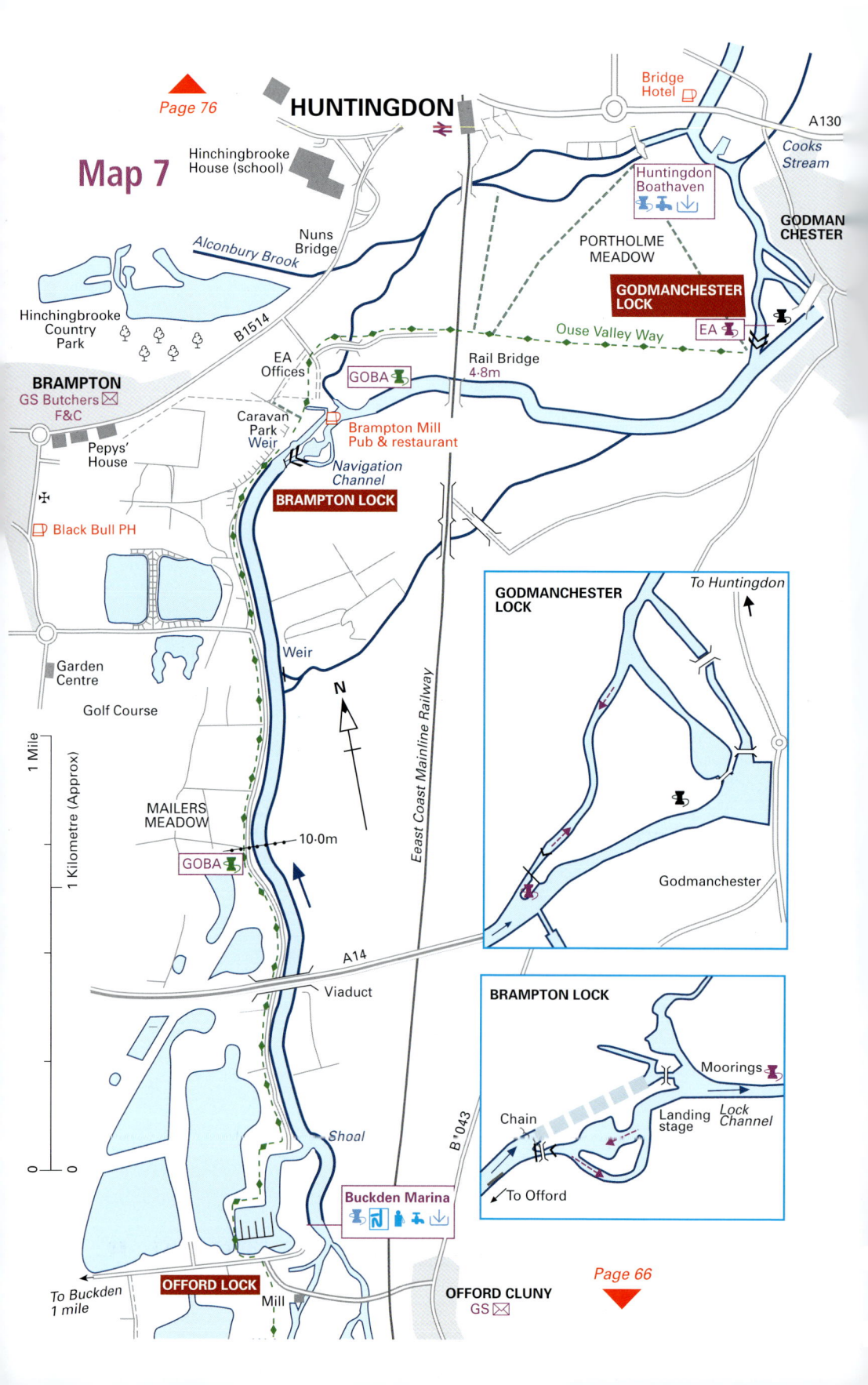

Map 7

Page 76

HUNTINGDON

Hinchingbrooke House (school)

Bridge Hotel

A130

Cooks Stream

Huntingdon Boathaven

GODMANCHESTER

Alconbury Brook

Nuns Bridge

PORTHOLME MEADOW

Hinchingbrooke Country Park

GODMANCHESTER LOCK

EA

Ouse Valley Way

B1514

EA Offices

GOBA

Rail Bridge 4.8m

BRAMPTON
GS Butchers
F&C

Caravan Park Weir

Brampton Mill Pub & restaurant

Pepys' House

Navigation Channel

BRAMPTON LOCK

Black Bull PH

Weir

Garden Centre

Golf Course

N

1 Mile
1 Kilometre (Approx)

MAILERS MEADOW

10.0m

GOBA

East Coast Mainline Railway

A14 Viaduct

Shoal

B1043

Buckden Marina

OFFORD LOCK

To Buckden 1 mile

Mill

OFFORD CLUNY
GS

GODMANCHESTER LOCK (inset)

To Huntingdon

Godmanchester

BRAMPTON LOCK (inset)

Moorings

Chain

Landing stage

Lock Channel

To Offord

Page 66

Map 7

Offord Lock to Huntingdon Bridge

Distance 4½ miles
Time 2 hours

Map 7 Offord Lock to Huntingdon Bridge

Lowest bridge Rail bridge 4·8m

Offord Lock L 30·5m, W 3·4m (11'1") D 1·05m, Head 2·7m

Brampton Lock
Electrically operated D shaped lock
L 31·7m, W 3·4m (11'1") D 1·45m, Head 2·8m

Godmanchester Lock (D shaped): L 30·5m, W 4·0m (13'1") D 1·1m, Head 2·75m

Location	Lock width	Moorings and facilities								Victualling		
		Overnight	48hr	Long stay	Water point	Chemical disposal point	Pumpout	Refuse	Fuel	Shops	Pub	Café/restaurant
Buckden Marina		⚓	⚓	⚓	🚰	⬇	🚽		Diesel & petrol			
Offord Lock	▯											
GOBA Mailer's Meadow			⚓									
Brampton Lock	▯▯▯											
Brampton Mill GOBA			⚓								🍺	🍴
Godmanchester EA moorings next to lock			⚓							🧺	🍺	🍴
Godmanchester Lock	▯▯											
Godmanchester town moorings			⚓							🧺	🍺	🍴
Huntingdon Boat Haven		⚓	⚓		🚰	⬇				🧺	🍺	🍴

River Great Ouse Kempston to Earith

Navigation notes

Half a mile below **Offord Lock** is the entrance to **Buckden Marine**, with long term moorings within a lodge complex. There is a commercial service point where visitors can obtain water, fuel (diesel and petrol) and a pump-out.

Cruising downstream, the rerouted **A14 trunk road** crosses the river on a mighty new bridge constructed from white concrete and self colour steel (it is easy to confuse 'self colour steel' with rust). The bridge construction caused regular delays to river traffic during 2018. I remember waiting once during a temporary closure and pondering the irony that I had bought a boat to get away from traffic jams, but here I was, held up by road works!

A quarter of a mile downstream of the bridge, on the left bank, are a long run of pleasant **GOBA moorings at Mailer's Meadow**. At this point the river is wide and calm and it can be no surprise that these moorings are popular with families.

> ### Moorings and facilities
> **Buckden Marine**, PE19 5BH
> Long term moorings, overnight if space. Self service diesel & petrol, pump-out
> ☏ 01480 812660
> **GOBA 'Mailer's Meadow' moorings** on left bank between Buckden Marine and Brampton Lock
> **GOBA moorings** left bank after Brampton Mill

Another mile brings you to **Brampton Lock**. Immediately below the lock there is an island with a one-way system around it, but I've rarely seen local boaters pay much heed to this. At Brampton Mill the river splits and a non navigable arm heads towards the historic Hinchingbrooke House. There are **GOBA moorings** on the left bank of the main river, popular with visitors to **Brampton Mill** pub and restaurant.

The navigable channel continues under a railway bridge where the East Coast line finally leaves the river.

Construction of new A14 bridge

Brampton Mill

Brampton
The Black Bull, 25 Church Lane, PE28 4PF
☎ 01480 457201
Brampton Mill, Bromholme Lane, PE28 4NE
☎ 01480 459758

Shops
Co-op, Nisa Local, Grieves off-licence, Measures Butchers, chemist

Restaurants
Brampton Fish Bar, 54 High St
☎ 01480 453030,
Hare on the Green, 40 The Green
☎ 01480 413592
Rumbles chip shop, 99 High St, Brampton PE28 4TQ
☎ 01480 455033

Godmanchester

Continuing to the right takes you into the pretty town of **Godmanchester**, much of which is clustered around a back water or pool of the Great Ouse. It features attractive old buildings, a museum and the picturesque Chinese Bridge. There are **moorings on the left bank**, and it is well worth stopping here.

The river below **Godmanchester Lock** is narrow and winding, but it gradually swells as the channels that have detoured via the pool of Godmanchester are reunited with it. The gardens of large houses run down to the river, several of which have boat houses.

The river winds around **Portholme Water Meadow**. Ahead you can see the spire of **Godmanchester's Grade I listed Church, St Mary the Virgin**. To the north, across the great meadow, you may be able to discern the modern, former **A14 fly-over**, and behind that the historic **14th-century bridge**. Godmanchester Lock forks off the left bank. There are **moorings adjacent to the lock** on the left bank of the right hand channel.

Godmanchester moorings looking east

Godmanchester Basin

RIVER GREAT OUSE

Godmanchester's Chinese Bridge

Cook's Stream also joins from the right, under an historic bridge just before the entrance to **Huntingdon Boat Haven** and a derelict site of former moorings, clearly awaiting redevelopment. After the next bend, the Hinchingbrooke arm of the Great Ouse rejoins the main channel just before you pass under the great **former A14 viaduct**. Shortly after you will pass under a metal footbridge and the old stone **Huntingdon Bridge**.

Lazy Days Boat Hire operate a small fleet of self-drive boats from the Huntingdon Boat Haven. These boats are amusingly named *Uncle Albert*, *Del-Boy*, *Boycee*, *Marlene*, *Raquel*, and *Cassandra* (one does wonder what fate befell poor old *Rodders*). Users often appear oblivious to the rules and etiquette of navigation, travelling on the wrong side of the river, making sudden and unexpected changes of direction, not fully opening guillotine gates, and leaving slackers open. Wariness around them is recommended.

Walking

Apart from a minor detour around the back of Buckden Marina, the **Ouse Valley Way** continues along the west bank of the river from **Offord Lock** to **Brampton Mill**, just above **Brampton Lock**.

From Brampton Mill the **Ouse Valley Way** runs parallel to, but not next to the river, across **Portholme Meadow**, until it crosses by a footbridge at the lock. Here it abandons the river for a while, but there is a footpath across the meadow into **Huntingdon**.

Huntingdon Old Bridge with the central concrete pier of the great A14 viaduct seen upstream through it

74 RIVER GREAT OUSE

Moorings and facilities
EA Godmanchester moorings next to the lock
Town moorings on the left bank approaching Godmanchester basin
Lazy Days Boat Hire
☏ 07951 785305
Huntingdon Boat Haven, Godmanchester PE29 2AF
Overnight/longterm moorings
☏ 07951 785305

Local history

Offord Lock - there has been a lock on this site since around 1620. This was necessary to enable navigation past the Brampton mills. Only one of the four mills now remains.

Brampton was the childhood home of the 17th century diarist **Samuel Pepys**, who attended Huntingdon Free School.

Portholme Meadow stretches between Brampton, Godmanchester and Huntingdon. William Camden wrote in the 16th century 'a meadow encompass'd with the Ouse, called Portholme, exceedingly large, and a more glorious one the Sun never saw'. It is believed to be the largest lowland meadow in England. It has been the site of horse racing in the 19th-century, and in WWI it was used as an airfield. It is now a SSSI and is home to many wildflowers including marsh dandelion, cowslip, brown sedge, great burnett and snakes head fritillary.

Godmanchester, situated on a ford over the Ouse, was the meeting place of three roman roads, Ermine Street (London to York), Via Devana (to Cambridge) and a military road to Sandy. A six arched bridge, built in 1332, carried the main road to the north over Cook's Stream.

Godmanchester
Pubs
The Exhibition, 3-5 London Rd, Godmanchester, PE29 2HZ
☏ 01480 459134
The White Hart, 2 Cambridge Rd, Godmanchester, PE29 2BW
☏ 01480 414050
The Royal Oak, 7 Causeway, Godmanchester, PE29 2HA
☏ 01480 453819,
The Black Bull, 32 Post St, Godmanchester, PE29 2AQ
☏ 01480 437638

There is a wide selection of eateries in **Godmanchester** to suit all tastes, including:
Planet Spice, 5 Causeway, PE29 2HA
☏ 01480 414426
Cinta, 12 Post St, Godmanchester, PE29 2BA
☏ 01480 450354
Riverside Restaurant, 10 Causeway, Godmanchester, PE29 2HA
☏ 01480 450413

Godmanchester shops
2 Co-ops, bakery and sandwich bar, One Stop Shop, Thomas Family Butchers

The current, much photographed, **Chinese** (or 'willow pattern') **footbridge** was built around 1958. The original was constructed in 1827.

During severe floods in 1894, Godmanchester Corporation opened the sluices at Godmanchester, Houghton and Hemingford to alleviate the flooding. The owner of the Ouse Navigation argued in Court that they were not entitled to touch the sluices, but lost his legal action. This will have helped form the precedent that led to the practice of 'lock reversal' where gates at both ends of a lock are left open to prevent the lock arresting peak flow.

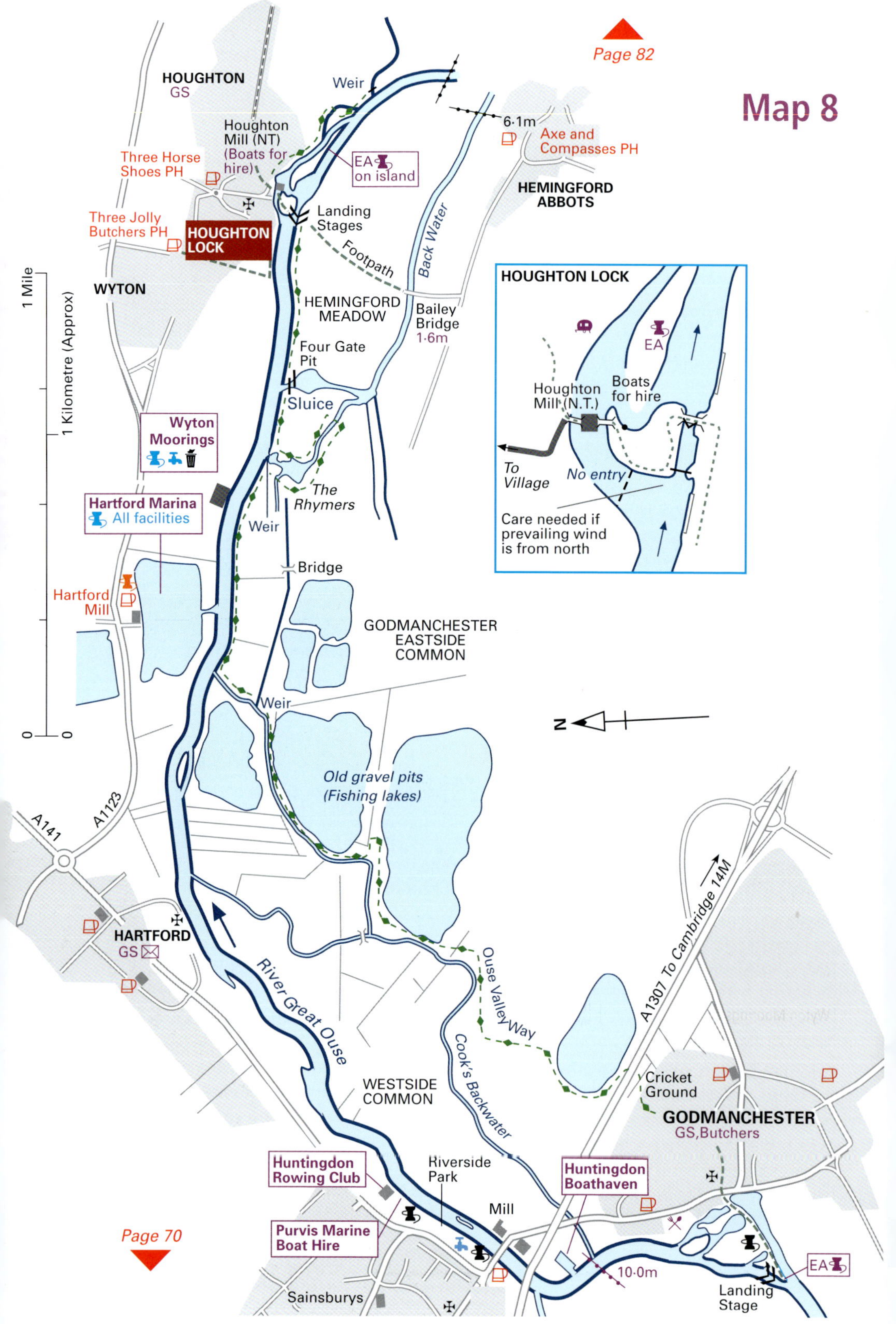

Page 82
Map 8
HOUGHTON
GS
Weir
Houghton Mill (NT) (Boats for hire)
Three Horse Shoes PH
EA on island
6·1m
Axe and Compasses PH
HEMINGFORD ABBOTS
Three Jolly Butchers PH
HOUGHTON LOCK
Landing Stages
Footpath
Back Water
WYTON
HEMINGFORD MEADOW
Bailey Bridge
1·6m
Four Gate Pit
Sluice
1 Mile
1 Kilometre (Approx)
0
0
Wyton Moorings
Hartford Marina
All facilities
The Rhymers
Weir
Bridge
Hartford Mill
GODMANCHESTER EASTSIDE COMMON
Weir
N
Old gravel pits (Fishing lakes)
A141
A1123
HARTFORD
GS
River Great Ouse
Ouse Valley Way
Cook's Backwater
A1307 To Cambridge 14M
Cricket Ground
GODMANCHESTER
GS,Butchers
WESTSIDE COMMON
Huntingdon Rowing Club
Riverside Park
Huntingdon Boathaven
Mill
Page 70
Purvis Marine Boat Hire
10·0m
EA
Landing Stage
Sainsburys
HOUGHTON LOCK
EA
Houghton Mill (N.T.)
Boats for hire
To Village
No entry
Care needed if prevailing wind is from north

Map 8

Huntingdon Old Bridge to Houghton Lock

Distance 2¾ miles
Time 1 hour approx

River Great Ouse Kempston to Earith

Map 8 Huntingdon Old Bridge to Houghton Lock

Lowest bridge 3·4m Huntingdon Old Bridge
Houghton Lock
(D shaped) L 37·5m, W 3·65m (11'11") D 1·5m Head 2·75m

Location	Lock width	Moorings and facilities								Victualling		
		Short stay/visitor	48hr	Long stay	Water point	Chemical disposal point	Pumpout	Refuse	Fuel	Shops	Pub	Café/restaurant
Town moorings Huntingdon Bridge			⚓		🚰					🛒	🍺	🍴
Riverside Park			⚓							🛒	🍺	🍴
Hartford Marina (and Hartford Mill PH)		⚓	⚓	⚓	🚰	⬇	⬆	🗑	petrol & diesel		🍺	🍴
Wyton Moorings		If spaces available		⚓	🚰			🗑				
Houghton Lock	000											
EA Houghton Island			⚓									🍴

RIVER GREAT OUSE

Huntingdon

Navigation notes

Unlike other local riverside towns, **Huntingdon** does little to welcome passing boaters and encourage visitors. There are hard moorings on the left bank immediately after the old bridge. There is a water point on the southern moorings (nearer the old bridge). The tap wasn't of the type that allowed you to connect a hose, but we understand that this has now been fixed. There is another short section of moorings on the side of **Riverside Park**, just before **Purvis Marine**.

Huntingdon Riverside Park runs along the left hand side of the meandering river for some distance, but sadly with no further mooring spots. **Huntingdon Rowing Club** is situated in the park and powered traffic should slow for rowers, many of whom are children. Open countryside lies to the southeast.

Hartford then arrives on the north bank. Formerly a village in its own right, it has now largely been subsumed into the town of Huntingdon. The pretty, late 12th century, **All Saints parish church** stands on the river bank. It boasts a late 15th century tower, a contrast to many of the soaring spires of other villages on the river. There can be few more picturesque riverside churches in the country.

The river turns east and, once again, the gardens of large properties run down to the river and many of them boast private boat houses.

About ½ mile further on is the entrance to the large **Hartford Marina**, with well stocked chandlery and popular Hartford Mill Pub and Carvery. Moorings are provided for restaurant customers.

From Hartford Marina it is about 1mile to **Houghton Lock**. Pronounced locally 'haw-tun', this is a very popular lock, both with walkers, and with local kids wanting a swim. During peak summer times it is manned by EA volunteers. There is often an audience watching you. There are **EA moorings on the island below the** lock and **Houghton Mill**, a National Trust-owned working flour mill, with tea room, is a popular visitor attraction.

In the distance, to the south from Houghton, you may spot the elegant spire of **St Margarets Church, Hemingford Abbots**.

All Saints Church, Hartford

Moorings and facilities

In **Huntingdon**, there are moorings on the left bank immediately downstream of the old town bridge. **Water point**.

Further moorings on the left bank on **Riverside Park** just upstream of Purvis Marine

Purvis Marine Riverside Car Park, Hartford Road, Huntingdon PE29 3RP
Boat hire and repair
☎ 01480 453628

Hartford Marina PE28 2AA
Overnight & long term moorings and all services including petrol and diesel, chandlery
☎ 01480 454677

Wyton Moorings, Wyton PE28 2AA
Long term moorings, overnight if available. Repairs
☎ 01480 455898

EA Houghton moorings on island forming left bank of main river downstream from Houghton Lock. No land access.

Other water users
Huntingdon Rowing Club

Regattas
Traditional July rowing regatta, not been held for a number of years

Huntingdon Head of the River generally last Sunday in October

Huntingdon is a vibrant shopping centre with a range of shops

Supermarkets in the town centre centre include Sainsbury's, Iceland, Aldi, Tesco Express and Lidl, and out of town Tesco Extra.

Central pubs serving food include **The Old Bridge Hotel**, Sandford House (Wetherspoon) Cromwells Bar, The George Hotel, The Falcon Tavern, Samuel Pepys and the Market Inn

Markets
General market Wednesdays and Saturdays, High Street

Places to visit
Hinchingbrooke House
Cromwell Museum and **Shakespeare at the George** (open air theatre in a pub courtyard - 'beer and The Bard') midsummer.

Public Transport
Huntingdon is on the East Coast mainline Railway

Hartford
Mill Pub and Carvery, Hartford Marina PE28 2AA
☎ 01480 414311
King of the Belgians, 27 Main St, PE29 1XU,
☎ 01480 52030
The Barley Mow, 42 Main St, Hartford PE29 1XU
☎ 01480 450557

The Three Jolly Butchers, 3 Huntingdon Rd, **Wyton** PE28 2AD,
☎ 01480 463228

Houghton
Three Horseshoes
PE28 2BE,
☎ 01480 462410,

Houghton Mill National Trust-owned working 18th century flour mill.
www.nationaltrust.org.uk/houghton-mill-and-waterclose-meadows

Walking

The **Ouse Valley Way** avoids Huntingdon, but **Huntingdon Riverside Park** borders the river on its left bank for much of its journey through Huntingdon.

Having left the Great Ouse at **Godmanchester Lock**, the Ouse Valley Way doesn't return to it until opposite **Hartford Marina**. From here it follows the right bank of the river to **Houghton Lock**, where it crosses the river once more.

Local history

Huntingdon is another of the Great Ouse market towns which grew up where a major Roman road, in this instance Ermine Street, forded the river. It was a staging post for Danish raids upstream, until they moved their camp to Tempsford in Bedfordshire before finally being defeated by Edward the Elder in AD878.

In 1332 the ford was replaced with a stone bridge. This was built from both sides of the river at the same time. The two halves didn't quite align, and there is a slight bend near the central pier. The bridge survives, somewhat battered, nearly 7 centuries on. Parallel to it runs a great concrete viaduct constructed in the 1970s to carry the A14. The A14 has been moved further south and this bridge already finds itself largely redundant.

In the 18th and 19th centuries Huntingdon was a major coaching centre and a legacy remains in several inns, most notably **The George Hotel** with its wooden galleries. Daniel Defoe wrote 'It is a great Thorough-fair on the Northern Road, and full of very good Inns'.

Its Members of Parliament have included **Oliver Cromwell** in the 17th century, and the former conservative Prime Minister **John Major** who represented Huntingdon between 1979 and 2001.

The annual **rowing regatta** was once such an important event in the town's calendar that the shops closed for the afternoon so that people could attend.

The river above the bridge was home to a number of industries, and Robert Simper (*Rivers to the Fens*) reports that the '...in the 1940s the river used to turn violet when the cotton mill had a clean up, and green when the pea factory released its waste'.

At **Hartford**, a chain ferry carried cattle to Westside Common from in front of

Huntingdon

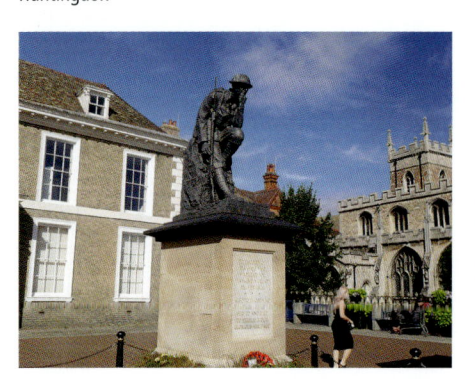

The George Hotel Huntingdon

the pub. This finished 1949. There was a smaller ferry quarter of a mile up river for anglers.

In 1964 two Huntingdon council workers were digging a new road in Hartford when they discovered a hoard of over eleven hundred silver coins dating back to the 15th century. These included Groats, half Groats, pennies, half pennies and French coins, covering the reigns of Henry VI, Edward IV, Richard III and Henry VII. The Richard III coins were of particular interest as there were few in existence because Richard only reigned for two years. They were all in near mint condition and are now in the British Museum where they are known as the Hartford Hoard.

The first record of a mill at **Houghton Mill** was in 969 when it was given to the Abbey of Ramsey. The current five story mill was built in the seventeenth century, and extended in the nineteenth. There was a movement to demolish it after it closed, but Lt Col. Louis Tebbutt gave it to the National Trust and it became a youth hostel. It is now, once again, a working watermill and the last surviving mill on the River Great Ouse able to produce stone ground flour.

Huntingdon converted mill

Houghton Mill
Richard Humphrey

RIVER GREAT OUSE

Map 9

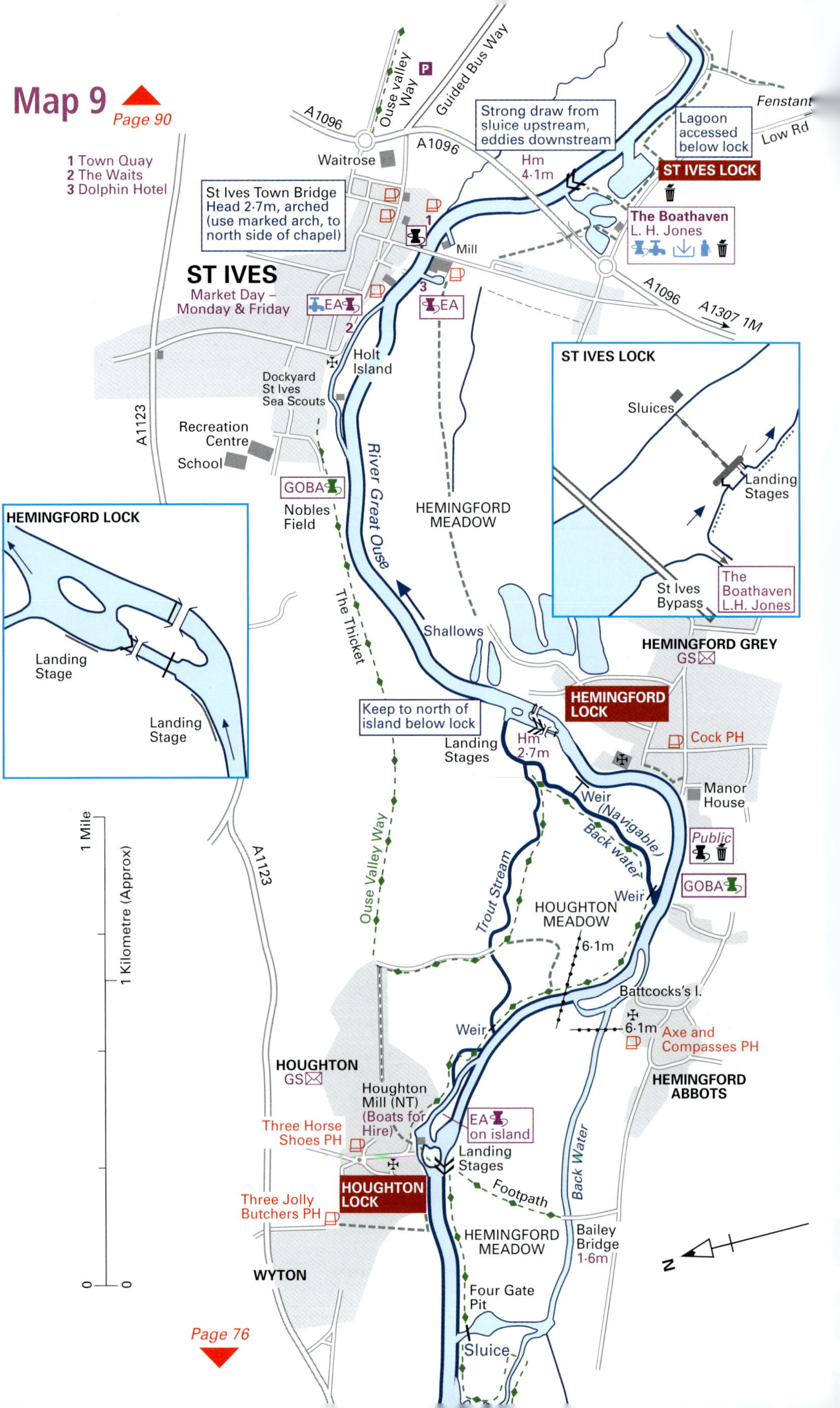

Page 90
1 Town Quay
2 The Waits
3 Dolphin Hotel
A1096
Ouse valley Way
Guided Bus Way
Waitrose
Strong draw from sluice upstream, eddies downstream
Lagoon accessed below lock
Fenstanton
Low Rd
Hm 4·1m
ST IVES LOCK
St Ives Town Bridge Head 2·7m, arched (use marked arch, to north side of chapel)
The Boathaven L. H. Jones
Mill
ST IVES
Market Day – Monday & Friday
EA
A1307 1M
Holt Island
Dockyard St Ives Sea Scouts
Recreation Centre
School
A1123
GOBA
Nobles Field
River Great Ouse
HEMINGFORD MEADOW
ST IVES LOCK
Sluices
Landing Stages
St Ives Bypass
The Boathaven L.H. Jones
HEMINGFORD LOCK
Landing Stage
Landing Stage
The Thicket
Shallows
HEMINGFORD GREY
GS
Keep to north of island below lock
HEMINGFORD LOCK
Landing Stages
Hm 2·7m
Cock PH
Manor House
Weir (Navigable)
Back water
Public
1 Mile
1 Kilometre (Approx)
A1123
Ouse Valley Way
Trout Stream
Weir
HOUGHTON MEADOW
6·1m
Battcocks's I.
Weir
6·1m
Axe and Compasses PH
HOUGHTON
GS
HEMINGFORD ABBOTS
Houghton Mill (NT) (Boats for Hire)
EA on island
Three Horse Shoes PH
Landing Stages
Back Water
Footpath
HOUGHTON LOCK
Three Jolly Butchers PH
HEMINGFORD MEADOW
Bailey Bridge 1·6m
N
WYTON
Four Gate Pit
Sluice
Page 76
0
0

Map 9

Houghton Lock to St Ives Lock

Distance 3 miles
Time 1 hour

Map 9 Houghton Lock to St Ives Lock

Lowest bridge 2·7m Hemingford Lock bridge
Houghton Lock (D shaped) L 37·5m, W 3·65m (11'11"), D 1·5m, Head 2·75m
Hemingford Lock (D shaped) L 28m, W 3·85m (12'7"), D 1·5m, Head 2·75m
St Ives Lock (D shaped) L 31·3m, W 3·35m (10'11"), D 1·5m, Head 4·0m

Location	Lock width	Moorings and facilities								Victualling		
		Short stay/visitor	48hr	Long stay	Water point	Chemical disposal point	Pumpout	Refuse	Fuel	Shops	Pub	Café/restaurant
Houghton Lock	🔒											
GOBA Hemingford Meadows			🏕									
Hemingford Grey town moorings			⚓					🗑			🍺	🍴
Hemingford Lock	🔒											
GOBA Noble's Field St Ives			🏕									
The Waits EA moorings St Ives			⚓		🚰					🛒	🍺	🍴
EA Dolphin Hotel moorings			⚓							🛒	🍺	🍴
St Ives Town Quay			⚓							🛒	🍺	🍴
Jones Boatyard (boats less than 40' only)		Overnight if spaces	⚓		🚰	⬇		🗑	petrol & diesel			
St Ives Lock	🔒											

Navigation notes

About ½ mile downstream from **Houghton Lock** the river splits around **Battock's Island** and a pretty back-water leads back to **Hemingford Abbots**.

Once the two arms of the river are reunited you find yourself approaching the picture postcard perfect village of **Hemingford Grey**. Every July this is the home to the oldest village regatta in the country (it started in 1904). This is not the hi-tech event of the modern rowing club, with fibre glass boats and carbon fibre oars, but a good old fashioned 'splash about' in skiffs, canoes and punts!

Hemingford Grey

St James' Church Hemingford Grey

Moorings and facilities

GOBA Hemingford Meadow moorings on right bank between Hemingford Grey and Hemingford Abbots.

Town moorings in Hemingford Grey, right bank. There are also **rubbish disposal facilities**.

GOBA Noble's Field moorings, left bank before arrival at St Ives.

There are **meadow-side GOBA moorings** and extensive **Parish Council hard moorings**, so if you are passing during regatta, why not stop and enjoy the spectacle and enjoy a cream tea or hot dog on offer? It is an absolutely quintessentially English event.

St James' Church, Hemingford Grey, is another attractive riverside church. Its spire collapsed during a hurricane in 1741 and was never replaced.

Pubs
Axe and Compass, High St, Hemingford Abbots PE28 9AH
① 01480 463605

The Cock, 47 High St, Hemingford Grey PE28 9BJ
① 01480 463609

Places to visit
The Manor, **Hemingford Grey**, was built in the 1130s and is one of the longest continuously inhabited houses in Britain. It is the former home to Lucy Boston and setting of her 'Green Knowe' children's books. The house has fine gardens and is open to the public

River events
Hemingfords' Regatta - around 2nd Saturday in July
www.hemingfordgreyparishcouncil.gov.uk

Leaving **Hemingford Lock**, the two spires of **All Saints Church St Ives** and **St Ives Free Church** appear across the flood meadow. This was the site of an infamously sodden IWA Festival in 2007.

On the left bank there are extensive **GOBA Noble's Field** moorings. These popular moorings are within reasonable walking distance of St Ives town centre.

The GOBA moorings are followed by **Holt Island**, a 7 acre nature reserve, after which you arrive in the centre of **St Ives**.

The Free Church, St Ives

RIVER GREAT OUSE

St Ives

St Ives offers three mooring areas. **Hard moorings in The Waits**, behind Holt Island, are accessed by turning left at the bottom end of the island, next to St Ives Rowing Club. **The EA provide 48h moorings** adjacent to the **Dolphin Hotel**, on the right bank a little above the bridge. Passing under the bridge, the old **Town Quay also offers mooring** in an historic setting.

I've moored here on a Saturday night, and despite warning from other boaters, suffered absolutely no inconvenience from late night revellers.

As you approach **St Ives Lock**, you can look back at the 55 arch causeway on the London road. Sometimes called 'the New Bridges', this description was more accurate in 1822 when first constructed. This provides a stark contrast to the modern concrete bypass bridge which you pass under before reaching the lock. St Ives Lock features unusual (for the River Great Ouse) restraining chains on the upper V gates for holding them open

St Ives old causeway seen under the modern bypass, looking upstream

St Ives old Town Quay

Moorings and facilities

Town moorings on **The Waits**, left hand fork, 150m upstream of Town Bridge

EA Moorings at The Dolphin Hotel in cut on right bank immediately upstream from the Dolphin Hotel.

LA moorings, town quay, left bank, immediately after Town Bridge.

Water point on The Waits

Jones Boatyard, PE27 5ET
Long term moorings and overnight, if availability, for boats less than 40'. All services, petrol & diesel, boat sales, chandlery
☏ 01480 494040

Other water users
St Ives Rowing Club

St Ives is a interesting shopping centre with a range of shops.
Supermarkets include a town centre Waitrose, Tesco Express (1 mile from town centre), and a large Morrisons and Aldi (1¼ miles from town centre)

There is a variety of **restaurants and takeaways** in St Ives town. There is a Wetherspoons (The Swan and Angel), and other town centre pubs serving food include The Dolphin, Floods Tavern, The Royal Oak, Nelsons Head, The White Hart and The Oliver Cromwell.

Markets
General market on Mondays and Fridays, Market Hill
Farmers' market 1st and 3rd Saturday every month in the Sheep Market

Launderette
The Wash and Dry Shop, 42 The Broadway PE27 5BN, near The Waits
☏ 07514 505602

Tourist Info Centre in the library,
4 Library Row, Station Rd, PE27 5BW
☏ 01736 796297

Places to visit
The Norris Museum, The Waits
www.norrismuseum.org.uk

Boat trips
St Ives Electric River Boat Company offer chauffered 12 person, one hour trips on their boats *Meander* and *Whisper,* or self-drive. From Town Quay Fri-Mon in season (weather permitting).
☏ 07906 257308
info@electricriverboat.co.uk

Public Transport
Connected to Cambridge by guided bus
Buses to Huntingdon

against the wind and is the last 'pregnant' lock (with a side bay) you will encounter heading downstream on the Great Ouse. It also features the last self-operated set of manual V gates.

On the south bank is **Jones Boatyard marina**. Sales, chandlery, and the workshop are all at the upper river level and accessed from above the lock. Below the lock an extension to the marina has been dug.

Walking

From **Houghton Lock** the **Ouse Valley Way** now heads off toward historic **St Ives**, but there are alternative footpaths to **Hemingford Grey**, and on to **St Ives**, approaching along the causeway and entering via the old town bridge with its chapel.

St Ives bridge

Local history

Hemingford Grey watermill was demolished around 1960. **St James' Church in Hemingford Grey** once had a spire, but this collapsed during a hurricane in 1741, and has never been rebuilt, leaving only the stump.

Hemingford Lock was the first on the Great Ouse to be fitted with an electric guillotine gate.

St Ives was originally the site of a ford, before a wooden bridge was built at the beginning of the 12th century. The current stone bridge was constructed in the 15th century. It boasts an extremely rare surviving chapel to St Leger on the bridge. The bridge had been built by the abbots of Ramsey Abbey. Travellers 'gave thanks' (in cash) for a safe journey and this was collected by a monk stationed in the chapel. Two extra floors were added to the chapel and it became a house, and then a shop, until the extra storeys were removed in the early twentieth century.

The bridge was constructed in Gothic style with pointed arches. During the English Civil War (1642-1651) two of the arches on the southern side were demolished and a drawbridge installed in 1645 to defend the town against Royalists. The drawbridge remained in use until 1716 when the Duke of Manchester ordered that two new arches were built. Unlike the existing Gothic arches these were formed in a rounded, Roman style. To this day the bridge retains this mixture of styles.

The Church of All Saints, St Ives, lost its spire in a gale in 1741, when it was rebuilt, and again in 1879, only to loose it for a third time when an aircraft flew into it in 1917/8. It was rebuilt, a third time, in 1924.

Converted mill building, St Ives

By 1916 **the quay at St Ives** was regarded as 'the highest point up to which barges can now be navigated'.

A well known riddle about St Ives poses the question:

As I was going to St. Ives,
I met a man with seven wives,
Each wife had seven sacks,
Each sack had seven cats,
Each cat had seven kits:
Kits, cats, sacks, and wives,
How many were there going to St. Ives ?

(Answer at the bottom of the page.)

In 1869 the captain of **St Ives Rowing Club** was **John Goldie**, son of the local vicar. John went on to captain Cambridge University Boat Club, stroking them for four successive years and ending an Oxford 9-year winning streak. The CUBC reserve boat has been called 'Goldie' ever since.

The six storey Victorian building on the south bank, now flats, was constructed in the 1850s as a corn mill for the Quaker milling magnate, **Potto Brown**. For many centuries milling had remained largely unchanged, with either water or wind driving great grinding stones. However with the advent of the industrial revolution, steam engines offered an alternative power source, and

The headquarters of **Imray Laurie Norie & Wilson Ltd**, the publishers of this guide, are located in St Ives in Wych House, a Grade II listed building, formerly The Globe Inn. Dating back to 1732 the building was re-fronted around 1840 in the Georgian Style.

The company was formed in 1904 by the merger of three chart publishing firms, each of whom had been producing nautical charts since the mid-1700s. In 1939 the company moved from central London to St Ives. It is still owned and run by descendants of the original founders.
www.imray.com

other technical advancements improved the process. This type of mill may have represented one of the 'dark satanic mills' blighting 'England's green and pleasant land' immortalised by William Blake in his poem 'Jerusalem'. In 1901 the building became a print works and its name changed to Enderby's, before being taken over in the 1970s by **Sir Clive Sinclair** to manufacture the world's first pocket calculator. Despite common belief, it was never the development base for Sinclair's remarkable failed transport revolution - the Sinclair C5.

The answer to the riddle (above) is 'one'. The narrator who poses the riddle was the only person going to St Ives - the man with seven wives must have been going in the opposite direction for them to meet. However it has been argued the the man with the seven wives may have also been heading in the same direction, and had caught up the narrator. In which case the total number of items mentioned is 2,802: the narrator, the man, his seven wives, forty nine sacks, three hundred forty three cats, and two thousand four hundred and one kits!

RIVER GREAT OUSE

Map 10

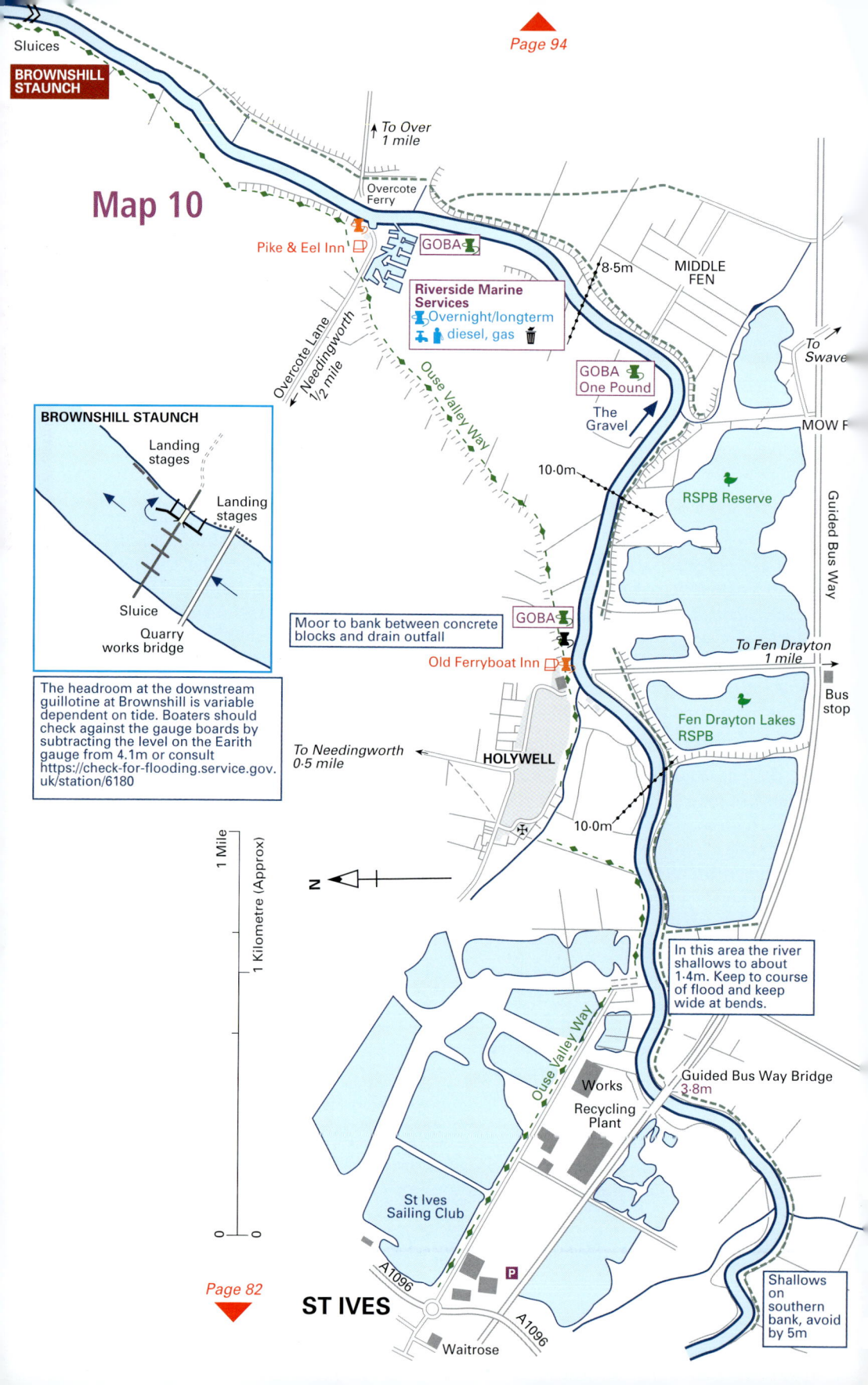

BROWNSHILL STAUNCH

Sluices

Page 94

To Over 1 mile

Overcote Ferry

Pike & Eel Inn

GOBA

Overcote Lane

To Needingworth ½ mile

Ouse Valley Way

Riverside Marine Services
Overnight/longterm
diesel, gas

8.5m

MIDDLE FEN

GOBA One Pound

The Gravel

10.0m

RSPB Reserve

To Swave

MOW F

Guided Bus Way

BROWNSHILL STAUNCH

Landing stages

Landing stages

Sluice

Quarry works bridge

The headroom at the downstream guillotine at Brownshill is variable dependent on tide. Boaters should check against the gauge boards by subtracting the level on the Earith gauge from 4.1m or consult https://check-for-flooding.service.gov.uk/station/6180

Moor to bank between concrete blocks and drain outfall

GOBA

Old Ferryboat Inn

To Fen Drayton 1 mile

Bus stop

Fen Drayton Lakes RSPB

To Needingworth 0.5 mile

HOLYWELL

10.0m

N

1 Mile
1 Kilometre (Approx)

In this area the river shallows to about 1.4m. Keep to course of flood and keep wide at bends.

Ouse Valley Way

Works
Recycling Plant

Guided Bus Way Bridge 3.8m

St Ives Sailing Club

Page 82

A1096

ST IVES

Waitrose

A1096

Shallows on southern bank, avoid by 5m

Map 10

St Ives Lock to Brownshill Staunch

Distance 5½ miles
Time 2 hours

Map 10 St Ives Lock to Brownshill Staunch

Lowest bridge St Ives guided bus bridge 3·8m
St Ives Lock L 31·3m, W 3·35m (10'11") D 1·5m
Brownshill Staunch L 30m, W 4m (13'1") D 1·5m, Head 3·0m, downstream guillotine headroom varies depending on tide (see note, Map 10)

Location	Lock width	Moorings and facilities								Victualling		
		Short stay/visitor	48hr	Long stay	Water point	Chemical disposal point	Pumpout	Refuse	Fuel	Shops	Pub	Café/restaurant
Old Ferryboat Inn PH		●									●	●
Ferryboat Inn GOBA			●								●	●
Holywell public moorings		●										
GOBA 'One Pound'			●									
GOBA 'Overcote Ferry'			●								●	●
Pike and Eel PH, Needingworth		●									●	●
Riverside Marine, Needingworth			●	●	●			●	Diesel			
Brownshill Staunch	⬭											

RIVER GREAT OUSE

Navigation notes

The river gently meanders eastwards from St Ives. In the distance, the spire of **St Peter and St Paul's Church, Fenstanton**, briefly appears to the south, before the river passes under the modern bridge which carries the guided busway to Cambridge. The guided busway was originally estimated to cost £86 million, but increased during construction to £147 million and has subsequently required £36 million in repairs. Many locals refer to it as the *mis*guided busway! The cycle track next to the busway is very popular with cyclists, but at only 16 miles long, and with an average construction cost for the busway of £11.4 million/mile, perhaps we should celebrate it as the world's most expensive cycle-way!

The next section of the river is really lovely, and it is no surprise that it's popular with boaters, with the twin destinations of **The Ferry Boat PH** at **Holywell** and **The Pike and Eel PH** at **Needingworth** both offering victualling opportunities to the hungry or thirsty boater.

In addition to **hard moorings on the left bank outside the Ferry Boat**, there are extensive **GOBA moorings** just downstream, and more at **'One Pound'**

Ferry Boat Holywell moorings

> Immediately upstream from Brownshill Sluice a covered conveyor transported aggregate from Needingworth Quarry across the river. This quarry is being transformed into a 1,700 acre nature reserve – the Ouse Fen. This will link up with RSPB nature reserves at Fen Drayton Lakes and the Ouse Washes creating a new continuous wetland of over 6,000 acres, The Great Ouse Wetland.

moorings, 1 mile further downstream. Similarly there are more **GOBA moorings** on the left bank shortly before **The Pike and Eel. The Pike and Eel** itself offers only a limited number of visitor moorings. **Riverside Marina**, next to the pub, is predominantly for long term berth holders.

There is a car park on the south bank opposite the Pike and Eel, popular with residents from nearby Over, so keep a sharp eye open for swimmers and youngsters messing about in the water, sometimes in small inflatables.
Just downstream of The Pike and Eel you cross the Prime Meridian (also known as the Greenwich Meridian).

One mile beyond the Pike and Eel is the next lock, **Brownshill Staunch**. This features guillotine gates at both ends, and that bane of the single-handed boater's life - a fixed bridge across the middle of the lock. Less of a problem when travelling downstream, when going up in the lock you climb the ladder at the back of the lock taking with you a middle or front rope. But because you can't pass the rope under the bridge, you can't secure the boat towards the middle or front of the lock. One of those conundrums that lock designers clearly enjoy setting!
Brownshill is the last self-operated lock travelling downstream on the Great Ouse - though there are others on the tributaries, including on the River Cam.

Moorings and facilities

48h public moorings in **Holywell** in front of the **Old Ferryboat Inn**.

GOBA moorings left bank, 130m downstream of Old Ferryboat Inn.

GOBA 'One Pound' moorings, left bank upstream of The Pike and Eel, Needingworth.

GOBA 'Overcote Ferry' moorings left bank just upstream of The Pike and Eel.

The Pike and Eel has moorings outside for patrons.

Riverside Marina, Needingworth, PE27 4TW
Long term and overnight moorings, diesel, sales, chandlery, repairs.
✆ 01480 463336

RMS Boat Hire, Needingworth, PE27 4TW
✆ 01480 463336

The Old Ferry Boat, Holywell
PE27 4TG
✆ 01480 463227

The Pike and Eel, Overcote Ln, Needingworth
PE27 4TW
✆ 01480 463336

Walking

After a diversion away from the river, the **Ouse Valley Way** rejoins on the left bank between the **Guided Busway bridge** and Holywell. The route then follows the river from Holywell until **The Pike and Eel at Needingworth/Over**, from where it continues to **Brownshill**.

On the right bank of the river there is also a footpath from **Hemingford Grey to Over**. This then joins the **Pathfinder Long Distance walk** along the Bedford Level Corporation Barrier Bank to Brownshill Staunch and Lock.

Local history

Holywell takes it name from a spring near the church of St John the Baptist with alleged healing powers.

The **Overcote ferry** was a chain ferry which carried animals and vehicles across the river, as well as people. It was lost in the great, post-thaw, flood of 1947.

The **chain ferry at The Pike and Eel in Needingworth** stopped in the early 1920s and was replaced by a punt passenger ferry which was also swept away in the floods of 1947.

Brownshill Staunch, was originally constructed in 1834. Now a double guillotine lock, it marks the end of the 'Bedford Ouse' and is the beginning of the River's journey through the Fens. In 1947 there was a pub at Brownshill Lock which was kept by the lock keeper. Its remote location permitted a disregard of licensing hours which made it popular with boaters.

Brownshill Staunch looking downstream onto the short central tidal section of the River Great Ouse

Map 11

Page 102

Willingham

A1123 To Haddenham 12 miles

Bridge Farm

B1050

Road bridge across Hermitage Lock restricts headroom at high tide or flood

Old West River

Note The New Bedford River is also known as the Hundred Foot River

B1381 to Ely

Hermitage Marina
Overnight/long stay No fuel

New Bedford River (Tidal)

10.0m

The Bulwarks

Shelford Farm

Landing Stages

HERMITAGE LOCK
Overnight Showers and WC at the lock

Old Bedford River

Earith Sluice

Chain

Hermitage Lock (inset)

A1123 to Haddenham — Old West River
B1381 to Ely
New Bedford River
Hermitage Marina
B1050 to Cambridge
Landing stage
Landing stages
A1123 to Earith
River Gt. Ouse

HERMITAGE LOCK

Crown PH

EARITH
GS

Westview Marina
Overnight/longstay
Diesel, lift out

EA 48hrs

Bury Fen

A1123

THIS SECTION IS TIDAL
Take care on mooring. During the summer season the rise and fall is only about 0.3m but at spring tides it may be about 0.75m. Heights are also affected by local rains. Measurements shown are for normal average conditions. Consult the lock keeper.

St Marys

BLUNTISHAM

The White Swan PH

To St Ives

River Great Ouse

Ouse Valley Way

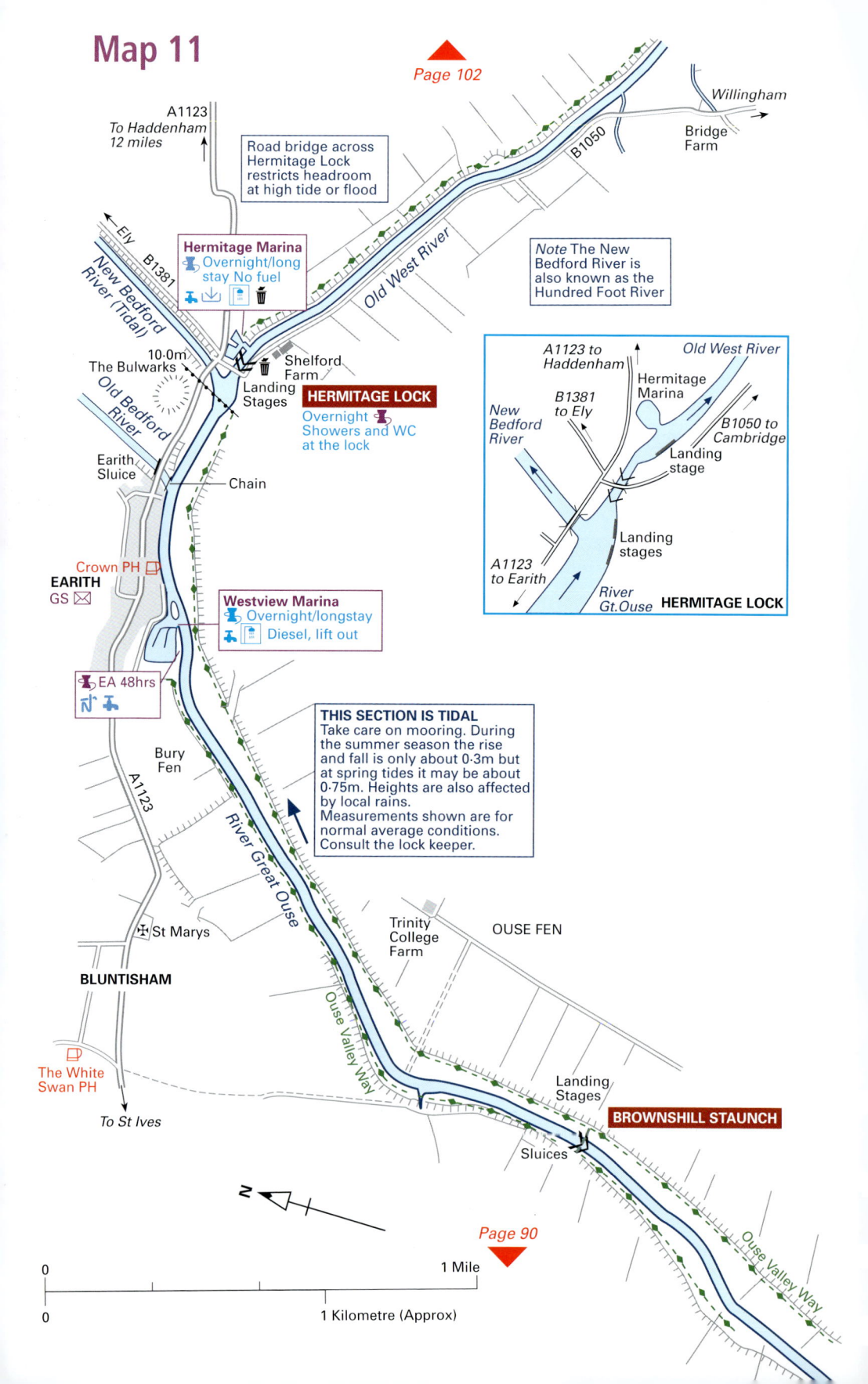

Trinity College Farm

OUSE FEN

Landing Stages

BROWNSHILL STAUNCH

Sluices

N

Page 90

0 — 1 Mile
0 — 1 Kilometre (Approx)

Ouse Valley Way

Map 11

Brownshill Staunch to Hermitage Lock (tidal)

Distance 2¼ miles
Time ½ hour

Map 11 Brownshill Staunch to Hermitage Lock

Lowest bridge: Hermitage Lock road bridge headroom varies depending on tides and flood levels

Tidal range: on a spring tide the difference between high tide and low tide is 0·75m (1' 6")

Brownshill Staunch and Lock
L 30m, W 4m (13'1") D 1·5m, Head 3·0m

Hermitage Lock (attended)
L 30·5m, W 4m (13'1") D 1.5m, H2·75m
Open April-Sept 0900 - 1900,
October-March 0900-1600
Closed daily 1300-1400
☎ 01487 841548

Location	Lock width	Moorings and facilities								Victualling			
		Short stay	Overnight/48hr	Long stay	Toilets/showers	Water point	Chemical disposal point	Pumpout	Refuse	Fuel	Shops	Pub	Café/restaurant
Brownshill Staunch	◊												
Earith EA			⚓			⚱		⛵					
Westview Marina			⚓	⚓	⚿	⚱	⬇	⛵		Diesel no petrol			
Hermitage Lock	◊◊		when lock closed		⚿				🗑				
Hermitage Marina			⚓	⚓	⚿	⚱	⬇		🗑				

RIVER GREAT OUSE

Navigation notes

Below **Brownshill Staunch** the river briefly becomes tidal and changes quite dramatically. Every river has different faces and moods, but if there is any wind here its effect on the Great Ouse is exaggerated by the tidal changes. This is also the reach where you are most likely to meet a seal (see p.98).

Approaching **Earith**, the river passes **Crane's Fen** and the substantial brick piers of a railway which once crossed the fen and the river. **Westview Marina** is situated just beyond these piers, on the north bank at Earith. Just upstream of the marina's service pontoon (diesel) is an **EA pontoon which provides water and a pump-out**. It is also signed as a **48 hour mooring** and is the only such public riverside mooring between Brownshill and Hermitage. This dual use, without separately defined areas, can cause problems. If you moor for 48 hours next to the pump-out you will inevitably find boats coming alongside and pumping out across your boat. If you plan to stop overnight it would be advisable to move to the east end, leaving access to the pump-out.

The EA provision of boaters' services is split between Earith and Hermitage Lock, the latter offering rubbish disposal, showers and a toilet.

Before you get to **Hermitage Lock** the back gardens of Earith run down to the river and a sign announces **The Crown PH**. Sadly its former moorings had, at the time of writing, collapsed, and were not useable.

Old and New Bedford Rivers

At the end of the houses a sluice flows into the **Old Bedford River**, and takes extra water from the Great Ouse, directing it onto the **Ouse Washes**, a 10 square mile area where up to 20,000 million gallons of water is stored, providing a nature reserve of international importance.

Shortly after the **Old Bedford River** is the open entrance to the **New Bedford River**, also known as the **Hundred Foot River**, which carries water from the Great Ouse in a 20 mile cut to below Denver Sluice, thereby bypassing the next sections of the Great Ouse, alternatively known as the Old West River (as far as Pope's corner) and then the Ely Ouse. The New Bedford is navigable with caution, but not for hire boats. The general recommendation is to navigate the New Bedford starting at Denver and travelling to Earith. (See Chapter 4 p.153.)

Hermitage Lock

Immediately beyond the entrance to the New Bedford River is **Hermitage Lock**. The lock is manned and cannot be self-operated out of hours. If you arrive after it is closed, overnight mooring on the lock moorings is allowed. It also closes for an hour at lunchtime. Traffic lights tell you when the lock keeper is ready for you to enter the lock.

Earith Bridge looking into the New Bedford River

Moorings and facilities

Hermitage Lock
Toilet and shower, rubbish disposal
☎ 01487 841548

EA 48h mooring floating pontoon, left bank, Earith.
Water and **pump out** on floating pontoon.

Hermitage Marina, Earith, PE28 3PR
Long term moorings and shorter stays subject to availability.
☎ 01353 664 622

Westview Marina, Earith, PE28 3PN
Long term moorings, diesel, sales, chandlery, repairs, Elsan emptying
☎ 01487 840089

The Crown PH
48 High Street, Earith
☎ 01487 843490

Earith Curry House serves takeaway food, 57 High Street, PE27 4TW
☎ 01487 740590

Places to visit
Ouse Washes nature reserve
www.ousewashes.org.uk

Hermitage Lock Opening Times
Summer Hours
April to September 9am - 6pm
Winter Hours
October to March 9am - 4pm*
*Please call Hermitage lock on 01487 841548 for winter operating details and to arrange passage through the lock.
Closed daily 1pm - 2pm for lunch

Hermitage Lock from the non-tidal Old West River

RIVER GREAT OUSE

Seals

If you are lucky you may meet a seal on the Great Ouse. A typical experience is spotting what initially looks like a dog swimming in the river, and just as you wonder where the dog's owner is (when actually you should be grabbing your camera), you realise that it is a seal.

The favourite section of river to spot them is the Great Ouse between Brownhill's Staunch and Hermitage Lock because they come straight from the tidal river up the New Bedford River. During the summer of 2020 boaters were treated to regular sightings of a mother seal with a young pup.

I've also seen them upstream of Denver Sluice, near Brandon Creek, on the Old West River, and just below St Ives. They get onto these non tidal stretches by sneaking though the locks in the company of boats. It must be a source of considerable frustration to the EA that they can neither collect a registration fee from these frequent river users, nor charge a rod licence to these prolific consumers of fish!'

Remarkably in late summer 2023 a pair of dolphins were spotted on this reach between Brownhill's Staunch and Hermitage Lock. Sadly they did not survive.

The resident seal, nicknamed 'Neil the Seal', who frequently sunbathes on the EA Windmill mooring (see p.134). In 2023 'he' surprised everyone by producing a healthy pup!

Walking

From **Brownshill**, the **Ouse Valley Way** follows the left bank of the river to Hermitage Marina at **Earith**. On the right bank the **Pathfinder Long Distance walk** along the Bedford Level Corporation Barrier Bank continues to **Hermitage Lock**.

Local history

Earith lies on the short tidal section of the river before it becomes **The Old West River**. At the beginning of the 20th-century there was a station at Earith Bridge on the Ely, Sutton and St Ives branch of the Great Eastern Railway. During cold winters special trains brought thousands of people from Cambridge to the flooded and frozen nearby **Bury Fen** where great skating matches took place. Iron posts on the south side of the river below Brownshill remain from where the railway crossed the river.

Hermitage Lock

It was common practice for 'hermits' to collect tolls on behalf of religious houses. The hermitage and chapel of St Mary lay in a loop of the West Water and belonged to the Diocese of Ely. The bridge and causeway over Haddenham Fen, then known as 'Earith Causey', were looked after by hermits in the 14th and 15th centuries. This is the origin of the name 'Hermitage' for the lock.

Earith was a busy port when water was the primary means of transporting goods. Its location at the end of the New Bedford, or Hundred Foot River, contributing to its growth. Its wharves and warehouses have now largely disappeared. In 1836 **George Jewson** and his son founded the builder's merchants 'Jewson & Sons' here.

The Ouse Washes

The Ouse Washes are a 10 square mile nature reserve of international importance. They are protected by an comprehensive series of classifications. They are a SSSI (site of special scientific interest), a Ramsar important wetland site (Ramsar is a 1975 intergovernmental environmental treaty), a SPA (special protection area) under the European Union Birds Directive, a Special Area of Conservation and a Grade 1 Nature Conservation Review Site.

The Washes form a flood-plain lying between the Old Bedford River/Delph River and the New Bedford River, stretching from St Ives in the south west to Downham Market in the north east. With the capacity to store a staggering 20,000 million gallons of water, they are fed from the river Great Ouse via the Old Bedford River (which becomes the River Delph) before the waters spill out onto the flood plain. When the waters are released at the northern end, they are let out into the New Bedford River through Welmore Lake Sluice back into the tidal Great Ouse where they finally flow out to sea.

The RSPB have observational hides at Purl's Bridge (accessed from Manea down what must surely be the bumpiest road in Cambridgeshire). Facilities are basic, but there are toilets.

Welney Wetland Centre (wwt.org.uk) is an altogether grander (and warmer) affair, with a restaurant and shop, and an enclosed bridge crossing the New Bedford River to the observation areas.

In winter the washes attract thousands of ducks and swans, and in spring they are a breeding ground for hundreds of snipe, lapwings and redshanks. Even a non-twitcher, like me, has been pleasantly surprised by what a fascinating and enthralling day can be had at the Wetland Centre.

As well as providing a varied and rich ecosystem, the Washes are a fantastic leisure resource. I've walked the banks of the New Bedford River in summer, paddled across the flooded washes in autumn, and hope one day to skate them.

As autumn turns into winter it is worth stopping at Salter's Lode and walking along the bank of the New Bedford River. You will be treated to the spectacle of flocks of birds arriving from Arctic Russia and Iceland. They land with an apparent sense of relief and exhaustion that can only result from flying several thousand miles in near freezing conditions.

The flooded Ouse Washes from the A142 Mepal Causeway

EA 'Windmill' moorings on the Ely Ouse at Ten Mile Bank, regular home to 'Neil the Seal' (see p.98)

2

RIVER GREAT OUSE EARITH TO DENVER

The Old West River and the Ely Ouse to Denver via Ten Mile Bank

Described travelling **downstream**

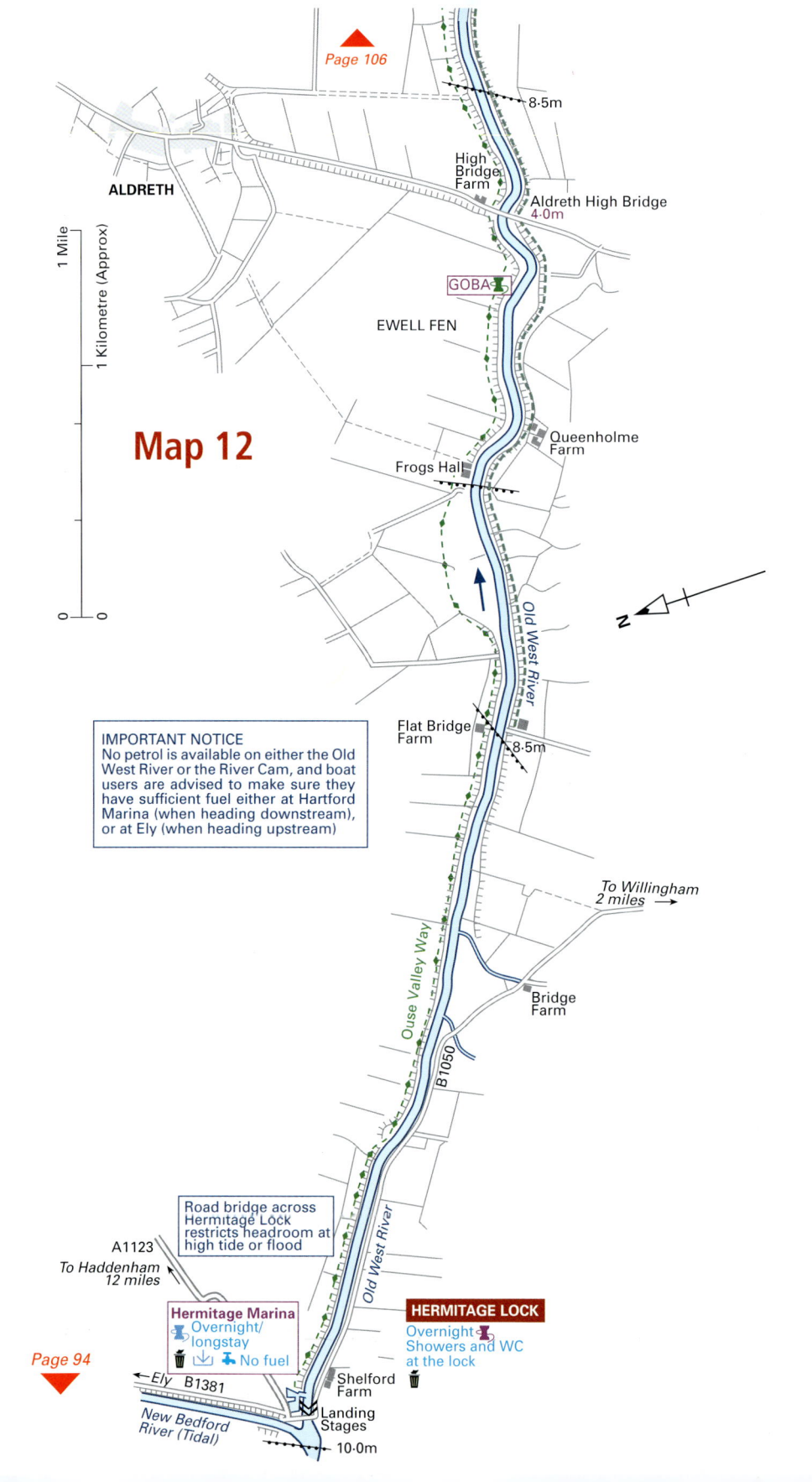

Map 12

ALDRETH

Page 106

8.5m

High Bridge Farm

Aldreth High Bridge 4.0m

GOBA

EWELL FEN

Queenholme Farm

Frogs Hall

Old West River

Flat Bridge Farm

8.5m

To Willingham 2 miles

Ouse Valley Way

Bridge Farm

B1050

IMPORTANT NOTICE
No petrol is available on either the Old West River or the River Cam, and boat users are advised to make sure they have sufficient fuel either at Hartford Marina (when heading downstream), or at Ely (when heading upstream)

Road bridge across Hermitage Lock restricts headroom at high tide or flood

A1123
To Haddenham 12 miles

Hermitage Marina
Overnight/longstay
No fuel

HERMITAGE LOCK
Overnight
Showers and WC at the lock

Shelford Farm

Ely B1381

Landing Stages

New Bedford River (Tidal)

10.0m

Old West River

Page 94

Map 12

River Great Ouse
Old West River
Hermitage Lock to
Aldreth High Bridge

Distance 3½ miles

Time ¾ hour (in favourable conditions)

Map 12 Hermitage Lock to Aldreth High Bridge

Lowest bridge 4m Aldreth High Bridge
Hermitage Lock (attended)
L 30·5m, W 4m (13'1") D 1.5m, Head 2·75m
Open April-Sept 0900-1800, October-March 0900-1600
Closed daily 1300-1400
Ring in advance ☎ 01487 841548

Location	Lock width	Moorings and facilities								Victualling			
		Over night	48 hour	Long stay	Toilets/showers	Water point	Chemical disposal point	Pumpout	Refuse	Fuel	Shops	Pub	Café/restaurant
Hermitage Lock	⏀⏀	⚓	Overnight only when lock closed		🚻				🗑				
Hermitage Marina		⚓	⚓	⚓	🚻	🚰	⬇		🗑				
Aldreth Drain GOBA			⚓										

RIVER GREAT OUSE

Navigation notes

The main waters of the Great Ouse having been diverted down both the Old Bedford river and then the New Bedford River, the river downstream of Hermitage Lock is comparatively narrow. The only water it receives from the Great Ouse is what comes through the lock. There is no weir or lock by-water.

As you emerge from **Hermitage Lock** into what is now known as the **Old West River**, it appears that you are on a radically different river to the one that entered the lock. Non-tidal once again, the river is dramatically reduced in size from the mighty river just upstream of the lock.

Hermitage Marina is on the north side of the river, immediately after the lock.

Apart from a small amount of river water coming through on every use of the lock, the Old West River's supply of water is all from land drainage, both natural run-off and pumped. This means there is very little flow. In high summer, and following periods of low rainfall, this section of the river can be so slow

Duck weed on the Old West River

Speed limit

The entire section from Hermitage Lock to Pope's Corner has a 4mph speed limit.

Few boats have speedometers and at both ends of the Old West the agency has erected timing posts. (see photo). If you travel between the posts in less than 30 seconds you are breaking the speed limit!

moving that it becomes carpeted from side to side in green duckweed (*Lemnoideae*). This floats on the surface of the water but, although appearing somewhat daunting to the boater, it doesn't negatively affect navigation unless your engine is water cooled and draws river water. In these circumstances you need to ensure that your water intake remains clear, to avoid your engine overheating.

Other years, blanket weed (*Cladophora glomerata*) or cott weed (*Vaucheria dichotoma*) thrive. These are far more of a problem to the boater. Although clearly visible, most of the plant is below the surface, and long filaments can foul and choke your propellor. It pays to steer from patch of clear water to patch of clear water, trying to dodge the weed, and if unable to avoid it, periodically put

Moorings and facilities

Toilet, shower and rubbish disposal at **Hermitage Lock**

Hermitage Marina, Earith, PE28 3PR Long term moorings and shorter stays subject to availability.
☎ 01353 664 622

GOBA Aldreth Drain moorings on Ewell Fen, 200 yards upstream of Aldreth High Bridge.

New Life on the Old West (NLOW) is a heritage lottery funded three year project creating new ponds, scrapes and wildflower meadows, and making the network of drainage ditches more wildlife friendly to create natural stepping stones between key Cambridgeshire wetland reserves. They run educational wildlife walks. Their website www.newlifeoldwest.org.uk is worth visiting and joining one of their walks highly rewarding.

Egret

---

your engine briefly into reverse to attempt to throw weed off the prop.

To their credit the Environment Agency regularly cut and clear the weed, but it sometimes appears to return almost as quickly as it was cut.

Downstream from Hermitage Lock, the river is closely shadowed on its south bank by the busy B1050 road for ¾ mile and you will be the subject of interest to passing motorists, looking across with apparent envy in good weather, and smug satisfaction in bad.

After the road turns away, the next 6 miles are some of the most glorious, nature filled boating to experience anywhere. On just one recent trip, on a dull grey day, the author spotted oyster catcher, egret, grebe, heron, an abundance of shag, a large hunting bird - possibly a buzzard or a marsh harrier. He was followed down the river by a tern, diving behind the boat after the fish he might have disturbed. The raised flood banks on either side of the river have been left to wild flower and offer a dazzling display.

On the north bank you pass **Haddenham Engine pumping station**, near Frog Hall. About ½ mile southeast of the hall is one of two sites put forward as the location for Hereward the Wake's defeat of the Norman troops in 1071. The only **visitor moorings** on the Old West River before Stretham are provided here by GOBA. So far, there have not been any reports of boaters being disturbed at night by the ghosts of slain Normans!

Around a bend, just downstream of the GOBA moorings, **High Bridge**, a farm access bridge, crosses the river northwards towards the small village of **Aldreth**.

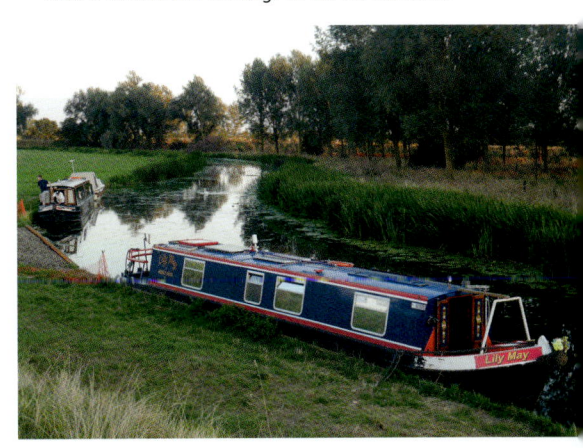

GOBA Aldreth Drain moorings on the Old West River

River Great Ouse Earith to Denver

RIVER GREAT OUSE   **105**

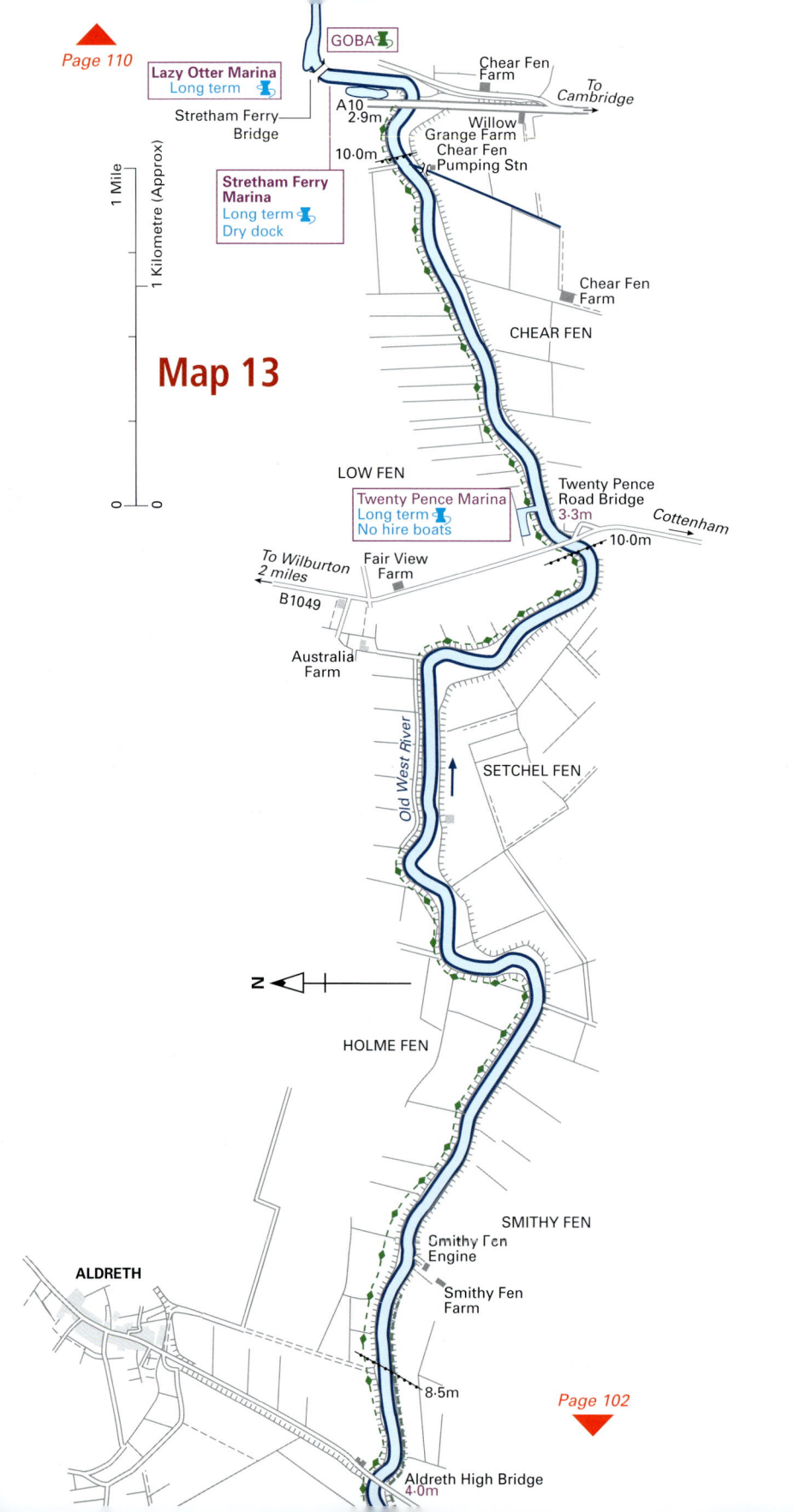

Map 13

Page 110 ▲

- **Lazy Otter Marina** — Long term
- Stretham Ferry Bridge
- GOBA
- A10 2·9m
- 10·0m
- Willow Grange Farm
- Chear Fen Pumping Stn
- Chear Fen Farm
- To Cambridge
- **Stretham Ferry Marina** — Long term, Dry dock
- Chear Fen Farm
- CHEAR FEN
- LOW FEN
- **Twenty Pence Marina** — Long term, No hire boats
- Twenty Pence Road Bridge 3·3m
- 10·0m
- Cottenham
- To Wilburton 2 miles
- B1049
- Fair View Farm
- Australia Farm
- Old West River
- SETCHEL FEN
- N
- HOLME FEN
- SMITHY FEN
- Smithy Fen Engine
- Smithy Fen Farm
- ALDRETH
- 8·5m
- Aldreth High Bridge 4·0m

Page 102 ▼

Scale: 1 Mile / 1 Kilometre (Approx)

Map 13

Old West River Aldreth High Bridge to Stretham Ferry Bridge

Distance 5 miles
Time 1¾ hours (in favourable conditions)

Map 13 Aldreth High Bridge to Stretham Ferry Bridge

Lowest bridge 2·9m (Stretham A10 bridge)

Location	Moorings and facilities									Victualling		
	Short stay/visitor	48hr	Long stay	Water point	Chemical disposal point	Pumpout	Refuse	Diesel	Shops	Pub	Café/restaurant
Twenty Pence Marina			⚓	Facilities for customer only							
Stretham Ferry Marina			⚓	Facilities for customer only							
Lazy Otter Meadows Marina			⚓	Facilities for customers only						🍺	🍴
GOBA 'Lazy Otter' moorings		⚓									

Navigation notes

Beyond **Aldreth High Bridge** a series of drains run next to the river on the south side. They transition seamlessly from First Sock Drain to Second Sock Drain to Third Sock Drain.

The **B1049 Twenty Pence Road** crosses the river next to an attractive thatched cottage. The Bridge PH was demolished in 2002 and houses were built on the site. The origin of the name 'Twentypence' is unclear, although the bridge used to be a toll bridge. It cost 1d per person to cross to Cottenham and 2d with a bike. **Twenty Pence Marina** lies on the left bank, just after the bridge. On the right bank there are the disappearing hulls of old wooden boats, a sort of unofficial graveyard.

The river returns to rural countryside for another 1½ miles until it is crossed by the **modern bridge carrying the A10**. Briefly, the river's character appears to change between the new A10 bridge and the old former A10 bridge, known as **Stretham Ferry Bridge**. It travels through a wooded area with side ponds. On the left bank is a dry dock, available for hire, and popular for DIY blacking, owned by the neighbouring **Stretham Ferry Marina**.

Just east of **Stretham Ferry Bridge**, on the north bank is the **Lazy Otter PH** which as at September 2023 had ceased to function as a pub. Planning permission had been refused to turn it into a domestic dwelling, and its future is sadly uncertain. There used to be popular GOBA moorings here, but these have been reclaimed by Lazy Otter Meadows marina and are no longer available to visitors. **GOBA have secured alternative moorings**, slightly further on, on the right bank.

An historic view of the punt and lift bridge across the Ouse at Twenty Pence Road wilburton.ccan.co.uk

Moorings and facilities

Twenty Pence Marina, Wilburton CB6 3PX
Long term moorings (hire boats not allowed)
☏ 01954 251118

Stretham Ferry Marina, CB6 3LU
Long term moorings
☏ 01353 648383
To hire dry dock, call Ken on
☏ 07581 458069

Lazy Otter Meadows Marina CB6 3FS
Long term moorings
☏ 01480 587121

GOBA moorings on right (south) bank opposite the The Lazy Otter (PH closed 2023).

The Old West River

Before the 17th century draining of the Fens, the Old West River used to run from east to west and was called either the 'West Water' or the 'Aldreth River'. Vermuyden linked it to the Cam reversing the direction of flow, causing it to run in the opposite direction, from west to east.

Understanding where the rivers went in Roman times is fascinating. The course of the Ouse was very different. It turned north instead of east at Earith and followed a now extinct course west of Chatteris and March to Upwell, Wisbech and the sea. The winding Chatteris to Somersham Road follows its course and is still reflected in the name Ferry Hill. This river was called the West River.

The Cam flowed from Cambridge past Ely and to Littleport before diverting from its present route and heading off through Welney and Upwell to join the Ouse (aka the West Water) and enter the sea at Wisbech. The channel between Littleport and Wisbech would later be known as the Well Stream.

In Roman times the Ouse and Cam were separate rivers until they met at Upwell.

The River Little Ouse always drained into the Wash at Lynn (until 1537 Bishop's Lynn, and latterly King's Lynn). Between 1215 and 1270 a short leam (less than 2 miles) was cut between Littleport and Stowbridge to connect with the Little Ouse flowing to Lynn.

As a result of Vermuyden's work in the mid 17th century the Aldreth river linked the main stream at Earith with the Cam near Stretham. With the construction of the Old Bedford River (1630 - 1636) and the New Bedford River (1652) the West Water gradually fell extinct. The diversion of the greater part of the water previously draining at Wisbech meant that such stream as was left could no longer scour out a channel through the sands which the incoming tide continually silted up. Wisbech became more and more shut off from the sea, and is now 10 miles from it. The inability of the water to escape quickly enough through these choking sands drove the river water at Wisbech to back up on itself and drown the neighbouring fens.

Nothing remains of the West Water as a living river, although what is now called the Old River Nene enters and leaves its former channel between Benwick and March. The bed of the former Wisbech Ouse is still occupied in its upper reaches by the Old Croft River (now little more than a drain), and between Outwell and Wisbech by the artificial Wisbech Canal dug in late 18th Century.

I have written in greater detail on the draining of the Fens in our companion volume *Fenland Waterways* and am enormously indebted to A. K. Astbury's 1958 work *The Black Fens*.

Walking

The **OVW** sticks close to the north bank of the Old West River. There is also a footpath along the southern flood bank which starts at **Flatbridge**, a couple of miles east of Hermitage lock. Both of these continue to **Stretham**. For anyone with a love of nature's flora and fauna this must be a delightful section of the Ouse to walk.

Local history

The Roman road **Akeman Street** crossed the river at **Stretham Ferry**. The ferry was replaced in 1763 by a turnpike road with a toll bridge. The bridge was narrow and steep and was in turn replaced in 1925 by the current bridge. It was load tested by driving either two or four traction engines over it (accounts vary). Until 1976 it carried the A10, until the road was straightened and the new bridge was built to the west of the old.

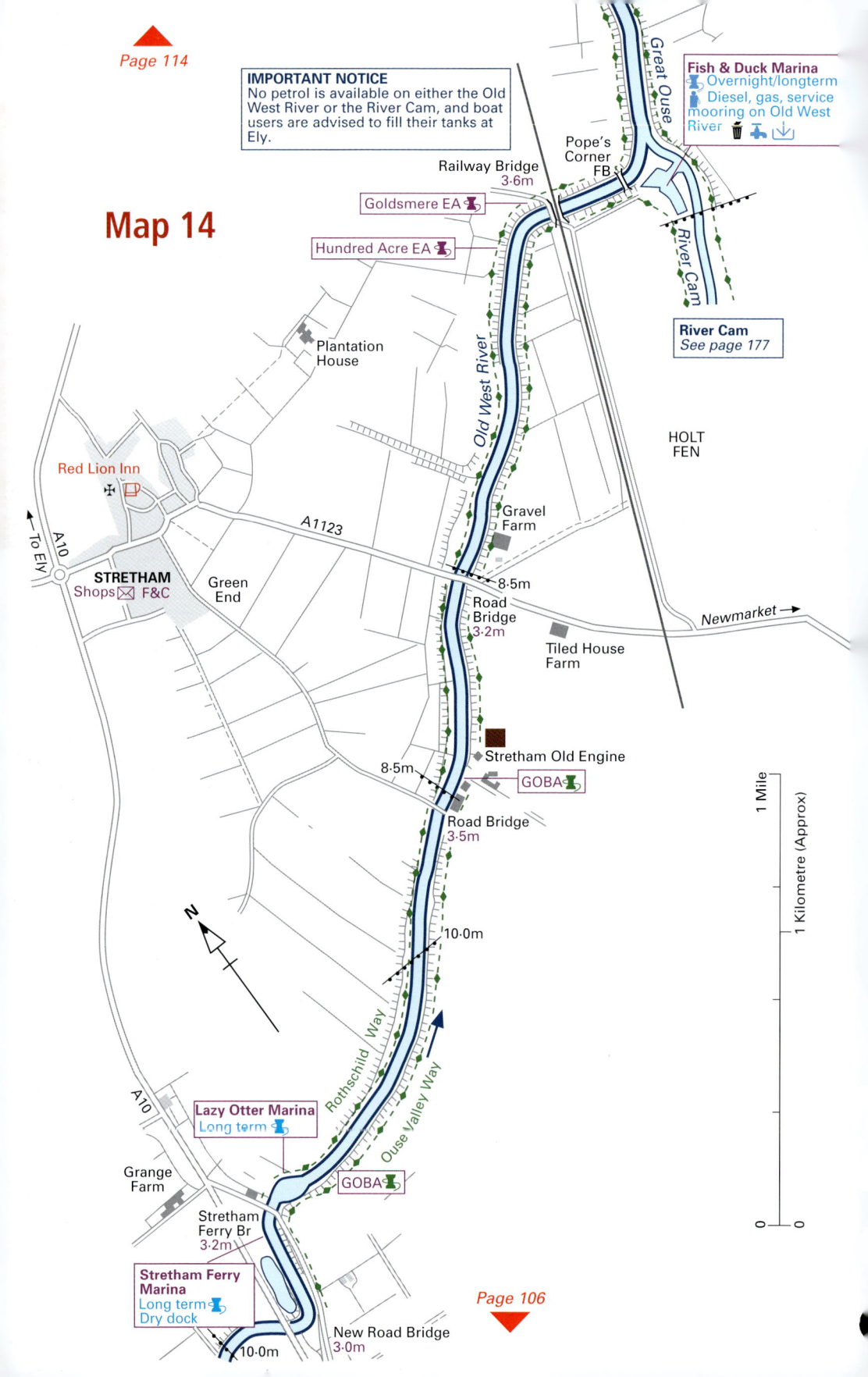

Map 14

Page 114

IMPORTANT NOTICE
No petrol is available on either the Old West River or the River Cam, and boat users are advised to fill their tanks at Ely.

Fish & Duck Marina
Overnight/longterm
Diesel, gas, service mooring on Old West River

Great Ouse

Pope's Corner FB

Railway Bridge 3·6m

Goldsmere EA

Hundred Acre EA

River Cam
See page 177

Plantation House

Old West River

HOLT FEN

Red Lion Inn

To Ely — A10

STRETHAM
Shops F&C

A1123

Green End

Gravel Farm
8·5m

Road Bridge 3·2m

Tiled House Farm

← Newmarket →

Stretham Old Engine

8·5m

GOBA

Road Bridge 3·5m

10·0m

1 Mile
1 Kilometre (Approx)

Rothschild Way

Ouse Valley Way

A10

Lazy Otter Marina
Long term

Grange Farm

GOBA

Stretham Ferry Br 3·2m

Stretham Ferry Marina
Long term
Dry dock

10·0m

New Road Bridge 3·0m

Page 106

Map 14

Old West River
Stretham Ferry Bridge to Pope's Corner

Distance 3 miles
Time 1 hour

River Great Ouse Earith to Denver

Map 14 Stretham Ferry Bridge to Pope's Corner

Lowest bridge 3·2m A1123 road bridge, Stretham

Location	Moorings and facilities							Victualling		
	48hr	Long stay	Water point	Chemical disposal point	Pumpout	Refuse	Diesel	Shops	Pub	Café
GOBA Stretham Old Engine	✓									
EA Hundred Acre moorings	✓									
EA Goldsmere moorings	✓									
Fish and Duck Marina	✓	✓	✓	✓		✓	✓			

RIVER GREAT OUSE

Navigation notes

Downstream of **Stretham** the reach is enriched by a profusion of european white water-lily (*Nymphaea alba*) - an indicator of excellent water quality.

There are several sections with moored boats between the old Stretham Ferry road bridge and Pope's Corner, and residential moorers will often request that you slow below the maximum 4mph in order to minimise your wash.

The towering chimney of **Stretham Old Engine** appears on the right bank. There are **GOBA moorings downstream of the bridge**, well located for visiting this popular attraction.

The landscape is now flat fen. Next you pass under the **A1123 road bridge**. To your north the tower and octagon of the distant Ely Cathedral, known as 'the ship of the Fens', appear. Less than a mile beyond the A1123 bridge there are two sets of **EA moorings on the north bank**.

An electrified **railway line** comes in from the east and **crosses the river downstream of the moorings**. Just beyond the railway bridge there is a **footbridge at Pope's Corner** and then, after the bend, on the right side, the mighty **River Cam** joins the modest Old West River from the south.

European white water lily

Moorings and facilities

GOBA moorings at **Stretham Old Engine**.

EA 'Hundred Acre' moorings left bank, approaching Pope's Corner, just upstream of railway bridge.

EA 'Goldsmere' moorings, left bank, just downstream of Hundred Acre moorings.

Fish and Duck Marina
Pope's Corner, CB6 3HR
Long term moorings, day boat hire, sales, diesel, chandlery.
☏ 01353 648081

The Fish and Duck Marina at Pope's Corner is the confluence of the Rivers Cam and Great Ouse. The service point is on the Great Ouse. The marina offers fuel, gas, chandlery, mooring, boat sales, and has a small fleet of day boats for hire.

Walking

The **OVW** swaps to the south side of the Old West river at the **A10 road bridge** just before Stretham, and continues riverside all the way to the **Fish and Duck Marina** at **Pope's Corner**. There is also a path along the north bank, the Rothschild Way, from the **Lazy Otter Marina** to **Pope's Corner**.

Confluence
The River Cam joins at Pope's Corner.

Places to visit

Stretham Old Engine, CB6 3LF
Museum containing a steam driven pump, generally open to the public Sunday afternoons and Bank Holidays from April to October (inclusive), check in advance:
www.strethamoldengine.org.uk

Local history

Stretham Old Engine is the sole surviving operational steam engine in the Black Fen (ancient peat fen). It was installed in 1831, replacing four windpumps. The first Fens steam pump arrived at Sutton St Edmunds in 1817. The former pumping station, is now a museum run by Stretham Engine Trust. It includes a steam powered beam engine, once one of a hundred steam engines draining the fens. The Old Engine worked from 1831 to 1924 when a Mirrlees diesel engine was fitted. The steam engine remained as a standby, and was brought back into service during the floods of 1939 and 1940. The diesel engine would in turn be removed and replaced by 5 electrical pumps. The Prickwillow Museum on the River Lark boasts a similar Mirrlees diesel engine (see p.227).

In 1925 a new road was constructed across the former **Stretham Mere** to a bridge over the Old West River that replaced a ford.

The inn at the **Fish and Duck** was closed and demolished in 2009. Built in 1850 its first recorded owner was a Richard Pope. The junction of the Old West river and River Cam is still called **Pope's Corner**. In 2018 permission was granted to build a new restaurant on the site, however there has been no futher progress.

A fuller history of the draining of the fens is included in our companion guide, **Fenland Waterways** (Imray).

Stretham Old Engine

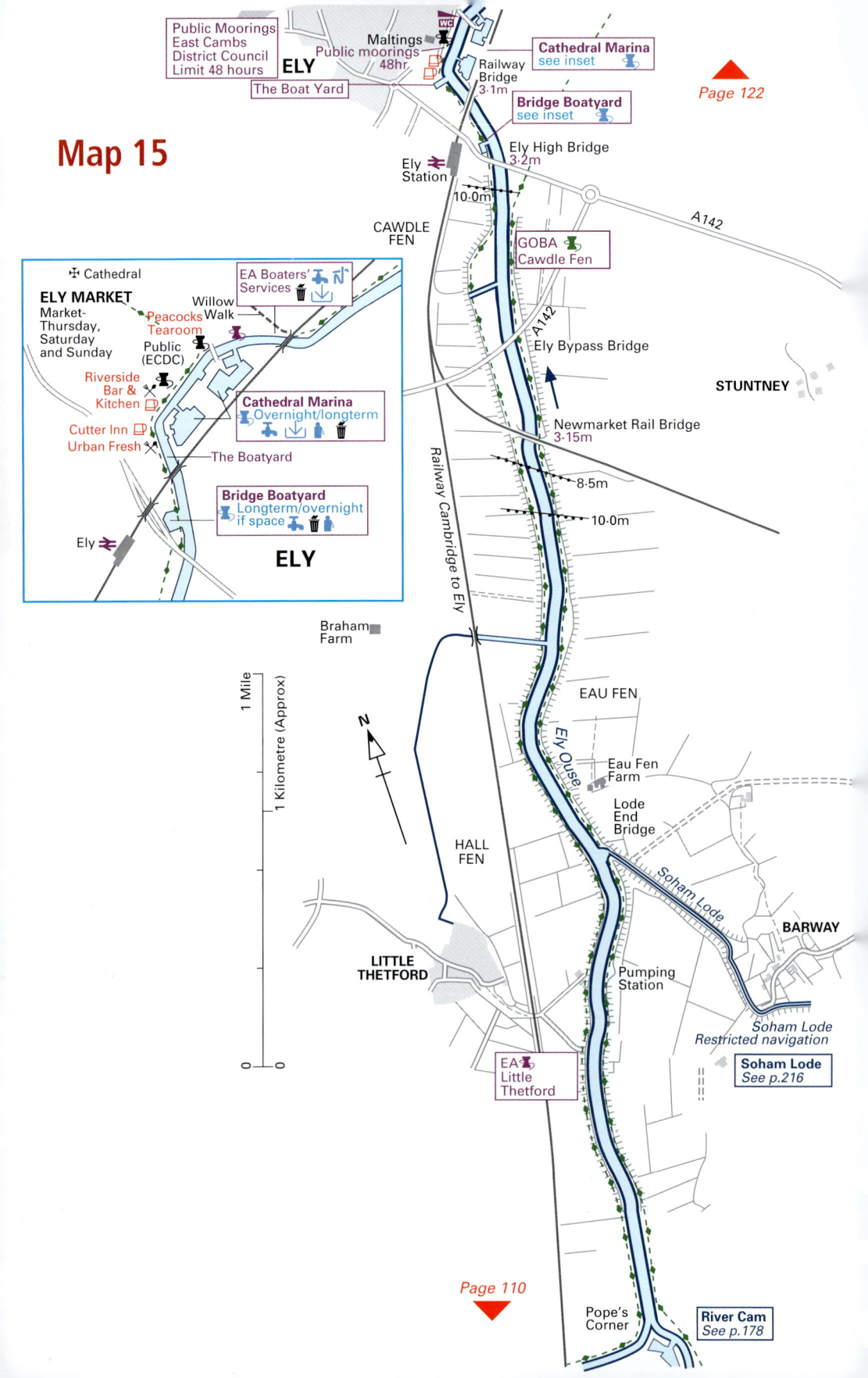

Map 15

Public Moorings East Cambs District Council Limit 48 hours

ELY

Maltings
Public moorings 48hr

The Boat Yard

Railway Bridge 3·1m

Cathedral Marina see inset

Bridge Boatyard see inset

Ely High Bridge 3·2m

Ely Station

10·0m

CAWDLE FEN

GOBA Cawdle Fen

A142

Ely Bypass Bridge

STUNTNEY

Newmarket Rail Bridge 3·15m

8·5m

10·0m

Page 122

Inset: ELY

✠ Cathedral

ELY MARKET Market-Thursday, Saturday and Sunday

EA Boaters' Services

Willow Walk

Peacocks Tearoom

Public (ECDC)

Riverside Bar & Kitchen

Cathedral Marina Overnight/longterm

Cutter Inn
Urban Fresh

The Boatyard

Bridge Boatyard Longterm/overnight if space

Ely

ELY

Braham Farm

Railway Cambridge to Ely

EAU FEN

Eau Fen Farm

Lode End Bridge

Soham Lode

BARWAY

HALL FEN

LITTLE THETFORD

Pumping Station

Soham Lode Restricted navigation

Soham Lode See p.216

EA Little Thetford

Pope's Corner

River Cam See p.178

Page 110

1 Mile / 1 Kilometre (Approx)

N

Map 15

The Ely Ouse Pope's Corner to Ely

Distance 3½ miles
Time 1 hour

Map 15 Pope's Corner to Ely

Lowest bridge 3·1m Railway bridge Ely

Location	Moorings and facilities							Victualling		
	48hr	Long stay	Water point	Chemical disposal point	Pumpout	Refuse	Fuel	Shops	Pub	Café
Little Thetford EA moorings	✓									
Cawdle Fen GOBA	✓							Short walk to Ely		
Bridge Boatyard	If spaces available	✓	✓			✓	Diesel	✓	✓	✓
Ely Town Quay ECDC moorings	✓					✓		✓	✓	✓
Ely Marine/Cathedral Marina	✓	✓	✓	✓		✓	Petrol & diesel	✓	✓	✓
EA Willow Walk moorings	✓							✓	✓	✓
Willow Walk Boaters' Services			✓	✓	✓	✓				

River Great Ouse Earith to Denver

RIVER GREAT OUSE

Navigation notes

Downstream of Pope's Corner, the River Great Ouse is known as the 'Ely Ouse' and will remain so for the rest of the river's nearly 20 mile non-tidal course to Denver Sluice. Because the waters of the Old West river are swelled by the far greater volume of water joining from the Cam, several people have asked why the Cam doesn't give its name to the Ely Ouse. Apparently, it's not volume of water that counts, but distance from source.

About a mile downstream from **Pope's Corner**, on the left bank of the Ely Ouse, are the pleasant, but remote, **EA Little Thetford** moorings. These can accommodate several craft. A track leads across **Holt Fen** and over a level crossing into nearby **Little Thetford** village. There is no pub or shop in the village, which is on the A10 busy trunk road, with Ely about 3 miles away. There is a path to Ely at the side of the A10, but it is narrow and walking or cycling to Ely is not recommended by this route. A much better alternative is the Ouse Valley Way which follows the river all the way into Ely.

The Ouse is now wide, generally reasonably fast flowing, and bordered by open fens. The cosy, sometimes tree lined, meandering character of the upper Ouse has now long gone.

About half a mile downstream of the Little Thetford moorings, on the right bank, are the gates and pumping station to **Soham Lode** (see p.220). This is navigable for about a mile early in the season, but by mid-summer there is a seemingly impenetrable build up of weed, both above and below the gates.

Moorings and facilities

EA 'Little Thetford' mooring, left bank.

GOBA 'Cawdle Fen' mooring, right bank shortly before Ely.

Ely Cathedral, known as the 'Ship of the Fens', emerging on the horizon

About a mile beyond Soham Lode the **railway crosses the Ely Ouse on a new bridge**. The previous bridge collapsed in 2007 before the IWA National Festival in St Ives. This closed the river, and boaters attending the festival were forced to use the alternative route along the New Bedford River.

The next bridge, a modern combination of pristine white concrete and 'self colour' steel carries the **Ely bypass**. Initially derided as ruining the historic views of **Ely Cathedral** across Cawdle Fen (and above the railway station), this road has removed the regular gridlock from the southern part of **Ely**, and done much to enhance the historic city.

Ely

New GOBA moorings have been recently established on the **right bank, opposite Cawdle Fen**, and provide a convenient alternative to the city centre moorings in Ely, which can be in great demand on summer weekends.

You enter the city under **Ely High Bridge**. The bridge sits on the old Stutney Causeway, proposed as the alternative location of Hereward the Wake's spirited, but sadly only temporary, defeat of the Normans.

In **Ely** there are **District Council public 48hr moorings** along the left bank of the river front, after a stretch of long term moorings let to Bridge Boatyard. Overstaying is monitored and time limits are enforced. The strict 48 hour mooring limit is now relaxed during severe weather conditions (see ECDC web site for Extreme Weather Warnings) and generally the mooring officers are

Ely riverfront from Lincoln Bridge leading to Ely Cathedral Marina

displaying a welcome more helpful approach. These are very popular moorings at weekends in season so get there early to avoid disappointment.

There is a boatyard, a boat hire business and two marinas and also the **EA boaters' services at Willow Walk**, just upstream of the railway bridge. There are further **council moorings** from the Babylon Art Gallery up to the boaters' services.

Walking

The river turns north at **Pope's Corner**. On the right bank the **Fen Rivers Way** runs along the flood bank, but as there is no bridge nearby it is inaccessible from the Fish and Duck marina without either a dip, or cadging a lift across the river from a passing boater. However the **Ouse Valley Way** continues along the left bank, all the way to **Ely**.

Ely runs down to the river and embraces it. The west bank of the river, with its public moorings, is accessible for its entire course through the city, from Bridge Road, Annesdale, Ship Lane, Pegasus Walk, and Willow Walk. The opposite bank is occupied by the private King's School boathouse and Cathedral Marina, and there is no access.

Local history

Ely was once an island (the Isle of Eels), where St Etheldreda built an Abbey Church in 672. The present cathedral was started in 1083 and granted cathedral status in 1109. **Ely Cathedral** remains one of the great medieval cathedrals. It has fought subsidence for most of its life. In February 1322 the central stone tower collapsed and was

> ### Moorings and facilities
> **EA boaters' services** at Willow Walk, water, pump-out, elsan disposal, rubbish (no recycling).
> **Bridge Boatyard**, CB7 4DY
> Overnight/ longterm moorings, boat hire, repairs, diesel, gas and coal.
> ☏ 01353 663726,
> **Ely Marine Ltd, Cathedral Marina** Waterside, CB7 4A
> Long term moorings, diesel & petrol, sales, repairs.
> ☏ 01353 664622
> **The Boat Yard** 1 Annesdale, Ely CB7 4BN
> Repairs and new builds.
> ☏ 01353 668551

replaced with the current octagon tower. This was constructed on twelve great oak beams (brought by river from Chicksands near Bedford) and is the 'greatest individual achievement of architectural genius at Ely Cathedral', according to the renowned architectural historian Nikolaus Pevsner. The guided tour up the Octagon Tower is a not-to-be-missed, never-forgotten experience.

Ely Cathedral's Octagon Tower

Traditional, former working boats, moored on Ely Town Quay

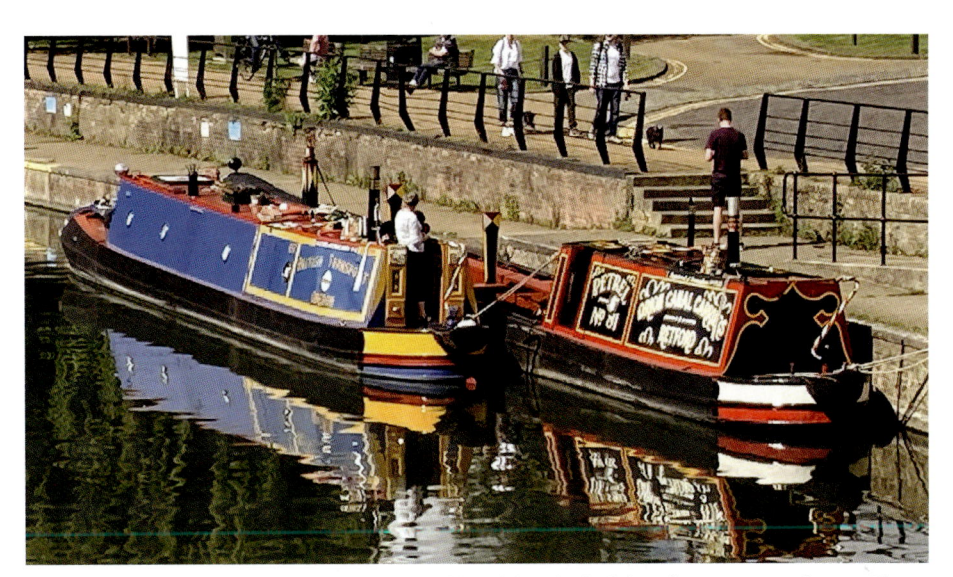

Boats painted in the old British Waterway's Colours (left), and the other built for Fellows Morton & Clayton with traditional livery of the Union Canal Carriers

In the 15th century the north east transept collapsed. Looking at the cathedral from Palace Green, the front of the building is dominated by the great Galilee porch, but it is not symmetrical on either side.

In 1689 Celia Fiennes, on a horseback tour of England wrote of Ely that it was 'the dirtiest place I ever saw'. William Cobbett wrote in 1830 'Ely is a miserable little town, very prettily situated, but poor and mean'.

The 2021 National Census confirmed Ely as the 9th smallest city in the UK by population.

The riverside **Cutter Inn in Annesdale**, is named, not after a type of sailing vessel (e.g. the tea clipper the 'Cutty Sark'), but after 400 navvies, many of whom drank in the inn, who, between 1827 and 1830, cut the new, straightened 3½ mile route between Queen Adelaide and Littleport. It is said that the landlord gave the Navvies credit between pay days by marking up their drinks on a blackboard with either a 'P' for Pint, or 'Q' for Quart. This gave rise to the expression 'mind your Ps and Qs'.

Ely Cathedral

The great Warrior Queen, **Boudicca** took on the Romans in AD61 and temporarily routed them, sacking Colchester and burning St Albans and London. **Hereward the Wake**, known as the 'last Englishman' led the sadly unsuccessful resistance to the Norman Invasion of 1066. Both hailed from the Fens north west of Ely.

The first religious foundation in Ely was established in AD655 by **Etheldreda**, later St Etheldreda, also known as **St Audrey**. In the Middle-ages a fair was held on her feast day, 23 June, outside the great Galilee Porch of Ely Cathedral. The word 'tawdry' (an amalgamation of 'Saint' and 'Audrey') is believed to derive from the practice of selling cheap shoddy knick-knacks at this fair.

The **Western Dock** at **Cawdle Fen** was built after 1845-47 when Ely became a main railway junction. This was once a large, 300 vessel capacity, dock where now the station car park stands. This was accessed by a short channel and lock, but any surviving evidence of this disappeared under the recent by-pass bridge. The dock was progressively filled in around 1914, during the 1940s, and finally in 1964.

Visit the medieval **Ely Cathedral**, known as the 'Ship of the Fens' and climb the Octagon Tower to marvel first hand at 14th-century engineering and enjoy commanding views across the countryside. The Cathedral's museum of stained glass also comes highly recommended.

Ely has a lively and individual High Street. Its range of **supermarkets** including Aldi, Sainsbury's, and Tesco, all only a short walk from the river. Waitrose is just off the market square.

Ely Leisure Village on the far edge of town has fast food restaurants and a cinema.

The Old Fire Engine House is a unique restaurant combined with an art gallery.
25 St Mary's St, CB7 4ER
① 01353 662582

Peacock's Tea Rooms, 65 Waterside CB7 4AU, evoke a lost age
① 01353 661100

Urban Fresh, 5 Annesdale, CB7 4BN
'A taste of South America in the heart of Ely'
www.urbanfreshely.uk
① 01353 240024

Central pubs serving food include The Hereward, The Cutter Inn, The Lamb Hotel, The Prince Albert, The Royal Standard, The Kings Arms, The Minster Tavern, The Townhouse, Riverside Bar and Kitchen. **The Drayman's Son**, 29a Fore Hill, Ely CB7 4AA is a unique 'micro' pub.
① 01353 662920

Octagon Tower, Ely Cathedral

Markets
Thursday, Saturday and Sunday in Market Square.

Tourist Information Centre
Oliver Cromwell's House, 29 St Mary's St
CB7 4HF
① 01353 662062

Launderette
J & R Launderette, 30 West End CB6 3AY

Babylon Arts, Babylon Bridge, Waterside, CB7 4AU

Boat trips
The 12 passenger *Liberty Belle* offers half hour cruises everyday of the week, weather permitting. Dog friendly.
Departs Ely Quayside outside RBK.
Captain Bob ① 07927 390380

The floating Vic
The Great Ouse has acquired its own vicar. The appropriately named Father David Goode can be found on his narrowboat *Grumpy* around Ely. He represents the Community of the Isle of Ely and The Fens in the Diocese of Eastern England (Open Episcopal Church). Dave often broadcasts services from his boat, and is always a supportive and friendly face.

Regattas
Great Ouse Marathon - Denver to Ely, late October/early November. A staggered start minimises inconvenience to other river users, but please slow down as you approach and pass boats - they may have just rowed over 12 miles.

Other water users
Isle of Ely Rowing Club
King's School Ely Rowing Club
Cambridge University Boat Club (elite 'blue' boats)

Public Transport train to Cambridge or Peterborough. X9 buses to central Cambridge.

RIVER GREAT OUSE

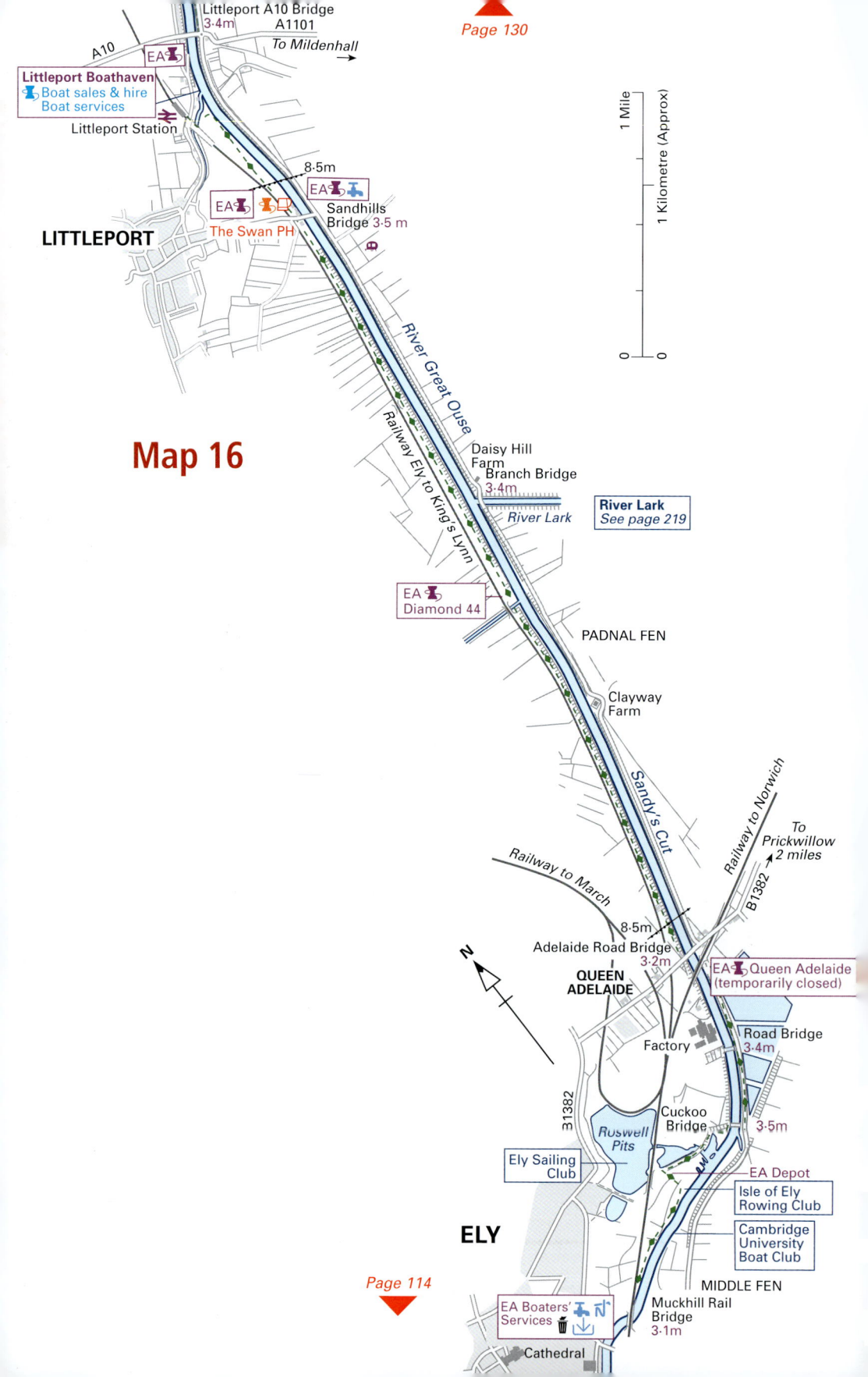

Map 16

LITTLEPORT

- Littleport A10 Bridge 3.4m
- A10 / A1101 To Mildenhall
- Littleport Boathaven — Boat sales & hire, Boat services
- EA
- Littleport Station
- The Swan PH
- EA
- Sandhills Bridge 3.5 m
- 8.5m

Page 130

River Great Ouse

Railway Ely to King's Lynn

- Daisy Hill Farm
- Branch Bridge 3.4m
- River Lark
- *River Lark See page 219*
- EA Diamond 44
- PADNAL FEN
- Clayway Farm
- Sandy's Cut
- Railway to March
- Railway to Norwich
- To Prickwillow 2 miles
- 8.5m
- Adelaide Road Bridge 3.2m
- **QUEEN ADELAIDE**
- B1382
- EA Queen Adelaide (temporarily closed)
- Factory
- Road Bridge 3.4m
- B1382
- Roswell Pits
- Cuckoo Bridge 3.5m
- Ely Sailing Club
- EA Depot
- Isle of Ely Rowing Club
- Cambridge University Boat Club
- **ELY**
- MIDDLE FEN
- EA Boaters' Services
- Muckhill Rail Bridge 3.1m
- Cathedral

Page 114

1 Mile / 1 Kilometre (Approx)

N

Map 16

The Ely Ouse
Ely to Littleport A10 Bridge

Distance 3½ miles
Time 1 hour

Map 16 Ely to Littleport A10 Bridge

Lowest bridge 3·1m Muckhill Rail Bridge, Ely

Location	Moorings and facilities								Victualling		
	Short stay/visitor	48hr	Long stay	Water point	Chemical disposal point	Pumpout	Refuse	Diesel	Shops	Pub	Café/restaurant
EA Queen Adelaide moorings		Closed temporarily									
EA Diamond 44 moorings		⚓									
The Swan PH	⚓								🛒	🍺	🍴
EA Black Horse (The Swan PH) moorings		⚓							🛒	🍺	🍴
EA moorings opposite PH		⚓		🚰					🛒	🍺	🍴
The Boat Haven Littleport	⚓ If available	⚓	⚓	🚰	⬇						
Littleport Station Road EA		⚓							🛒		🍴

Navigation notes

Continuing downstream, you leave Ely under the low **Muckhill railway bridge**. Immediately on your left is a meadow, popular with dog walkers and fishermen. Then, on your right you pass the newly built **headquarters of Cambridge University Boat Club** and on your left you will pass the home of the fledgling **Isle of Ely Rowing Club**. This is little more than a collection of boats kept in a field, an old steel container and a temporary 'loo'. Comparison with CUBC's state-of-the-art facilities starkly illustrates where the wealth lies in British rowing.

The River Cam in Cambridge is too crowded for 'serious' training, so oarsmen and women training for the annual Oxford v Cambridge boat races come here to practice. They are generally followed by small catamarans carrying their coaches. Both types of boat pay little heed to speed restrictions, claiming an exemption for 'marine racing craft'. University rowing slows down after the Easter Boat Race and only really resumes in the autumn (Michaelmas) term. Both

Cambridge University crew

Ely cathedral

the King's School Ely and the Isle of Ely rowing club put junior, less experienced, rowers out on this stretch of water, so once again care and consideration of other water users is required.

Ely Cathedral still stands sentinel on the sky line.

Next on the left is the entrance to the great **Roswell Pits**. The pits are now a SSSI (Site of Special Scientific Interest) and form an 8 hectare nature reserve (see Local history p.127).

Shortly after this the river is spanned by **two prefabricated sectional bridges**. The first only accommodates foot traffic, but the second, serving the former beet factory, carries 40 tonne lorries! When an 'artic' passes over me as I float underneath, I instinctively duck! It's quite remarkable that such a slender bridge can carry so much weight - and is testimony to the phenomenal strength of that simple geometric shape - the triangle.

The mighty wharves of the **Queen Adelaide sugar beet factory** (on your left) indicate the former importance of this industry. Local beet is generally now processed at Wissington on the River Wissey (see p.253), but in the 1930s the

Moorings and facilities

EA 'Queen Adelaide' moorings on right bank just upstream of the railway bridge (temporarily closed).

EA 'Diamond 44' moorings halfway down Sandy's Cut on the left bank.

Confluence

The **River Lark** joins from the south east. (See p.223)

factory at Queen Adelaide ran 7 tugs and 150 dumb barges collecting beet.

On the **right hand (opposite) bank beyond the factory** there are **EA moorings,** sadly currently closed and awaiting restoration (October 2023). Next **after another railway bridge** is **Queen Adelaide road bridge** which carries the B1382 Ely to Prickwillow road. During the 1920s there was a local spate of bridge building to replace the ferries which had once provided the only means of crossing the rivers. In the administrative area called the 'Isle of Ely' a number of new bridges were constructed in concrete, including Stretham Ferry bridge and Dimmock's Cote bridge, but prettiest of all is this road bridge. It demonstrates a design pride in detail and overall appearance which had sadly been abandoned by the time the subsequent crossings were built in Littleport.

You now enter a great man-made straight, known as 'Sandy's Cut'. Half way down, on the left bank are the **EA 'Diamond 44 moorings'** (see The Boat Race, p.129). Shortly after, on the right bank the **River Lark** joins. This great cut, from Queen Adelaide Bridge to Sandhills Bridge at Littleport, runs for 3¼ miles NNE, almost dead straight. In summer this is a calm and comparatively tranquil reach, but in winter, when a cruel wind blows from the north-east, it is in direct opposition to the flow of the river. Waves are whipped up, and as you pass the

Queen Adelaide sugar beet factory, 1926

Queen Adelaide EA moorings

The pretty Queen Adelaide road bridge

RIVER GREAT OUSE

confluence of the River Lark on your right, even white-topped breakers. I've been down this straight on an unforgiving winter's day huddled over my tiller with spray breaking over my bows and soaking me on the stern!

The Cambridge University rowing VIII's who train on this piece of water have earned themselves the well deserved nick-name within the rowing world of the 'hard men (and women) of the Fens'. I've seen rowing VIII's turn around above Littleport and when square to the sea-like waves, wondered if they will stay afloat during this precarious manoeuvre. The concerned looks on the faces of crew suggest that they too are worrying about the same thing!

Littleport is book marked at either end by modern concrete bridges. The first, **Sandhills**, announces your arrival, with the popular **Swan PH on the left bank**. The **EA moorings on either side of the river** here are the closest point for walking into Littleport.

Progressing downstream, **Littleport Boat Haven** on your left is under new ownership and has added several new services to the existing mooring

> ## Moorings and facilities
> **The Swan PH**, Littleport has customer moorings, public moorings can be found next to the pub moorings.
>
> **EA moorings** opposite **The Swan PH**.
>
> **Water point** at the EA moorings opposite The Swan PH. No dedicated space for water point access.
>
> **The Boat Haven**, Littleport, CB6 1QG Long term moorings, short stay & 48h if available, slipway for hire, repairs and servicing, boat cleaning, boat sales and hire.
> www.theboathaven.co.uk
> ☎ 01353 863763
>
> **EA Moorings Station Road**, Littleport (convenient for railway station).

provision. This unassuming collection of boats occupies the **former confluence of the Old Croft River** (also known as the Well Stream) which joined with Well Creek and was once the major trade route that transported, amongst many

The Swan PH moorings

EA moorings opposite The Swan PH

126 RIVER GREAT OUSE

The Swan PH, **Littleport**, is a gastro pub and a popular summer boating destination. It can be busy.
☎ 01353 861677

The Crown PH in **Littleport** (10 min walk from EA moorings).
☎ 01353 862700

There are several eateries in Littleport including Chinese take-aways, two Indian restaurants, chip shops and a pizzeria.

Littleport has two Co-ops, the larger is 1 mile from EA moorings, the other just over half a mile.
Chemist, 22 Main St.

Public Transport
Littleport - train to Cambridge or March (Peterborough). X9 bus to central Cambridge via Ely and Little Thetford

Littleport station road moorings

other goods, the Barnack stone from Northamptonshire which was used to build Ely Cathedral.

Just past the Old Croft River, still **on the left bank, there are further EA moorings** which are close to the **railway station**. This was the location of the quay which served the port of Littleport. It can be quite difficult getting off these moorings in windy conditions.

Just below these moorings you can make out the site of the former bridge, both from its abutment, and the old road which now only leads to the river's edge.

Just as your arrival in Littleport was a marked by a concrete bridge, so too is your departure, the **A10 crosses the river on a modern bridge**, opened in 1976.

Walking

The **Fen Rivers Way** crosses under the Muckhill railway bridge and continues NE out of Ely across a meadow sandwiched between the left bank of the river and the railway. It leaves the river briefly as it deviates behind some industrial buildings, before it crosses the entrance to **Roswell Pits SSSI** by Cuckoo Bridge. It merges briefly with **Hereward Way** and crosses the river on a 'Meccano' style bridge. **Hereward Way** immediately departs but the **Fen Rivers Way** continues north along the right bank of the Great Ouse for about a mile. It passes under another railway bridge, before it crosses back over the river on the elegant concrete Queen Adelaide bridge. From here it runs along the top of the western floodbank, next to the river, all the way to **Littleport**. This section of the path is popular with dog walkers.

Local history

Downstream of the City of Ely lie **Roswell Pits**. Kimmeridge clay, known as 'gault' was dug here for 300 years. It was transported by lighters to repair and seal the riverbanks. Men loading the barges were called 'gaulters' and those putting clay on the river walls 'bankers'. When dug, the clay is dark blue/black. As it

Roswell Pits nature reserve

dries it turns more yellow, and is responsible for the general yellow brick colour of old Cambridge. The remains of several abandoned and sunken lighters can be sometimes be spotted, early in the year, under the waters of the pits. Black Prince, one of the lighters sunk in Roswell Pits, was recovered in 1974 and taken to Cambridge Museum of Industrial Technology for conservation.

1½ miles northeast of Ely the river passes the village of **Queen Adelaide**. The village took its name from a pub, which in turn was named after Adelaide of Saxe-Meiningen, wife of the 'Sailor King', William IV, one of Britain's more popular, but now sadly generally forgotten, kings. Although the name survives, sadly the pub doesn't. Adelaide also lent her name to an Australian town which would become the capital of the territory of South Australia. During William's seven year reign, slavery was abolished in the Colonies, and the Great Reform Act passed.

The **electrified Littleport to Ely railway line** runs close by on the left bank. In 1870 a race was staged between a train travelling on this line, and a skater on the frozen Great Ouse which runs parallel. It is claimed that hot coals from the train's firebox were thrown onto the ice in an attempt to sabotage the skater, but never-the-less he finished the winner by half a minute! Entertaining though this story is, it is worth considering whether the railway is ever quite close enough to the river for the thrown hot coals to have actually reached!

The legendary founder of Littleport was **King Canute**. A fisherman gave the king shelter one night, after drunken monks had denied him hospitality. After punishing the monks, the king made his host the mayor of a newly founded village.

The Ely and Littleport riots of 1816, occurred between 22 and 24 May 1816. In the aftermath of the end of the Napoleonic wars, unrest grew throughout England as a result of high unemployment and rising grain costs. The riots started in Littleport, but soon spread to Ely. A militia formed from the citizens of Ely, and backed by the 1st Royal Dragoons rounded up the rioters. They were tried in the assizes at Ely in June 1816, and 23 men and one woman were condemned, of which five were subsequently hanged. They were buried in St Mary's Church, Ely. A stone plaque was installed on the west side of St Mary's Church, which concludes, 'May their awful Fate be a warning to others'.

William Harley, who was born in Littleport in 1835, emigrated to the U.S.A. in 1859. His son, William Sylvester Harley teamed up with a childhood friend, Arthur Davidson to build motorcycles. One of the World's most famous brand of motorcycle, the Harley Davidson, was born. There is a statue in Littleport which commemorates this link.

The Boat Race

The world-famous Oxford v Cambridge University Boat Race has, over the years, had a number of connections with Ely.

The first boat race, held in 1829 at Henley was the result of a challenge between two old friends from Harrow School; Charles Wordsworth (nephew of the poet William Wordsworth), of Christ Church College, Oxford, and Charles Merivale of St. John's, Cambridge. Charles Merivale went on to become Dean of Ely Cathedral. His many years of service are commemorated in the Cathedral.

The second race was held on the tidal Thames in London, over the now familiar Putney to Mortlake Course. It became an annual feature of London life. It was suspended during WWII and no races are recorded as having taken place during the years 1940-1945.

However, in 1944 It was decided to hold the race on the safer waters of the Great Ouse below Ely. Oxford were the winners on this occasion, but their win isn't recorded in the overall tally of total wins, and the participants weren't awarded a 'Blue'.

To mark the 60th anniversary of the wartime race the fledging Isle of Ely Rowing Club staged a recreation of the event with veteran oarsmen. Half way down the great Queen Adelaide straight, known as Sandy's Cut, the Environment Agency installed new moorings, called Diamond 44 to commemorate this event.

Cambridge have trained in Ely for a number of years and in December 2016 they opened a purpose built facility on the river just north of the city.

A number of different crews race in a modern University Boat Race. Both Universities enter 1st and 2nd men's VIIIs, and women's VIIIs and lightweight crews.

In 2020 the Covid-19 pandemic led to the cancellation of the race. In April of the same year engineers found hairline fractures in the cast iron Hammersmith Bridge which was then closed to road traffic. The river below was also closed to all boat traffic.

Problems repairing the bridge, and continuing 'lockdown' Covid regulations again prevented the race being held in London in 2021, so it was decided to return the race to the Great Ouse and again hold it between Littleport and Ely. This time the 'light blues' (Cambridge) triumphed.

1944 boat race on the 'Ely Ouse'
Mike Petty

Map 17

Page 132

Little Ouse Moorings
Boat hire & other services
Long term
Chargeable visitor moorings

Black Horse Drove

Picnic sites

EA 48hr
Black Horse Farm

Bank Farm

Little Ouse River

Little Ouse River
See page 233

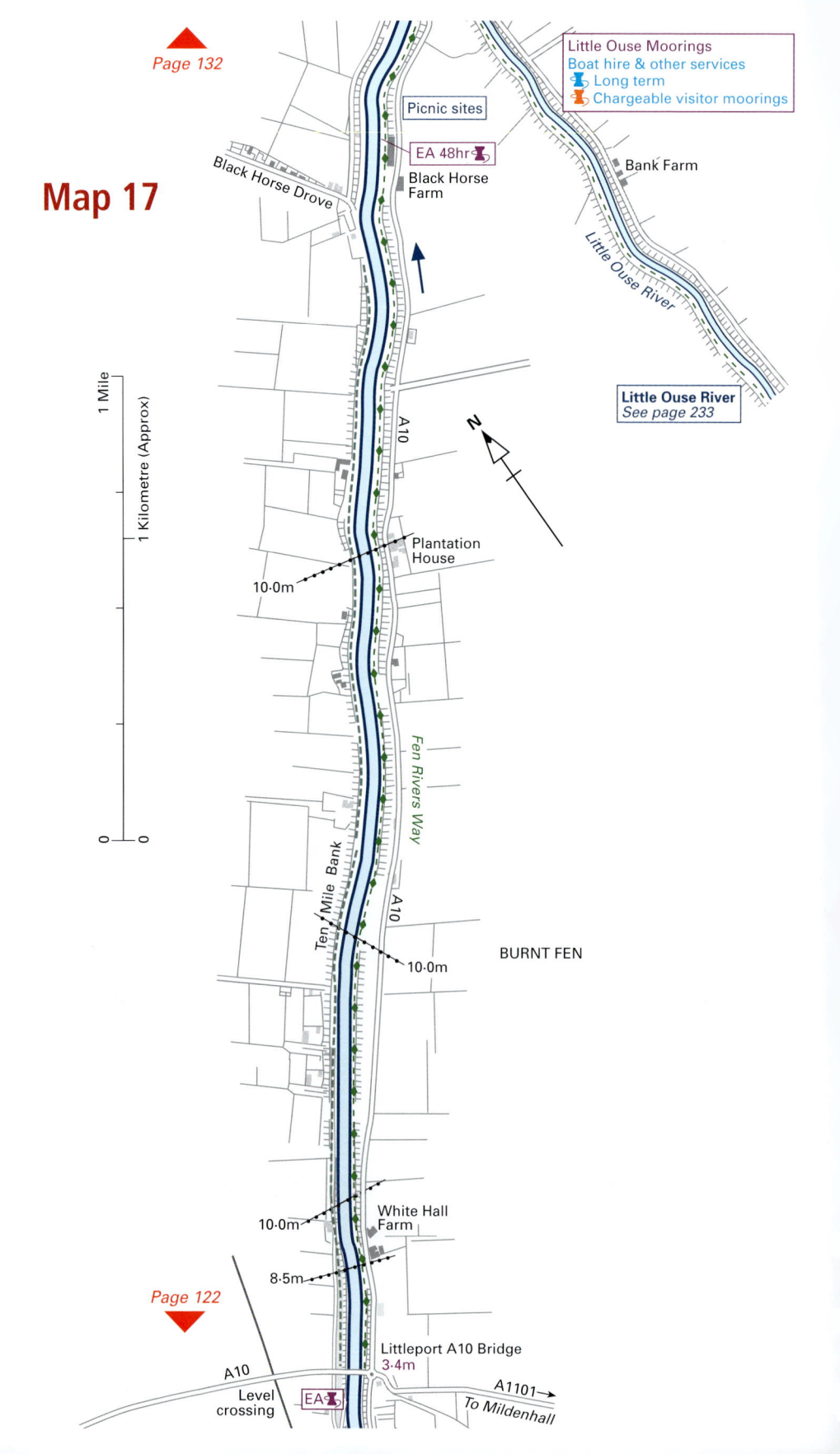

1 Mile
1 Kilometre (Approx)
0

A10

N

Plantation House

10·0m

Fen Rivers Way

Ten Mile Bank

A10

10·0m

BURNT FEN

10·0m

White Hall Farm

8·5m

Page 122

A10

Level crossing

EA

Littleport A10 Bridge
3·4m

A1101 →
To Mildenhall

Map 17

Littleport A10 Bridge to Black Horse Farm

Distance 2½ miles

Time 1½ hours

Map 17 Littleport Bridge to Black Horse Farm

Lowest bridge 3·4m Littleport A10 Bridge

Location	Moorings and facilities								Victualling		
	Visitor	48hr	Long stay	Water point	Chemical disposal point	Pumpout	Refuse	Diesel	Shops	Pub	Café/restaurant
Black Horse EA moorings	Not suitable for overnight mooring due to traffic noise from A10										
Little Ouse moorings	🔶		🔷								

Navigation notes

Downstream of Littleport Bridge, the river widens, and the banks grow higher. On the **right bank the A10 follows the river** for the next 4 miles. You can see the drivers of passing lorries, but only the roofs of cars. On the left bank the upper windows of occasional houses are visible, seemingly standing on tip-toes to peep over the high bank and see the river. Much of this land has moved as the peat has shrunk and dried, and a few of the houses lean at drunken angles.

There are **EA moorings** close to a picnic area off the A10 **on the right bank,** but these probably aren't suitable for overnight mooring, and you will be best advised to continue half a mile to the moorings at **The Ship PH** (at Brandon Creek).

Heading downstream from the confluence of the Ely Ouse and the Little Ouse

Map 18

Page 132

River Great Ouse
Pumping Station
GOBA
Ten Mile Bank
10.0m
Denver Cruising Club HQ
Ferry Farm
Pumping Station
SOUTHERY FENS
Fen Rivers Way
A10
Horse Fen Farm
River Farm
10.0m
Chain Farm
Road Bridge
2.8m
Ship Inn
EA
Brandon Creek
Black Horse Drove
Creek Farm
Picnic sites
EA 48hr
Black Horse Farm
River Great Ouse
Little Ouse Moorings
- Longterm
- Chargeable
Bank Farm
A10
Little Ouse River
Little Ouse River
See page 233

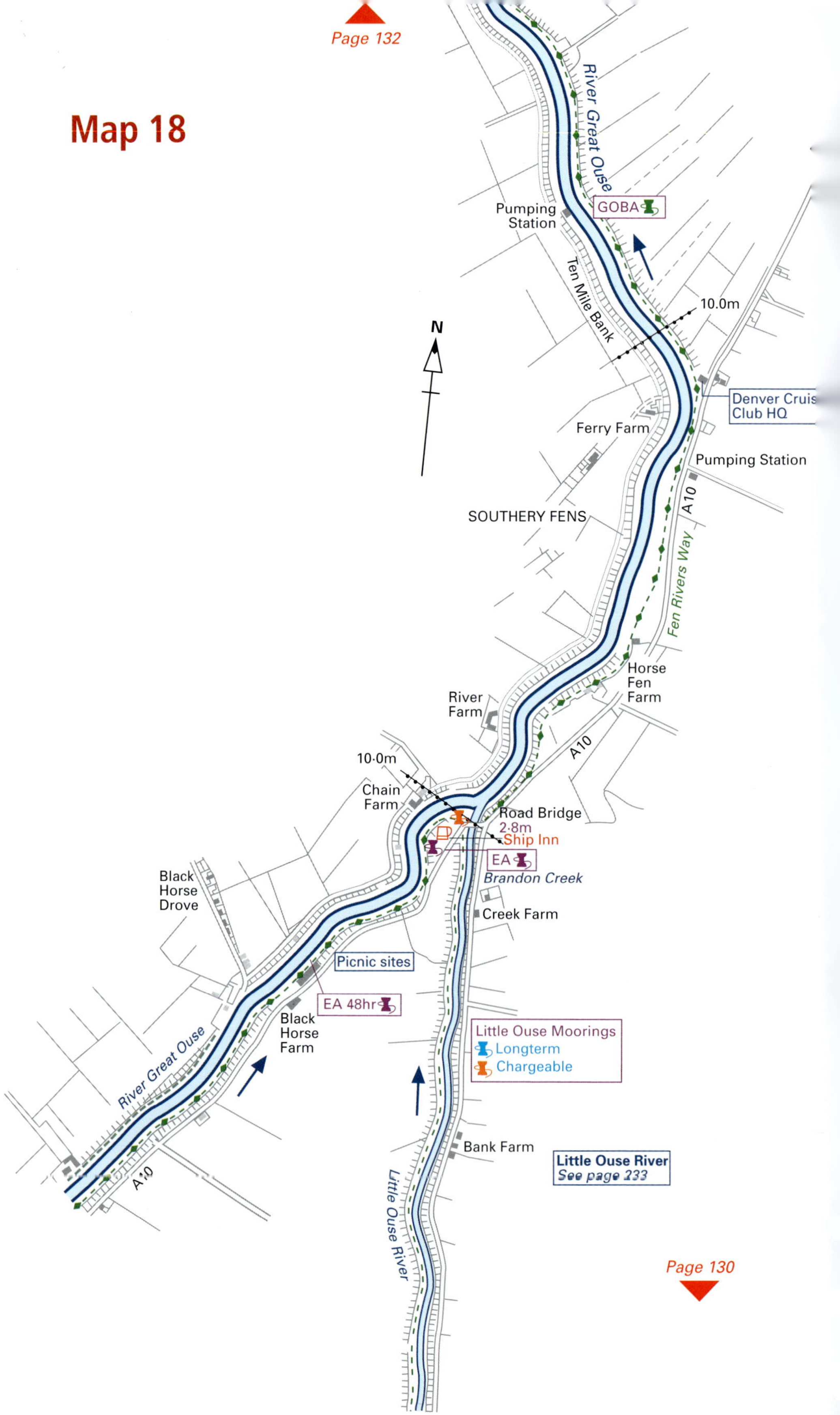

Page 130

Map 18

Black Horse Farm to Southery

Distance 2 miles
Time ½ hour

Map 18 Black Horse Farm to Southery

Location	Moorings and facilities								Victualling		
	Short stay	48hr	Long stay	Water point	Chemical disposal point	Pumpout	Refuse	Fuel	Shops	Pub	Café/restaurant
The Ship EA moorings		■								■	■
The Ship PH	■									■	■
Little Ouse moorings	■		■								
GOBA Ten Mile Bank moorings		■							PH in Southery	■	■

River Great Ouse Earith to Denver

Navigation notes

Brandon Creek is where the **River Little Ouse** joins its big brother the Great Ouse. There are **EA moorings and then some pub moorings on the right bank outside The Ship PH. Brandon Creek Boat Hire** have recently taken over the attractive steel day boat *Matilda* and she is based at Brandon Creek.

Less than a mile beyond Brandon Creek, a line of moored cruisers on the right bank announces your arrival at **Denver Cruising Club**. The brick building stands on the corner, **formerly The Old Ferry Boat Inn**, and marks the point when the busy A10 road finally departs from the river. The river breached its banks here in 1947 and nearly 60 miles of agricultural land were inundated (see photo p. 143). Just upstream of the Denver Cruising Club you pass one of the area's most attractive former **pumping stations on the right bank**, this pleasant yellow brick building includes an enormous cast iron tank at first floor level on a flat roof. The sheer weight of this, before it is even

Ten Mile Bank moorings

filled with water, must be huge! Presumably it was a steam pumping station and the tank fed water to the engines.

Three quarters of a mile further on, downstream of the pumping station, there are **remote GOBA moorings on the right bank**. These are called **Ten Mile Bank moorings** - although they are on the opposite bank, facing the Ten Mile Bank itself, which borders this section of the Ouse between the A10 bridge at Littleport and Denver.

Southery pump

Moorings and facilities

EA moorings just upstream of **The Ship PH at Brandon Creek**, right bank

Customer moorings outside **The Ship**, right bank

GOBA Ten Mile Bank moorings on right bank.

Little Ouse Moorings
PE38 0PR
Chargeable visitor and longterm moorings
Restricted opening hours
☎ 07713 465791
www.littleousemoorings.co.uk

The Ship at **Brandon Creek** serves pub grub
☎ 01353 676000

The Old White Bell PH in **Southery** is a short walk from the Ten Mile Bank moorings.
☎ 01366 378843

Confluence The **River Little Ouse** joins from the east at Brandon Creek (see p.236).

Dawn on the Great Ouse at Brandon Junction

RIVER GREAT OUSE

Map 19

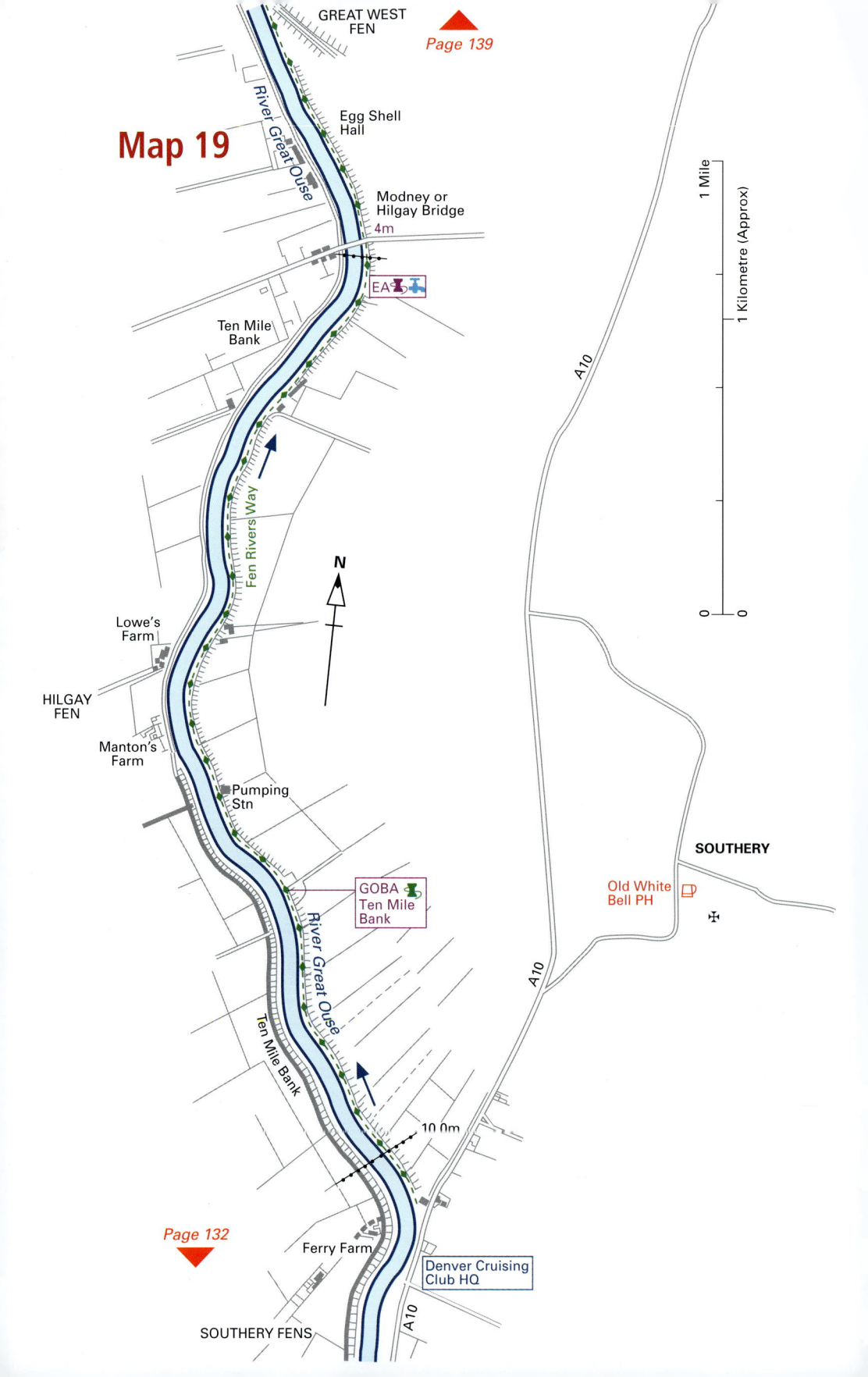

GREAT WEST FEN

Page 139

Egg Shell Hall

River Great Ouse

Modney or Hilgay Bridge
4m

EA

Ten Mile Bank

Fen Rivers Way

N

Lowe's Farm

HILGAY FEN

Manton's Farm

Pumping Stn

GOBA Ten Mile Bank

River Great Ouse

Ten Mile Bank

A10

SOUTHERY

Old White Bell PH

10.0m

Page 132

Ferry Farm

Denver Cruising Club HQ

SOUTHERY FENS

A10

1 Mile / 1 Kilometre (Approx)

Maps 19 and 20
Southery to Modney and Modney to Denver

Distance 4½ miles
Time 1 hour

Maps 19 and 20 Southery to Denver

Lowest bridge 4·0m Modney/Hilgay Bridge

Location	Moorings and facilities							Victualling		
	48hr	Long stay	Water point	Chemical disposal point	Pumpout	Refuse	Diesel	Shops	Pub	Café
Map 19										
GOBA Ten Mile Bank moorings	⚓									
EA 'Windmill' moorings at Modney/Hilgay Bridge	⚓		🚰							
Map 20										
EA visitor moorings	Temporarily closed									
2x EA Denver Complex moorings (left bank)	⚓									
EA Denver moorings (right bank)		⚓	1st temporarily closed							
Denver Lock moorings						🗑				
A.G. Wright Sluice services			🚰	⬇	🚰					
Relief Channel Lock moorings						🗑				

RIVER GREAT OUSE

Navigation notes

In summer months the river wanders on, unhurriedly. By now it appears almost as wide as the sky. 2½ miles downstream from the old pumping station at Southery brings you to **Modney/Hilgay Bridge**. As you approach the bridge you pass the **old engine house of Ten Mile Pumping Station on the left bank**. This has been first the site of horse driven pumps, then wind pumps, before the current building was constructed to house a steam pump. In turn this gave way in 1912 to diesel engines built by the prominent Bedford Engineering company W H Allen. Two of these engines can now be found at Prickwillow Museum of Fenland Drainage (see p. 227). **Modney Bridge** (variously called Hilgay Bridge) is the last road bridge to cross the Great Ouse before Denver Sluice. There are **EA moorings upstream of the bridge, and a water point**. **Ten Mile Bank village** lies at the west end of the bridge. The village is without a pub or shop.

Just past the bridge on the left bank is a curious house painted pink, with an unusual configuration of two dormer windows opening from the same room, but at right angles to each other. These will have been constructed to give views both up and down the river.

On the opposite bank the gable end of a yellow brick building is the intriguingly named Egg Shell Hall.

Another mile further on, the very last bridge before Denver is the **Fordham railway bridge** (named as Ouse Bridge on OS map). This green bridge is formed from riveted wrought iron and features three rather unusual arches across the tracks, between the two sides of the bridge.

Moorings and facilities

EA Windmill moorings at Modney/Hilgay Bridge right bank when travelling downstream

Waterpoint at Hilgay/Modney Bridge

Confluence

The **River Wissey** joins the River Great Ouse just downstream of the attractive 'Meccano' style Fordham railway bridge. See p.247.

Ten Mile Pumping Station

Fordham Railway Bridge

138 RIVER GREAT OUSE

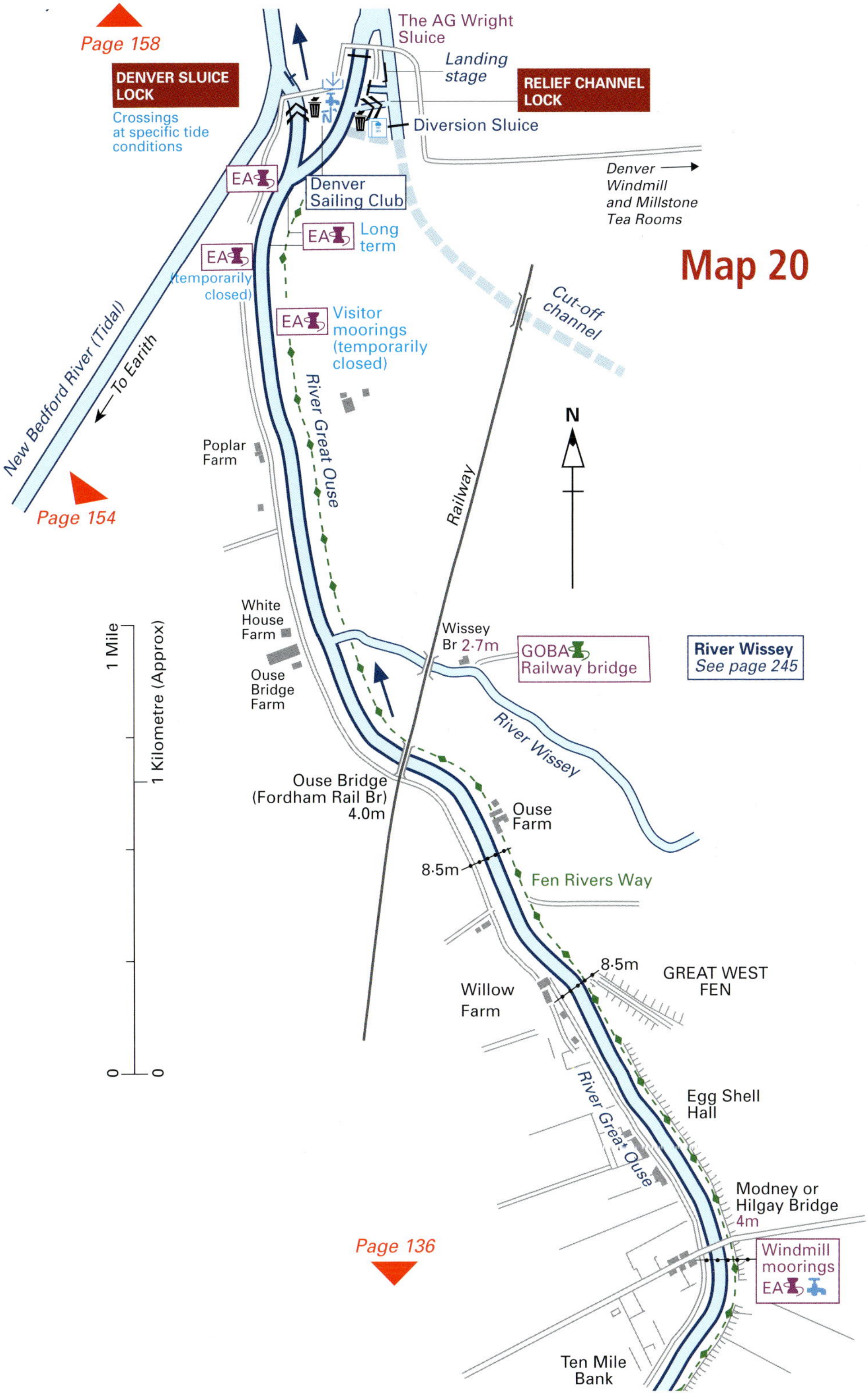

Map 20
Page 158
DENVER SLUICE LOCK
Crossings at specific tide conditions
The AG Wright Sluice
Landing stage
RELIEF CHANNEL LOCK
Diversion Sluice
Denver Windmill and Millstone Tea Rooms
Denver Sailing Club
EA
EA
Long term
EA
(temporarily closed)
EA
Visitor moorings (temporarily closed)
Cut-off channel
New Bedford River (Tidal)
To Earith
River Great Ouse
Poplar Farm
N
Railway
Page 154
1 Mile
1 Kilometre (Approx)
0
0
White House Farm
Ouse Bridge Farm
Wissey Br 2·7m
GOBA
Railway bridge
River Wissey
See page 245
River Wissey
Ouse Bridge (Fordham Rail Br) 4.0m
Ouse Farm
8·5m
Fen Rivers Way
8·5m
GREAT WEST FEN
Willow Farm
River Great Ouse
Egg Shell Hall
Modney or Hilgay Bridge 4m
Windmill moorings
EA
Page 136
Ten Mile Bank

Half a mile downstream of the Wissey confluence, you come to **EA** visitor **moorings on the right bank** (temporarily closed). Another half mile brings you to the first of the newly refurbished **EA Denver Complex moorings on the left bank**. From here, the outline of two great sluices appear on the horizon. Although these mark the end of the non tidal Great Ouse, your journey downstream isn't necessarily finished. You can continue through **Denver Sluice**, to the left, to either the Middle Level or King's Lynn, or through the **Relief Channel Lock**, to your right, to Downham Market. There are three sets of **visitor moorings at Denver**. Rubbish disposal is by the moorings for both locks, and pump-out and water on the left just before the other, righthand sluice, the A G Wright sluice.

Moorings and facilities

Denver Complex

Two EA Denver Complex moorings on left bank (first upstream visitor mooring temporarily closed)

Long term EA moorings on right bank (first upstream visitor moorings temporarily closed)

Pump out and **water** near the AG Wright Sluce, **rubbish** next to both locks, no recycling. **Toilet, shower and elsan emptying** in refurbished building.

Temporarily closed upstream right hand bank visitor moorings

Looking upstream at Denver before the construction of the new EA residential moorings

140 RIVER GREAT OUSE

Denver Complex

There are three main sluices at Denver, from West to East:

1. **The Main Sluice**, consisting the 'Big Eye', three 'Little Eyes' and a lock, the sluice controls the flow of water from the non tidal Great Ouse into the tidal Great Ouse

2. **A G Wright Sluice** (commissioned in 1964) which controls the flow of water from non tidal Great Ouse into the Relief Channel. This is also know as the 'Head Sluice' and the outlet sluice, 11 miles downstream, at the north eastern end of the Relief Channel, is called the 'Tail Sluice'.

3. **The Impounding Sluice** (at a lower level than the other two) controls the flow of water between the Relief Channel and Cut-Off Channel.

There are also two smaller sluices called the 'Diversion Sluice', and the 'Residual Flow Sluice':

A. **The Diversion Sluice** (immediately south of the 2001 Relief Channel Lock) diverts water from the non tidal Great Ouse into the Cut-Off Channel. This is used in summer to send water back up the Cut-Off Channel to Essex.

B. **The Residual Flow Sluice** (immediately north of the Relief Channel Lock) diverts water from the non tidal Great Ouse into the Flood Relief Channel (in effect duplicating the function of the A G Wright Sluice).

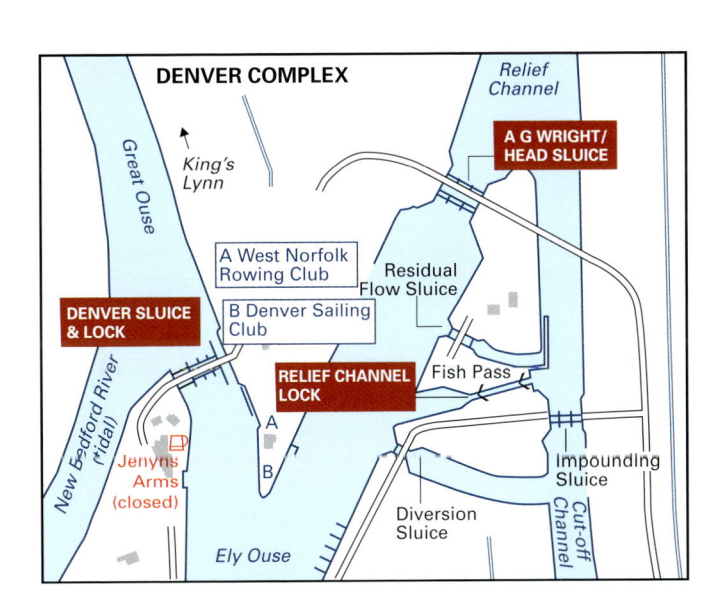

Walking

The Fen Rivers Way continues to follow the west bank of the Ouse through **Littleport**. At the top of Littleport the path crosses the river on the **A10 road bridge**. From here it follows the east bank, along the top of the flood bank to **The Ship at Brandon Creek**. The path is sandwiched between the busy A10 road and the river. I can't recall ever seeing anyone walking it, and it is difficult to imagine that it can be very pleasant, running so close to a major trunk road.

The opposite flood bank is extensively grazed and doesn't include a right of way. This is a shame because it would be far more pleasant walking than next to the road. It may be that creating a path there was deemed impractical because of the distance to the next bridge crossing the river, which is **Modney/Hilgay Bridge**.

The **Fen Rivers Way** continues along the west bank of the Great Ouse until **Modney/Hilgay Bridge**. However the traffic filled A10 leaves at the cruising club (former Ferry Boat Inn) and peace is thankfully restored. It crosses back to the west bank on the road bridge, and continues to **Denver Sluice**.

A.G. Wright Sluice

Other water users
West Norfolk Rowing Club, Denver Sailing Club, both located at Denver Complex

Regattas
Great Ouse Marathon - Denver to Ely, late October/early November. A staggered start minimises inconvenience to other river users, but please slow down as you approach and pass boats - they will be in the process of rowing 12 miles!

Local history

The winter of 1947 was a severe winter, and when the snow finally melted it generated more water that the Ouse, specifically Denver Sluice, could deal with. Much of Fenland was flooded. One of the major breaches was to the east bank of the river between Hilgay and Southery and large swathes of countryside were flooded. Troops were sent in to help staunch the breach. This natural disaster would lead to the construction of the **Great Ouse Cut-off Channel** and the **Great Ouse Relief Channel**, designed to prevent further recurrences.

The author and historian Andrew Hunter Blair observes: '...between Southery and Littleport, the river passes through countryside which has been described as the loneliest within 100 miles of London. Its massive flood banks stand high above the vast low-lying rich agricultural fenland, criss-crossed by straight roads, straight railways and straight drainage ditches. It is a hard country. In dry weather winds can whip up soil and seeds into huge black clouds which sweep across the fen like a sandstorm,

Information
Denver Complex Interpretation Centre
www.ousewashes.org.uk/explore/denver-sluice-complex/

Places to visit
Denver Windmill and tea room approx 1 mile walk from Denver Complex.

Plugging the breach during the floods of 1947

known locally as a 'fen blow'. In wet weather pumps struggle to empty full drainage ditches into rivers which themselves are brimful, and threaten the surrounding land with flooding. Whilst winters can be bitter and summers roasting, the ever changing skyscape is magnificent'.

Mr Hunter Blair's words powerfully evoke the never ending battle to keep the landscape drained, however the opening of the **Great Ouse Relief Channel** in the mid 1960s significantly reduced pressures on the infrastructure and the risk of flooding.

The **first sluice at Denver** was built by **Cornelius Vermuyden** in 1652, and improved in 1682. It blew up in 1713 (violent tides rushing up the river met floodwaters coming down, undermining and 'blowing-up' the sluices and dam). Originally passage through by boat was made 'on the level' when the water on both sides of the sluice was at equal heights. When the sluice was rebuilt in 1750 a lock was added. It was reconstructed 1832 by **John Rennie** and

Denver main sluice with (L-R) Denver Lock, 3 'Little Eyes' and 'Big Eye', viewed from the tidal Great Ouse

a larger sluice, known as the 'Big Eye' was added in 1923 to increase flow. The 'Big Eye' hasn't been opened for many years, its function having been relieved by the AG Wright Sluice and the Great Ouse Relief Channel. The three 'Little Eyes' between the 'Big Eye' and lock can still operate.

In the 1960s the **Great Ouse Cut-off Channel and Great Ouse Relief Channels** were dug (see p. 157), and the **AG Wright Sluice** and **Residual Flow and Impounding Sluices** were constructed. In 2001 the Relief Channel Lock was opened, permitting navigational access from the non tidal Great Ouse on to the Relief Channel for the first time.

The quiet beauty of the Great Ouse

3

TIDAL CROSSING TO THE MIDDLE LEVEL NAVIGATIONS
Denver Sluice to Salter's Lode

Crossing to the Middle Level navigations requires a short tidal, or estuary, crossing of approximately half a mile between **Denver Sluice** on the **River Great Ouse** and **Salter's Lode Lock** on the **Middle Level**.

Phone the Denver lock keeper in advance to obtain that day's crossing times. They are generally made close to either high tide, or low tide (when the tidal flow is relatively slack). The lock cannot be self-operated. You can't just turn up and expect to go through.

If you are travelling from Denver call either ☎ **01366 382340** or **382013**, and travelling from Salter's Lode call ☎ **01366 382292**.

Arrive a minimum of half an hour before the time given for your crossing window. Prevailing weather conditions affect tide times, and predicting them is not an exact science.

Estuary crossings are by definition 'tidal' and should be treated with respect, and demand consideration and preparation. This doesn't mean that they're not fun, so please don't be put off by the following checklists – just stick to them!

Make sure you have a copy of the Imray *Fenland Waterways* guide - you are about to enter them.

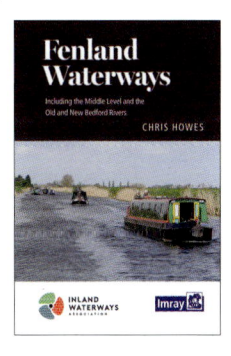

Map 21

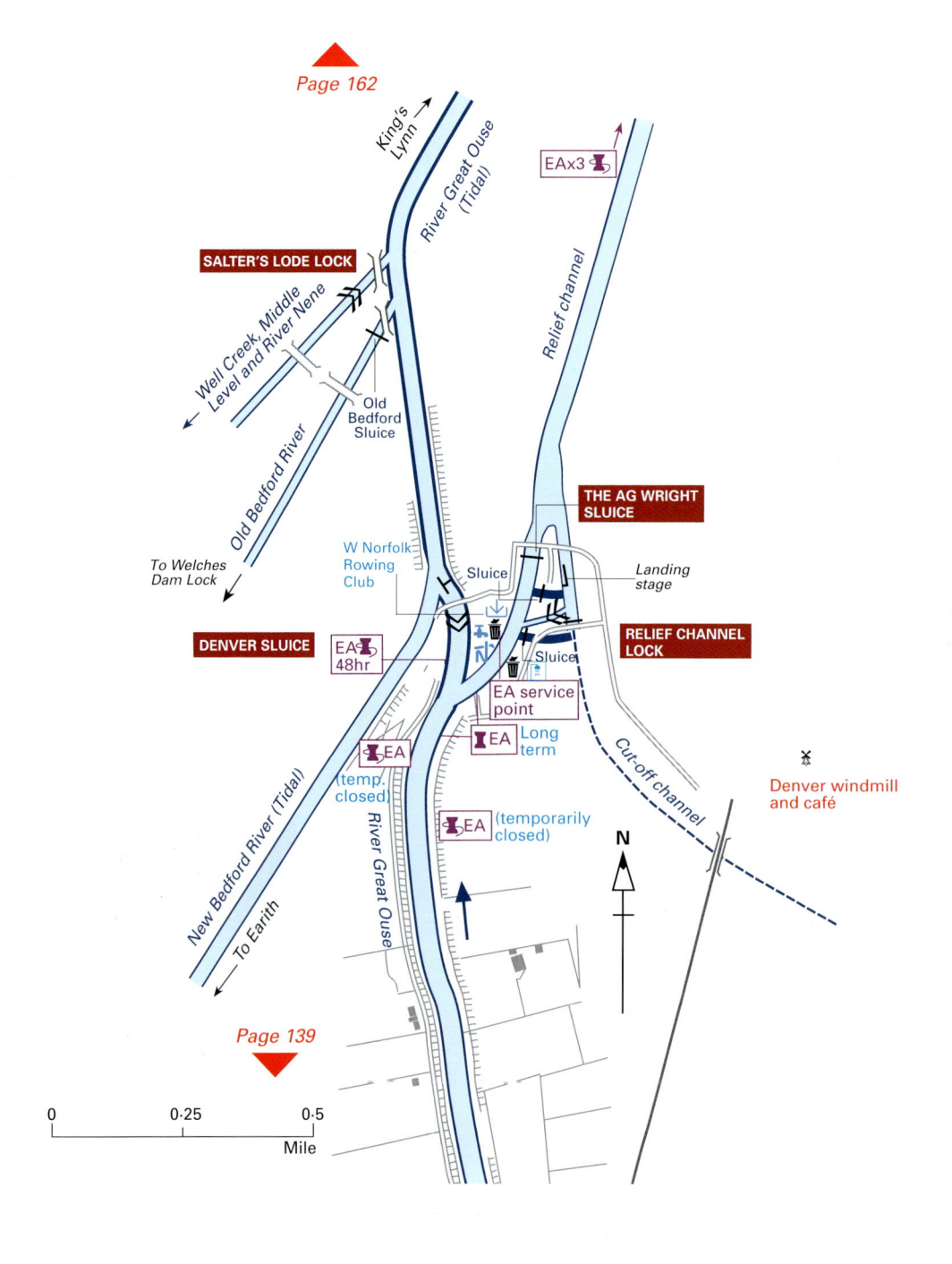

Map 21

Denver Sluice to Salter's Lode

Tidal Crossing: Denver to Salter's Lode

Map 21 Denver Sluice to Salter's Lode

Denver Lock
L 29·5m, W 5·4m (17'7") D 2·05m

Phone in advance
Denver Lock ☎ 01366 382340
Denver Complex ☎ 01366 382013
VHF radio channels 16/73

Salter's Lode Lock
L 24·4m, W 3·8m (12'5")
Lock keeper ☎ 01366 382292
The lock keeper at your departure lock will phone through to your arrival lock to warn them to expect you.

Salter's Lode Lock
Longer boats can pass 'on the level' (both gates open at once).

Floating lock moorings on tidal side of Denver Sluice, only to be used when waiting for lock.

Hard mooring on tidal side of Salter's Lode - **avoid using if at all possible**.

A Fox hireboat crossing from Denver to Salter's Lode. The crew are all suitably wearing lifejackets

RIVER GREAT OUSE   147

Preparation for the estuary crossing

- Avoid undertaking the crossing single handed if at all possible
- Check your boat's insurance covers you for tidal waters
- Check the weather forecast and talk to the lock keeper. If it is too windy, postpone your crossing
- Ensure you've got a reasonable level of fuel. Rougher tidal waters can shake up sediment in the bottom of the tank, so being at least half full is a good idea. I always try to have a full tank
- Tidal waters generate strong currents so check your propellor is clear from weed (allowing your prop to operate at maximum efficiency)
- If you've just checked your propellor, now check your weed hatch is securely refastened before you close your engine hatch – undertake a visual check by running your engine in both forward and reverse for short vigorous bursts while still moored
- Check your anchor is available for immediate deployment (not buried at the bottom of a hatch)
- Ensure you have sufficient life jackets for all on board
- Make sure your mobile phone is charged (for communicating with lock keepers) and that you have contact phone numbers for both Lock Keepers
- If you are undertaking a crossing at low tide, have a look at the tidal side of the lock before you enter it, and note the position of any sandbanks
- Undertake anti bio-contamination measures to prevent the spread of invasive species as necessary
- Always seek and pay heed to the Lock Keeper's advice before undertaking the crossing. He will inform you at what time that day's crossing is.

General estuary crossing advice

- **Ensure everybody on the boat is wearing a life jacket**
- Keep pets inside the boat cabin
- Understand whether the tide is coming in or going out
- Follow all advice the Lock Keepers may have given you
- Don't be tempted to cut corners at lock entrances, there may be a sandbank just below the surface
- Travel with sufficient, but not excessive, engine revs
- Post a look out in the bows to watch for floating debris
- If something unexpected happens, react calmly (don't panic!)
- If you become unable to control your vessel, drop anchor and alert the Lock Keeper
- If you do 'ground' on a sand bank, wait patiently for the tide to lift you off it.

Siltation

The Denver crossing has become increasingly affected by siltation on the tidal section. The Environment Agency used to dredge annually, now it needs dredging 4 times a year. Different theories endeavour to explain this increase - global warming / differing water release patterns at Denver and Wellmore Sluice / different dredging techniques. Even with this increased frequency of dredging there is a real risk of grounding around neap tides. The EA have restricted crossings around the time of neaps and boaters are strongly advised to check their web site to find when crossings are permissible. You can't simply arrive at either Denver or Salter's Lode and expect to cross the same (or next) day!
Check www.visitanglianwaterways.org > useful information > tidal windows

Crossing times are also published on the GOBA website each year
www.goba.org.uk/a-guide-for-visitors-to-the-east/the-denver-crossing/

Whereas dredging used to involve the removal of arisings to a different land location, the current technique digs out and returns the arising into the main stream. Coincidentally (or not?) silt has been appearing at the next downstream bend, outside Salter's Lode lock.

There is also a debate as to whether the same silt is also being carried back up river on the next full tide and causing the same problem again, in the same place!

Lining up for the difficult entrance to Salter's Lode on the tidal Great Ouse

The author aground on a sandbank just below Denver sluice. Even an experienced boater, who has done the crossing many times, can be caught out by tide and wind
Dan 'The Man'

Denver to Salter's Lode

- Be prepared for water coming down the New Bedford River on your port side (left) pushing your boat to starboard (right). The New Bedford joins immediately after Denver. During summer months this effect is minimal, but after heavy rain the volume of water will significantly increase and may override the tidal flow

- Be prepared to steer around sand banks (see p.151)

- Give a wide berth to the new floating moorings on the starboard (right) bank

- The entry to Salter's Lode Lock is tight. Don't cut the corner above it - there's a sandbank just waiting for you! You need to start to turn before you reach the lock, and enter it in a straight alignment. Keep an eye on the direction of flow as this may push you sideways. You will need to steer to compensate.

looking into Salter's Lode lock from the tidal side. At high tide you may need to wait for clearance below the horizontal beams

Approaching Salter's Lode from the tidal Ouse with the sand bank hidden beneath the water. Keep aligned with the lock

150 RIVER GREAT OUSE

Salter's Lode to Denver

- Make sure you have cleared the sandbank on your right at the lock exit before you start to turn (see photo below)
- Don't turn so sharply that your stern hits the high bank on your port (left side)
- The lock is at the left hand side of Denver sluice. The traditional advice of sticking to the left-hand side of the river has been made redundant by the construction of the floating tidal mooring and changing patterns of sandbank. I now travel toward Denver on the right of the river (in the increased flow from the New Bedford River), keeping a safe distance away from the tidal mooring, and turn across the face of the sluice as late as possible. The large sandbank rarely extends right up to the sluice. I recommend positioning a look-out in the bows 'spotting' for the sand bank.

Looking upstream from the new floating moorings towards Denver Sluice with the New Bedford River flowing in on the right

The exit from Salter's Lode, looking out towards the tidal River Ouse at low tide with sand bank exposed

RIVER GREAT OUSE 151

The A142 Mepal Causeway crossing the New Bedford River

4

THE NEW BEDFORD RIVER
Denver to Hermitage Lock (tidal)

Distance 20 miles
Approximate travel time 4¼ hours (depending on tides)

The **New Bedford River** (also known as the Hundred Foot River) is a man-made tidal cut, forming a direct link between **Earith** and the estuary of the Great Ouse immediately below **Denver Sluice**. Although it offers something of a 'short cut' between Denver and Earith, advice should be taken from the lock keepers at either Salter's Lode, or Denver before boating it. The journey is best done on specific tides as advised by the lock keeper.

It is recommended to make the journey upstream, from Denver to Earith, on a rising tide. If you try boating downstream on a falling tide, waiting for the tide to fall sufficiently to get under the A1123 road bridge at Earith will probably mean 'running out of water' before reaching the A1101 road bridge at Welney. It is quite common for boats to get temporarily stuck thereabouts, either as a result of the tide going out too quickly and 'beaching' a boat, or the tide coming in too quickly through 'the Narrows' and just bringing the boat to a halt. In either case waiting patiently for tidal conditions to change is the only option. Any time saving from this apparent short cut is easily lost.
I wouldn't say 'don't navigate the New Bedford River', but it's not for the faint hearted!

Map 22

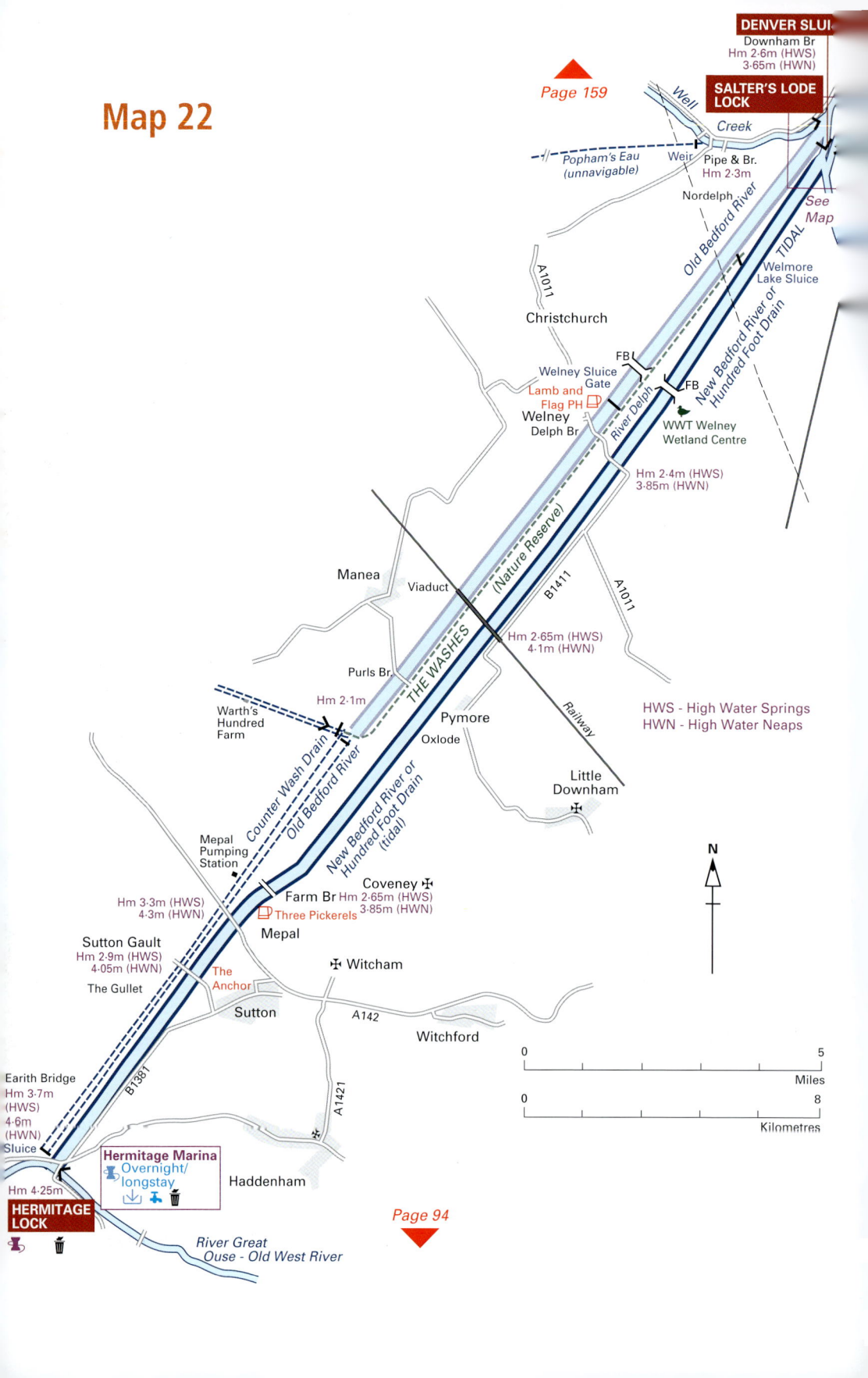

Map 22 New Bedford River: Denver to Hermitage Lock (tidal)

Lowest bridge 2·4m (high water, spring tide)

Salter's Lode Lock
L 24·4m, W 3·8m (12'5")
Lock keeper ☏ 01366 382292

Denver Lock L 29·5m, W 5·4m (17'7") D 2·05m
Phone in advance:
Denver Lock ☏ 01366 382340 or
Denver Complex ☏ 01366 382013
VHF radio channels 16/73

Hermitage Lock (attended)
L 30·5m, W 4m (13'1") D 1.5m, H 2·75m
Open April-Sept 0900-1900,
October-March 0900-1600
Closed daily 1300-1400
☏ 01487 841 548
For Hermitage Lock moorings see p.92

This journey is susceptible to the changing nature of tides and weather.

The times and conditions described below record one particular journey the author made in September 2019 in the company of Mike Daines and John Revell on John's boat *Olive Emily*, a 43' 43hp steel narrowboat, and are not typical of all journeys.

We left **Salter's Lode Lock** at the bottom of a spring tide, as soon as there was sufficient depth of water. (Had we left from Denver Lock we would have been delayed by having to wait for the water to clear the sand bar below the sluices.)

When we entered the New Bedford River the tide was coming in quite fast and we were travelling at 7mph on low (1200rpm) engine revs. There was a lot of floating debris in the water around us, but it was flowing on the tide in the same direction as us, so it didn't cause a problem.

We passed **Welmore Lake sluice** after 1½ miles, taking care to avoid the sandbank below the sluice. One and half miles later we passed under the pylons and and in a further mile and a half passed

Welney Wetland Centre and under their pedestrian bridge (which is covered to conceal visiting humans from birds).

By the time we reached the **A1101 road bridge**, another 1¼ miles, we had been travelling just over 2 hours. Just under another hour later we passed under the **'Meccano' railway bridge** a further 3¼ miles on. The water was by now largely debris free, and the tide had stopped coming in.

Welmore Lake sluice

RIVER GREAT OUSE

Meccano style railway bridge

*Six miles on we passed under the **old bridge at Mepal** by the 'Three Pickerels'. Sadly there are no proper moorings to facilitate accessing the pub, but determined boaters have been known to improvise! Be aware that water levels can alter significantly during the time it takes to enjoy a meal.*

Shortly afterwards came the modern concrete causeway carrying Ireton's Way (A142). The eponymous Ireton's Way was built on the instruction of Cromwell's General Ireton. Immediately west of the bridge are the remains of a grass sided lock which once linked the Old and New Bedford Rivers.

***Two miles on we passed by the The Anchorn PH at Sutton Gault**, again, unfortunately no moorings (in 2023 the pub had closed and is now a hotel and restaurant).*

If by now the tide was beginning to turn, it was barely noticeable, the river being wide and full.

*3¾ miles later we passed under the **A1123 bridge at Earith** and came to rest on **Hermitage Lock moorings** (see p.106).*

The entire 20 mile journey down the Old Bedford River (or Hundred Foot Drain) had taken just over 4 hours. In comparison the alternative route along the Great Ouse and Old West River is a total distance of 30 miles, and on average takes 8 hours.

Moorings and facilities

Improvise moorings outside **The Three Pickerels PH** at **Mepal**.

Toilet, shower and rubbish disposal at **Hermitage Lock**.

The Three Pickerels at **Mepal**
Riverside pub serving food.
☏ 01353 777777

Old Bridge at Mepal looking upstream

A1123 bridge at Earith looking north into the New Bedford River from the River Great Ouse

156 RIVER GREAT OUSE

5

THE RIVER GREAT OUSE RELIEF CHANNEL

The **River Great Ouse Relief Channel** is 11 miles in length, 60m (200') wide and 4·5m (15') deep. Construction started in the late 1950s to allow floodwaters in the Cut-off Channel and the Ely Ouse to discharge more quickly to the mouth of the River Great Ouse. It achieves this by acting as a by-pass to the tortuous and silted channel of the Tidal River between Denver Sluice and King's Lynn.

The Relief Channel can only be accessed at **Denver** through the **Relief Channel Lock** (added in 2001). There is no northern access where its waters join the Tidal Great Ouse through the **Tail Sluice**. Boaters must turn round and return the same route they came.

The Relief Channel is an excellent way to 'recce' (reconnoitre) the tidal river if you are planning to navigate all the way to King's Lynn. You can moor up and walk the banks of the tidal Great Ouse at low tide to note the current position and extent of the sandbanks.

Stowbridge rising moorings

RIVER GREAT OUSE

Map 23

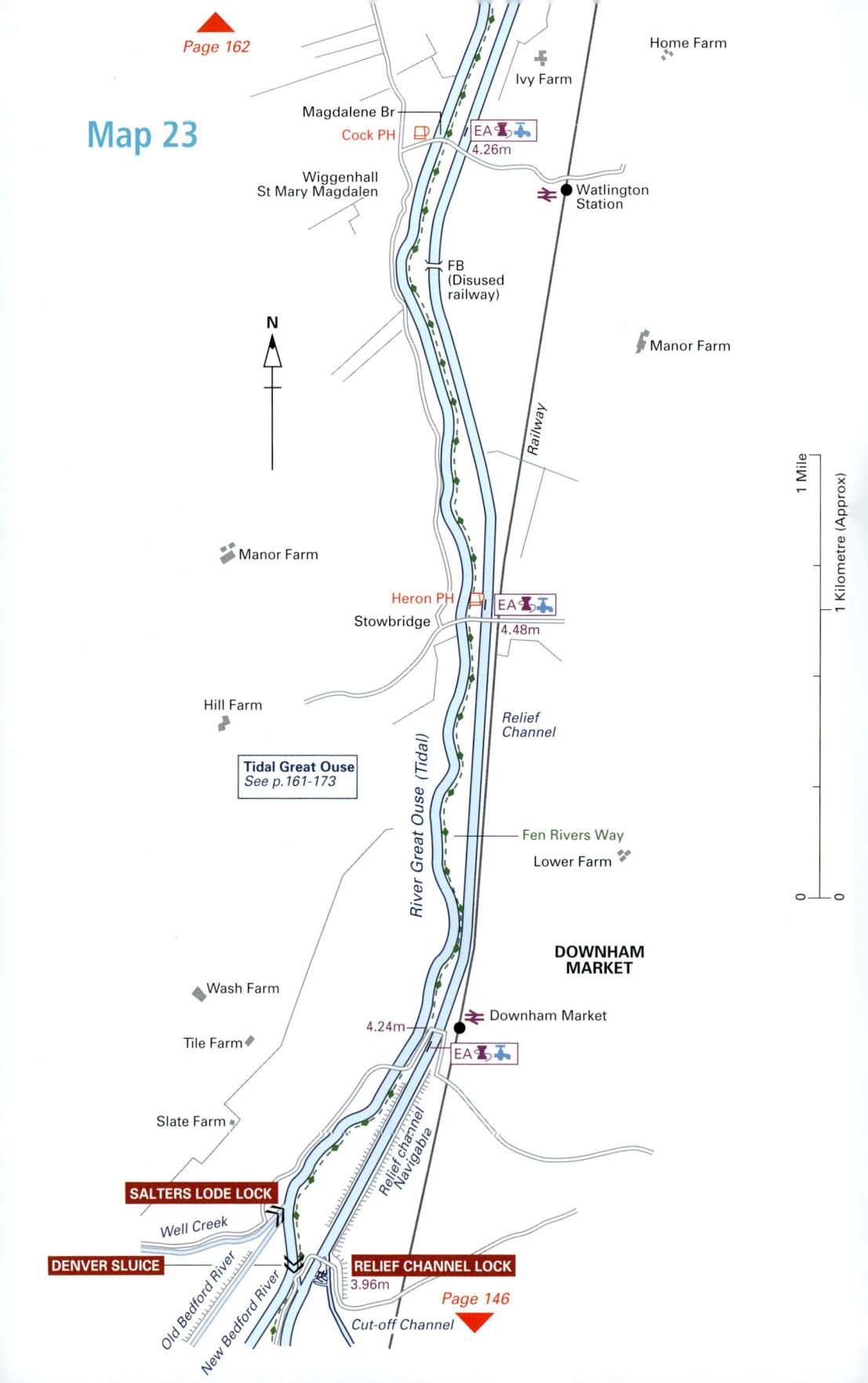

Page 162

Home Farm
Ivy Farm
Magdalene Br
Cock PH
EA 4.26m
Wiggenhall St Mary Magdalen
Watlington Station
FB (Disused railway)
Railway
Manor Farm
N
Manor Farm
Heron PH
EA 4.48m
Stowbridge
Hill Farm
Tidal Great Ouse See p.161-173
River Great Ouse (Tidal)
Relief Channel
Fen Rivers Way
Lower Farm
1 Mile
1 Kilometre (Approx)
DOWNHAM MARKET
Wash Farm
Tile Farm
4.24m
Downham Market
EA
Slate Farm
Relief channel Navigation
SALTERS LODE LOCK
Well Creek
DENVER SLUICE
Old Bedford River
New Bedford River
RELIEF CHANNEL LOCK
3.96m
Cut-off Channel
Page 146

Maps 23 and 24

The Relief Channel Lock to Relief Channel Tail Sluice

Distance one way 11 miles
Time 3½ hours

River Great Ouse Relief Channel

Maps 23 and 24 The Relief Channel Lock to Tail Sluice

Lowest bridge: 3·96m Relief Channel Lock bridge
Relief Channel Lock L 30m, W 4·6m, D 2m

Location	Lock width	Moorings and facilities								Victualling		
		48hr	Long stay	Toilets/showers	Water point	CDP	Pumpout	Refuse	Fuel	Shops	Pub	Café/restaurant
Relief Channel Lock	◊◊											
Downham Market EA moorings		♆			⊤					🛒	🍺	🍴
Stowbridge EA moorings		♆			⊤						🍺	🍴
Wiggenhall St Mary EA moorings		♆			⊤						🍺	

RIVER GREAT OUSE 159

Navigation notes

The Great Ouse Relief Channel is not the most romantic sounding name, and could suggest that these waters may not be worth visiting. In fact, this wide, straight piece of water provides an 11 mile, lock free, non-tidal river with three places to moor, two pubs and access to two attractive market towns (Downham Market and King's Lynn).

The Relief Channel is accessed through the lock of the **A G Wright Sluice** (which feeds the Relief Channel) (see p.141).

The access lock is to the right of the sluice, and the **lock moorings** are in the lock approach, not before you turn into the channel (see p.141).

The access lock features mitre gates top and bottom, and both gates and slackers are electrically powered. The lock both fills and empties slowly.

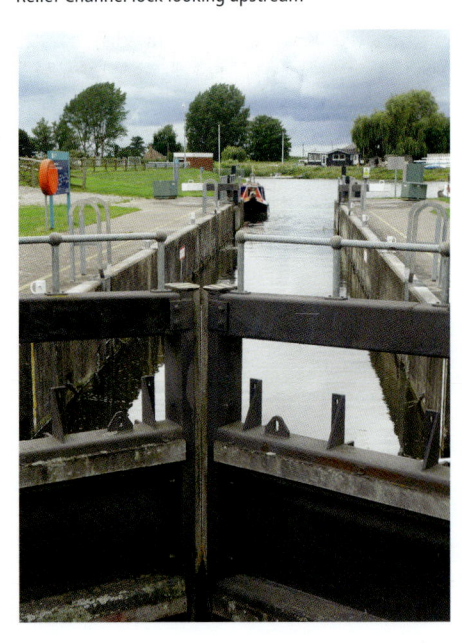

A.G. Wright Sluice, looking back up from the Relief Channel

On leaving the lock the channel turns to the left (north) away from 'Impounding Sluice' which connects the Cut-Off Channel to the Relief Channel. If the water in the Cut-Off channel is at a higher level than in the Relief Channel, it generally means that water from the Great Ouse is being collected and pumped to Essex.

As soon as you pass below the **AG Wright Sluice**, the outline of **Heygates' great mill** appears. There are good **rising moorings at Downham Market** just above the bridge, opposite Heygates 'Eagle Roller' mill. The mill processes more than 90,000 tons of wheat per year. However, unlike similar mills, (for example Whitworth's at Wellingborough on the River Nene) the mill is generally quiet.

Relief Channel lock looking upstream

Heygate's mill

Moorings and facilities

EA 48 hour moorings opposite Heygates mill, Downham Market

EA 48 hour moorings Stowbridge

EA 48 hour moorings Wiggenhall St Mary Magdalen

Water at all three moorings

Downham Market is an attractive market town, only a short walk across the bridge from the moorings. Sadly it is rather dominated by cars, and there appears little (if any) provision for pedestrians to cross its busy roads.

Downham was renowned in the past for its butter market. During the spring and summer months large quantities of butter were sent up river to Cambridge, and onto London by train, acquiring the name 'Cambridge Butter'. The butter market eventually moved to Swaffham.

It is less than 2½ miles on to the **Stowbridge** moorings outside the family and boater friendly **Heron PH**, just below the bridge on the left bank. The pub has deservedly become a visitor destination in its own right.

Downham Market moorings

The Heron, Stowbridge is a popular family pub with moorings which serves food. A popular destination with boaters.
☏ 01366 384040

The Cock, St Mary Wiggenhall
More frequented by locals than visiting boaters.
☏ 01553 811154

The Crown and Anchor, Wiggenhall St Germans
☏ 01553 617340

There is a chip shop in **Wiggenhall St Mary**.

Downham Market has a range of shops and **supermarkets** including **Morrisons, Iceland** and **Tesco Superstore**. **Restaurants and takeaways** include Chinese, Indian, fish and chip shops, kebab shops and a pizza shop. There is a Wetherspoons (The Whalebone), and pubs serving food and restaurants include **Arbuckles** and **The Chequers**.

Places to visit
Downham Heritage Centre, Priory Rd, Downham Market PE38 9JS
Tourist Information Centre at the Priory Centre, Priory Chase, Downham Market PE38 9JS.
☏ 01366 383287

Transport
Railway stations at Downham Market and Watlington (near Wiggenhall St Mary Magdalen)

Stowbridge is a key point on the tidal River Great Ouse for viewing sandbanks at low tide. If you are planning to go all the way to King's Lynn on the tidal river, take this opportunity to stand on the bridge at low tide, look upstream and downstream and take some photos as reminders.

River Great Ouse Relief Channel

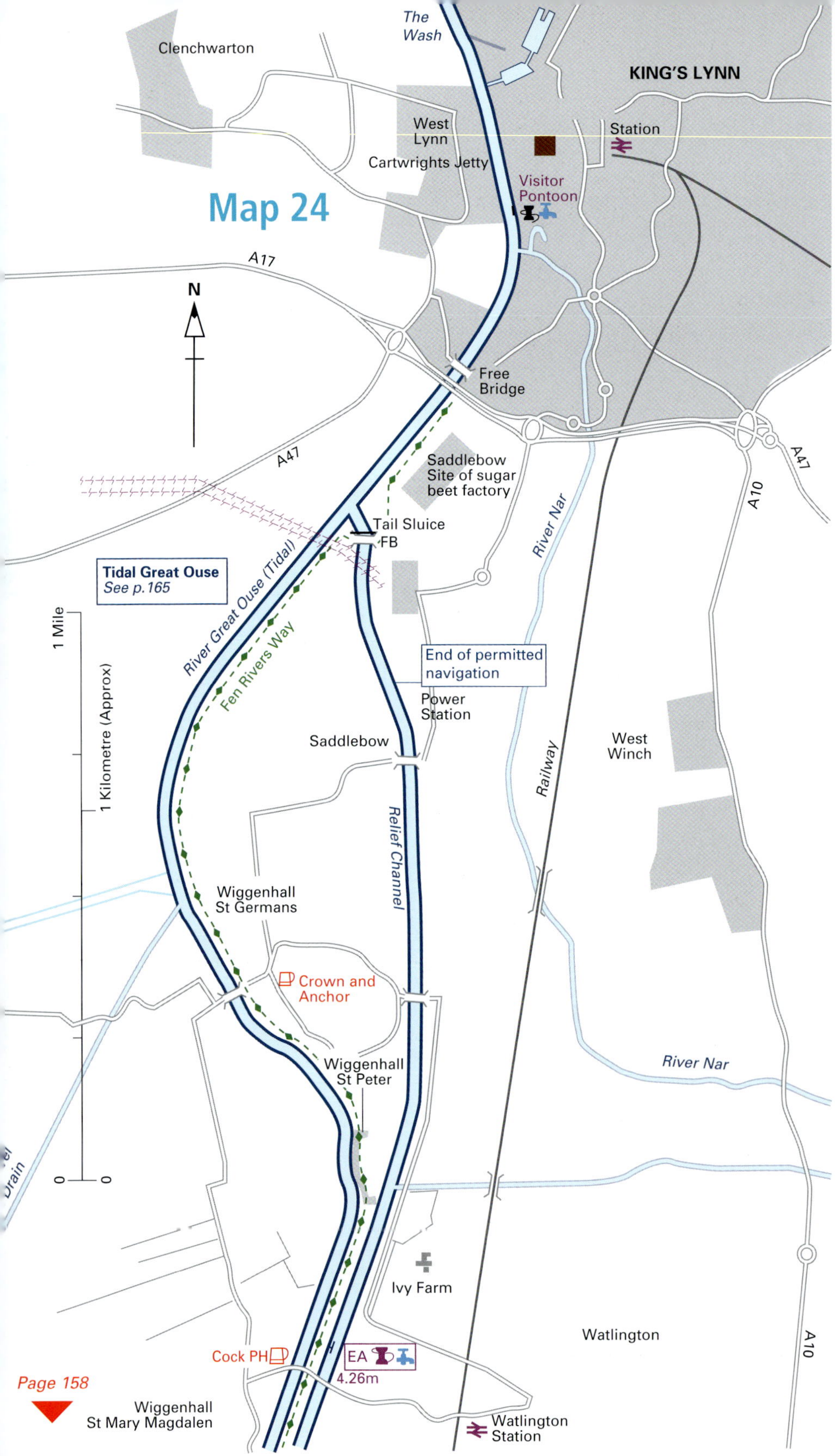

The Wash
Clenchwarton
KING'S LYNN
West Lynn
Station
Cartwrights Jetty
Visitor Pontoon
Map 24
A17
N
Free Bridge
A47
Saddlebow Site of sugar beet factory
A47
A10
Tail Sluice FB
River Nar
Tidal Great Ouse
See p.165
River Great Ouse (Tidal)
Fen Rivers Way
1 Mile
1 Kilometre (Approx)
End of permitted navigation
Power Station
Saddlebow
West Winch
Railway
Relief Channel
Wiggenhall St Germans
Crown and Anchor
Wiggenhall St Peter
River Nar
0
0
Drain
Ivy Farm
Watlington
A10
Cock PH
EA
4.26m
Page 158
Wiggenhall St Mary Magdalen
Watlington Station

Another 2½ miles takes you to the **EA moorings at Wiggenhall St Mary**. In summer the local kids here have been known to gather on the bridge over the Relief Channel and jump off, getting back onto land via the moorings. Friendly and generally polite, they are more of an entertainment than any sort of nuisance.

From the Wiggenhall St Mary moorings you are only 5½ miles away from the centre of King's Lynn. It's a great shame that neither of the proposed boating links to King's Lynn ever happened, but one of the attractions of the Wiggenhall St Mary moorings is the proximity of **Watlington railway station** and the short train ride to **King's Lynn**. The town can also be accessed by the Fen Rivers Way along the side of the nearby tidal Great Ouse (see Walking, p.175).

Wiggenhall St Mary mooring

Watlington station

The Relief Channel continues from Wiggenhall St Mary for nearly 4 miles further until it terminates at the Tail Sluice. The end of permitted navigation is signed before you reach the Tail Sluice. There are no fixed moorings and EA signs prohibit mooring to the bank here. There is a waterskiing club on this stretch, and it is advisable to avoid these waters when they are skiing.

Relief Channel history

As early as the 1640s **Cornelius Vermuyden** was proposing extra works to relieve the volume of water entering the Ely Ouse. In 1964 the **Relief Channel and Cut-Off Channel** were constructed, completing his vision. It was modified in the early 1970s, and made accessible for boating with the construction of an access lock and visitor moorings in 2001.

When the **Relief Channel Lock** was opened there were a couple of proposals to link the Relief Channel to King's Lynn. One was to put in a lock next to the Tail Sluice at the bottom of the channel. This would have still required venturing out onto the tidal river, but now only for less than two miles, and would have been restricted to specific tide conditions in a manner similar to the Denver to Salter's Lode crossing. An

Relief Channel Tail Sluice, marking the end of the navigable waterway

RIVER GREAT OUSE

alternative proposal was to lock down onto the River Nar from the Relief Channel, and follow the river until it joins the tidal Great Ouse about 1·5 miles below the Tail Sluice.

The project included the construction of a 460 berth marina accessed from the Relief Channel and was part of a proposed regeneration for King's Lynn. Sadly this didn't progress.

Walking

The Relief Channel does not have an accompanying public path. However it closely follows the course of the Great Ouse (tidal). **The Fen Rivers Way** follows the right bank of the tidal Great Ouse all the way to **King's Lynn**.

What's the point of the Relief Channel?

The Relief Channel reduces the possibility of flooding on the Ely Ouse.

How does this work?

To understand how the Relief Channel functions, first you need to be introduced to the even more imaginatively named 'Cut-off Channel'.

The Cut-Off Channel was dug (and opened at the same time) as the Relief Channel in 1964. Its function is to divert the waters of the rivers Lark, Little Ouse and Wissey from the River Great Ouse. Guillotine gates and syphons are positioned on the Little Ouse and Wissey and at time of a flood they partially close these rivers. At the same time a second sluice opens and diverts the water previously heading towards the Great Ouse into the Cut-Off Channel.

The Cut-Off Channel flows towards Denver. Via the great Impounding Sluice it joins the Relief-Channel below Denver Sluice and having bypassed the upper reaches of the tidal Great Ouse, finally joins the tidal Great Ouse through the Relief-Channel Tail Sluice, 11 miles downstream of Denver Sluice. In this way the flood waters of the rivers Lark, Little Ouse and Wissey don't join the Great Ouse until near King's Lynn.

The Christmas floods of 2020 demonstrated the effectiveness of the Great Ouse Relief and Cut-off Channels for flood alleviation on the Ely Ouse. Upstream of Earith, Bedford, St Neots and St Ives all suffered extensive flooding. The Ely Ouse, although it rose two foot, was largely contained. Sections of the rivers Cam and Old West rose above bank height, but were quickly brought under control.

The Cut-Off Channel has one more trick up its sleeve. Its winter job is flood alleviation, but in Summer its flow is reversed and it takes water from the Great Ouse into Essex. It can transfer up to 120 million litres per day!

The Cut-Off Channel is an open channel between the river Lark and Denver. Although a haven for wildlife, sadly navigation is prohibited. Above the river Lark, its journey to Essex is in a closed tunnel.

The tidal Great Ouse between Denver Sluice and King's Lynn is prone to the formation of sand banks. This may in part be compounded by the Relief Channel lessening the rivers natural scouring effect by taking some of its water away.

The Relief Channel transports the water from the Cut-off channel on from Denver to the tidal Great Ouse just above King's Lynn.

The Relief Channel was designed by the great 20th Century civil engineer Sir Murdoch MacDonald. MacDonald had previously worked on damming the river Nile and building the mighty Aswan Dam.

The Relief Channel was also intended to act as a reservoir as it is supplied with non saline water. Currently anticipated water shortages are preventing proposed developments in Cambridge, particularly a new cancer hospital. Surprisingly the firm which now carries Sir Murdoch's name, Mott MacDonald, who are designing the new Fens Reservoir, have turned down this readily available source of water.

6

THE TIDAL RIVER GREAT OUSE DENVER TO KING'S LYNN

It's all too easy to think that the River Great Ouse finishes at Denver, but it is a mistake to confuse the end of the non-tidal section with the true end of the river. King's Lynn has as much history to offer as the other towns on the river and shouldn't be forgotten. Its position on the coast made it a key trading link between river and sea and it was one of the Hanseatic League ports, networking merchants to ports in Norway and through the Baltic Sea.

King's Lynn is the last town on the River Great Ouse before it enters the Wash. Downstream of Denver Sluice to King's Lynn the river is tidal and is a very different river to navigate. For centuries boats have navigated up and down the tidal Great Ouse but it does need some forward planning.

The incoming tides, particularly spring tides, bring sediment up the river and deposit it as sandbanks in the river channel. In the opposite direction, the volume of water coming downriver scours the channel and sends sediment back downstream and out to sea. The effect of the contradictory flows means that the position of the sandbanks in the tidal river is constantly shifting.

Since opening in the mid 1960s, the Great Ouse Relief Channel (and its sister - the Great Ouse Cut-off Channel) take much of the water from the Great Ouse, and its tributaries, and send them down the Relief Channel through either the AG Wright Sluice or the Diversion Sluice.

The tidal Great Ouse is now only fed by water coming down the New Bedford River, (boosted in winter by water from the Ouse Washes entering the NBR through Welmore Lake Sluice) and small amounts of water being released through the 'little eyes' at Denver Sluice. With the greater volume of water diverted to the Relief Channel, less natural scouring occurs on the tidal Great Ouse itself, which results in more sedimentation.

Tides

Compiled by Imray from information provided by King's Lynn Port and Denver Lock Keepers

Average tidal range at King's Lynn on a spring tide is 5·8 metres (19') but can be as much as 8·5m, or even higher in a winter storm surge.

Average tidal range at King's Lynn on a neap tide is about 3·2m (10'6").

Tidal heights given are heights above King's Lynn Dock Sill, which is 0·7m below Chart Datum King's Lynn.

At King's Lynn the flood tide runs for about 4 hours and the ebb tide runs for about 8½ hours.

Bridge heights between Denver and King's Lynn can be calculated by subtracting the height of the tide from 9·15m.

If you are unused to tidal waters it is worth remembering that spring tides have a much bigger tidal range and a much faster flow, whereas neap tides have a smaller tidal range and a slower tidal flow. At the smallest neaps you will risk running aground before getting to King's Lynn, so it's usually better to aim for a period when there will be more water.

Tidal information is published at www.kingslynnport.co.uk/shipping/tides/

The Lock Keepers at Denver and Salter's Lode will also know the expected tide times and tidal flows.

Taking into account the river flows, the Lock Keepers' advice is usually to lock out at Denver as follows:

On a neap tide At about HW King's Lynn (i.e. about 1 hr before HW at Denver).

On a spring tide At about 1-3 hrs after HW King's Lynn (i.e. about HW to HW+2).

Heading back up river you will be carrying the flood. You should think about air heights as you get closer to High Water. Aim to be at Denver at High Water if air height allows.

If you are travelling down river on a spring ebb the speed of the flow can be as much as 5 knots. At this flow rate you are likely to lose some steerage (also see 'Crabbing' p.168).

Something else to take into account is that on the tidal Ouse a strong south or southwest wind can push back against the incoming tide, slowing the flow, delaying and reducing the height of High Water at Denver – then accelerating the outgoing tide. Conversely, a strong north or northeast wind can accelerate the incoming tide and make High Water at Denver earlier and higher – then slowing the outgoing tide. These effects can be considerable.

When the wind direction is opposite to the tidal flow it can create steep standing waves which may be dangerous to small boats.

Further advice on boating on the tidal Great Ouse can be found at www.kingslynnport.co.uk/leisure/ with a further link to 'Paddling on the Great Ouse' which is relevant for any small boats, not just paddlers:

www.kingslynnport.co.uk/wp-content/uploads/2021/01/Paddlers-user-quide-2021.pdf

Preparation for the tidal journey between Denver and King's Lynn

Going on a recce

It is worth making a recce before setting out on the trip, by walking the bank at low tide, noting where the sandbanks are. This helps in understanding what lurks under the brown, swirling waters when you navigate them. A mental picture of what's underneath is of considerable value when you come to make the journey. A really good way of doing this is to head down the Great Ouse Relief Channel before you try the tidal section. You can moor along the relief channel and walk the banks of the tidal river at low tide. Make some notes on the maps or take some photos to remind you where the sand banks are.

Timing your trip

Clearing sandbanks v getting under bridges

Higher spring tides give you greater clearance over sandbanks at the 'top of the tide', but less room under bridges. The decision when in the tide cycle to go is a balancing act between these two considerations. Ask for advice from the lock keepers and other experienced boaters who have made the journey. If in any doubt, employ a pilot familiar with the waters.

Differing requirements for different boats

I made the return journey in my steel narrowboat with 0·6m (2') draft and 1·8m (6') air clearance. With only one moderately powerful engine and no bow thruster, this was perhaps the least resilient boat for the journey. My pilot recommended we make the journey close to a spring tide. He was more concerned about clearing sandbanks than fitting under bridges. With a comparatively low air clearance of 1·8m, by the time we reached the first bridge at Downham Market, heading downstream, the tide had already fallen so far, that getting under the bridge was no problem.

Some fibreglass cruisers have an extra top deck, known as the 'flybridge', with radar added on top. These can require up to 3-3·7m (10-12') air clearance, and generally draw around 0·9m (3'). These boats often avoid travelling around spring tides because of concerns about getting under the bridges. Equipped with powerful twin engines and bow thrusters, they are better suited for these tidal waters than my narrow boat.

I've spoken to several captains of Dutch barges about the journey. They tend to be less choosy about when in the tide

SPRING TIDE

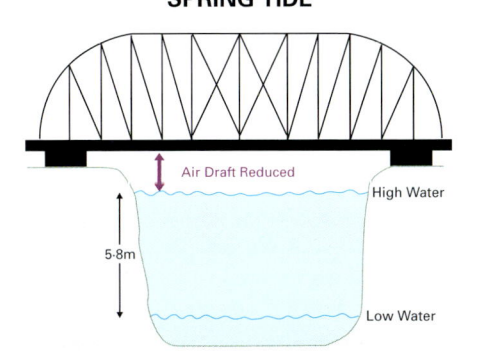

Air Draft Reduced
High Water
5·8m
Low Water

NEAP TIDE

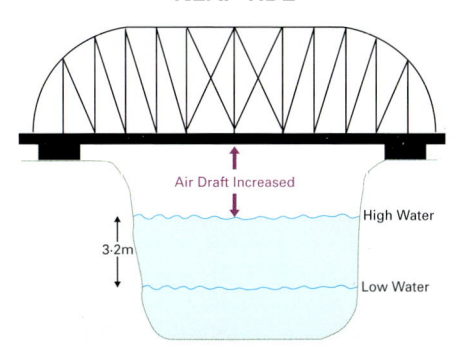

Air Draft Increased
High Water
3·2m
Low Water

RIVER GREAT OUSE 167

cycle they make this trip. All of them used the expression "dragging the bottom (of the boat) all the way up" when describing their journey. Dutch barges are built flat-bottomed for estuary work. Traditionally they would 'beach', settling on the bottom, load or unload their cargo, before they floated off on the next tide. Grounding isn't a problem to a Dutch barge, more an inconvenience. Typical draft on a Dutch Barge is about 1·8m (6') and air clearance 2·5m (8') (with the mast down!).

Plotting a route

Depending on recent tides and river flows, the shallows can sometimes form counter-intuitively on the outside of the bends rather than on the inside. This is why it is so important to do a 'recce' beforehand (see p.163). Your route will zig-zag from one side of the river to the other, taking the longest possible course. It may bring to mind the image of a recalcitrant child dragging their feet on their reluctant way to school; never quite leaving the route, but crossing from one side of the road to the other, prolonging the journey and postponing arrival as much as possible.

Potential Hazards

'Crabbing'

On tidal waters you can make a minor adjustment to your steering, which on non-tidal waters would redirect your boat, but on tidal waters has little more effect than causing your vessel to point on a different line, but to continue on the same course, now sideways. This can also be described as 'crabbing'. In a strong stream it is advisable to 'over steer' and increase power if initial use of the rudder has little effect on the actual trajectory of the vessel. In the 2020 season a narrowboat hit a bridge on the tidal Ouse sideways on, suffering considerable damage as a result. This may well have been as a result of 'crabbing'.

Catching a sand bank

If your bows ground on a sandbank your boat will almost inevitably spin 180 degrees, with your stern leading off downstream, and your bows only releasing when you are now facing the wrong way. Heading backwards on a strong stream with little or no steering is to be avoided at all costs! Turning in these circumstances is difficult and you will travel a considerable distance while performing this manoeuvre.

Missing the pontoon at King's Lynn and getting swept out to sea

Before I made this trip, boating friends fed me alarming stories that I would be travelling so fast on the falling tide, that when we got to King's Lynn I would only have one fleeting chance to get a mooring rope on the pontoon, before being swept out to sea! As it was, when we got to the pontoon, the flow was slowed enough to provide ample opportunity to turn, stem the tide, and moor.

Making sure you're insured

Your boat insurance provides cover within defined geographical limits. If your policy is effective within inland waters you should talk to your insurers about extending cover to tidal (estuary) waters. It is possible that you might overshoot the Kings Lynn moorings and then have to go out into the sea to turn around. Your insurers should agree to extend your policy to keep you covered should this occur.

Adhere to all the points described on p.167-168, plus:

- Simply don't do this single handed

- Advise the lock keeper 24 hours in advance of your intent to make the journey. The lock keeper will discuss with you what time of day and state of the tide is favourable

- Give serious consideration to employing a pilot familiar with the waters (your insurer may require you to do so)

- Try to walk as much of the route as possible at low tide, familiarise yourself with the position of sandbanks and other hazards. This will be much easier if you have opted to use the Great Ouse Relief Channel in order to familiarise yourself on foot with the tidal section. It's possible to do this from the moorings on the Relief Channel (see p.159). Remember that sandbanks can shift position from week to week

- Your pilot will bring a short range marine radio (VHF) with them. If you are not employing a pilot, you are strongly advised to have your own radio. If you do get a radio you cannot use it unless you first obtain a certificate of competence issued by the RYA on behalf of the Maritime Coastguard Agency

- If you are stopping at King's Lynn, book a place in advance on the floating pontoon

- If you are continuing to The Wash and beyond, a VHF radio is recommended to be able to notify Humber Coast Guard of your time of leaving King's Lynn and your recommended arrival at your next port.

17th-century Custom House, King's Lynn

Map 25

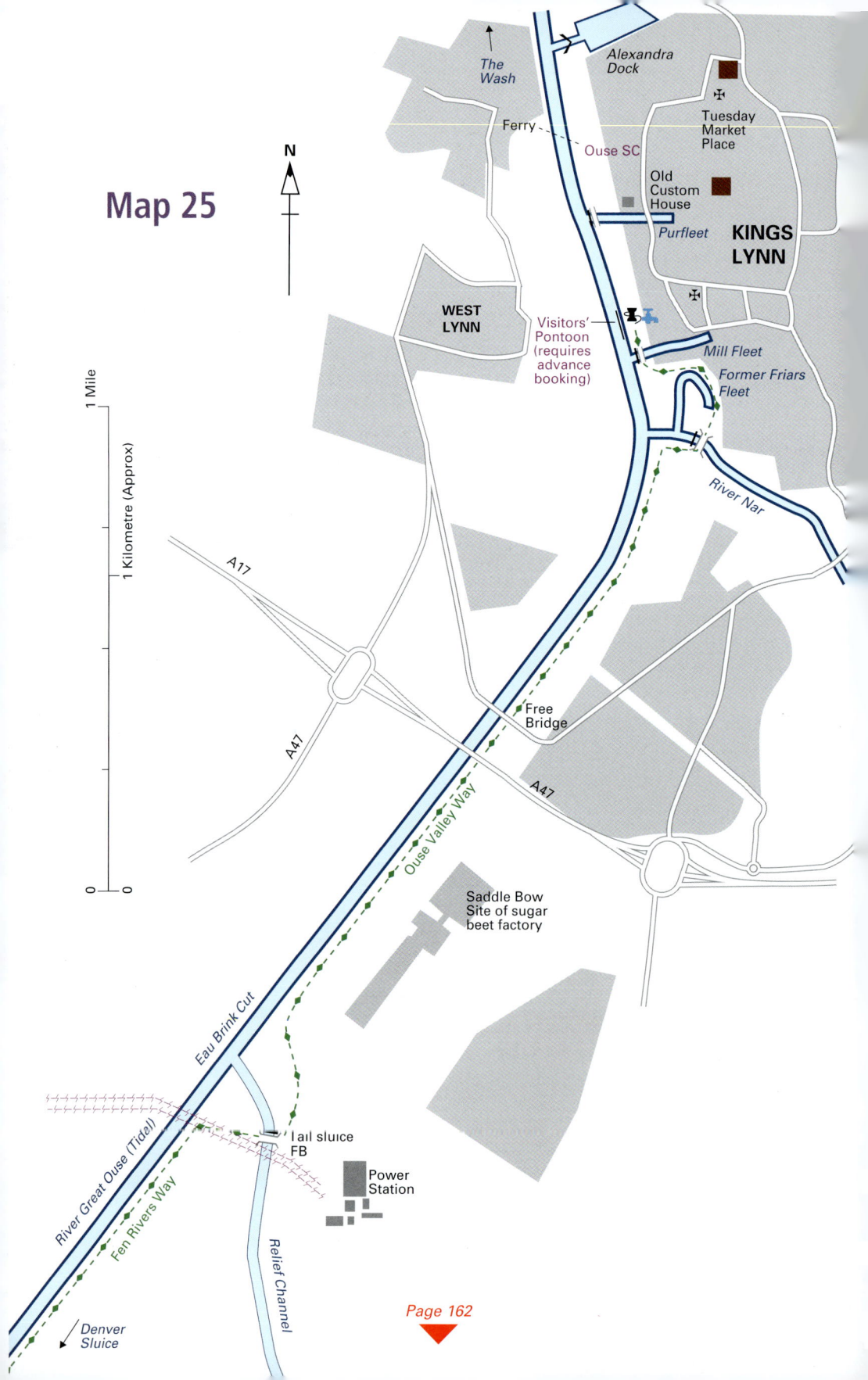

The Wash

Ferry

Ouse SC

Alexandra Dock

Tuesday Market Place

Old Custom House

Purfleet

KINGS LYNN

WEST LYNN

Visitors' Pontoon (requires advance booking)

Mill Fleet

Former Friars Fleet

River Nar

N

1 Mile
1 Kilometre (Approx)

A17

A47

Free Bridge

A47

Ouse Valley Way

Saddle Bow Site of sugar beet factory

Eau Brink Cut

River Great Ouse (Tidal)

Fen Rivers Way

Tail sluice FB

Power Station

Relief Channel

Denver Sluice

Page 162

Maps 23, 24 and 25

The Tidal Great Ouse Denver to King's Lynn

Distance 13 miles

Approx. time 2 hours (dependent of wind and tide)

Tidal River Great Ouse

Map 23 (p.158) / Map 24 (p.162) Tidal Great Ouse Denver to King's Lynn
Map 25 King's Lynn

Denver Lock
L 29·5m, W 5·4m (17'7") D 2·04m
Denver Lock ☎ 01366 382340 or
Denver Complex ☎ 01366 382013

Navigation Authority
Denver to Stowbridge: EA
Stowbridge to the Wash:
King's Lynn Port Authority

VHF radio
Denver Complex Ch 16/73
Kings Lynn Port Authority Ch 14

Tidal Range at King's Lynn
On a neap tide the average rise between high and low tide is 3·2m. On a spring tide this can increase to 5·8m or more

King's Lynn Port website gives accurate tide times and tidal heights
www.kingslynnport.co.uk/shipping/tides/

or see Imray **Tides Planner** app.
www.imray.com/tides-planner-app/

High Water at Denver is approximately 1-1·5h after HW King's Lynn

The widening estuary of the Great Ouse as it approaches King's Lynn, with Lynn Minster in the background

RIVER GREAT OUSE 171

Description of a journey made by the author to King's Lynn and back to Denver, August 2020.

Heading downstream

Our plan was to depart **Denver Lock** *at the top of the tide (or at least as soon we could squeeze under the tidal guillotine gate). High tide had been forecast for 09.23 at King's Lynn, which meant that it would happen one hour later, around 10.30, at Denver. It was a spring tide with a 6·5m (21ft) fall.*

We entered the lock at 11.10 and were locked straight through. We emerged into brown swirling water. It was immediately obvious to me that this was rather more 'serious' boating than I experienced on 'normal' days, and full concentration would be a must. The EA were constructing a down stream **mooring pontoon***. Attached to this was a large working platform, which served to block over half the river. A wave was breaking alarmingly over the outside corner of the steel deck. I endeavoured to steer round this obstacle but quickly realised that although I had turned the bows of the boat I was now travelling sideways (crabbing) still in the same direction, still heading for the threatening obstacle. I increased my*

Pilot Sid Fisher guiding the author out of Denver, with the New Bedford River sweeping in at top of photo
Kate Gipson

Working platform attached to mooring pontoon on the day of our trip

throttle and over steered, managing to 'side step' the platform. The speed at which we passed it brought home to me the seriousness of the journey, and the importance of quick reactions.

I hardly had time to glance at the mouth of the **Old Bedford River***, somewhere I've been a number of times, before we swept past the entrance to* **Salter's Lode***, the entrance point for the Middle Level. I was relieved that I wasn't trying to turn into the Lode. In those conditions I wondered if I would have actually succeeded! Crossings between Salter's and Denver are generally made on slack tides, but we were travelling on the ebb at 6 knots.*

We passed under **Stowbridge** *bridge at 11.56. My engine was reading 2,000 revs and we were travelling at 7 knots.*

We shot **St Mary Magdalen bridge** *at 12.19 still doing 2,000 revs at 7 knots.*

As we passed **Wiggenhall St German church** *it is quite clear from the 'tide-mark' on my photo below how much the height of the water had already dropped.*

We passed the outlet for the **Middle Level's Main Drain** *at 12.37.*

We were under the busy **A47 Bridge***, just above King's Lynn, at 12.57. I've frequently driven across the bridge and* marvelled how the gentle river I grew up with in Bedford could possibly have swollen to become this gargantuan monster. I had finally travelled the whole navigable extent of the Great Ouse, but until we had successfully moored I delayed any celebration!

At 13.05 we arrived at the **visitors' pontoon at King's Lynn**, where I had booked a mooring in advance. Getting onto the pontoon was considerably easier than I had been told to expect. My pilot sent me to the bows and turned the boat into the flow, stemming the tide, and gently ferry glided onto the pontoon. I jumped off with the rope and secured the boat. My fears about the speed of the outgoing tide past the pontoon had been unfounded, mainly because the increasing width of the estuary had diluted the speed of flow. As it was we came in on 'tick-over'. The only 'fly in the ointment' was a cruiser already moored there who maintained they were reserving the whole of the rest of that side of the pontoon for friends.

Only two hours after we had left Denver we were safely tucked up on the pontoon, and ready to explore King's Lynn.

Moorings and facilities

Denver tidal moorings solely for waiting for the lock.

King's Lynn moorings
A serviced visitor pontoon (water and electricity) is available at South Quay.
Must be advanced booked from King's Lynn Borough Council.
visitorpontoons@westnorfolk.gov.uk.
In 2020 moorings capacity was extended. This facility is charged. Combination for pontoon gate lock required to get back on pontoon.

Tidal Range at King's Lynn
On a neap tide the average rise between high and low tide is 3·2m. On a spring tide this can increase to 5·8m or more.

King's Lynn visitor pontoon

Wiggenhall St German church and the significant tidal drop is already evident

RIVER GREAT OUSE

Heading upstream

We had planned to make the return journey the next morning on the rising tide. We were aiming to get to Salter's Lode at high tide which was forecast in King's Lynn at 09.58 and Denver about 11.00 (6.12m tide). Our original plan had been to leave at 08.00am as the journey would take about 2 hours. However in the morning there was a fresh northerly wind blowing about 17mph which would hasten the high tide, so we left a bit earlier, at 07.36.

*We passed the **Relief Channel Tail Sluice** at 07.46, **St German's Bridge** at 08.02 and **St Mary Magdalen bridge** at 08.13. We were making 8 - 9 knots at 2,000 revs.*

*We reached **Stowbridge** at 08.32. We were making good time, so Sid instructed me to drop the revs to 1200, however we were still travelling at 7 knots. Just above the bridge is '**Stowbridge Hump**'. This is a sand bar running across the river. It is caused by deposition when the fluvial waters flowing downstream meet the incoming tide, and is generally regarded as the point on the tidal Ouse where you are most likely to ground. We passed over the 'hump' without any difficulties, but it was noticeable that my bows went up and down as we crossed it.*

*At 08.55 we passed under **Downham Bridge**.*

*Everything was going smoothly until we got to **Denver**. We had aimed to get there at the 'top of the tide', but we were early, and the tide was still coming in. On the regular Salter's Lode to Denver Crossing you approach Denver Lock near the eastern bank, in line with the lock. However, because of the new moorings and temporary work platform occupying much of the river, I was approaching from a position far further out in the river. Once clear of the working platform, I turned towards the lock. The incoming tide was sweeping the boat upstream, but the New Bedford River, running in the opposite direction to the tide, grabbed my bows, and turned them downstream, in the opposite direction to the one I wanted. I was powerless to stop the boat turning! With some trouble I brought my boat around for a second attempt. Wishing to avoid the sandbank I had spent eleven hours on earlier in the year (see photo p.145) immediately below Denver Sluice, I 'punched' the New Bedford and attempted to cross close, and parallel to, the sluices. I managed this, but in front of the lock the stream once again wrenched my bows away from the lock and turned them downstream again. Undeterred I simply entered the lock backwards. The time was 09.14, half an hour earlier than we had been aiming for.*

The tidal Great Ouse at Wiggenhall St Mary

Walking

The **Fen Rivers Way** continues along the east bank of the now tidal Great Ouse, all the way to **King's Lynn**. It only leaves the floodbank, briefly, to cross the outflow of the Relief Channel on the Tail Sluice. This is a popular route with both walkers and mountain bikers, both for its dramatically changing terrain, and abundant avian wildlife. This is an approximately 12 mile walk. Refreshment can be found at **The Heron, Stowbridge**, and **The Crown and Anchor, Wiggenhall St Germans**, but almost everyone I've seen on this path carries a small back-pack.

Local history

The **A47 bridge** is made up of three 37m (120') spans and two 21m (70') spans. In 1975 it replaced the 'New Bridge' constructed in the mid 1920s of concrete, which in turn superseded an iron bridge, constructed in 1873, this in turn replaced a wooden bridge known as the Free Bridge or Cut Bridge which opened in 1821. At over 800' long this was one of the longest wooden bridges in England. The current A47 bridge is immediately upstream of the site of the iron bridge, whose columns remain. It is common practice to build a new bridge close to, but not on the same footprint, as an older bridge it replaces, ensuring continuity during construction.

Alternative ways of getting to King's Lynn

If you don't want to take your own boat to King's Lynn, an alternative is to moor up and catch the train. The nearest station on the Great Ouse is at Littleport, and on the Relief Channel there are connecting stations at Downham Market and near Wiggenhall St Mary. There are moorings close to each of these.

The A47 bridge, and in front of it the Free Bridge, the last two river crossings before the Great Ouse finally meets the sea

King's Lynn Quay

King's Lynn

King's Lynn is an historic market town steeped in maritime history. In medieval times it was a member of the Hanseatic League, a trading association of towns across the the Baltic and North seas. It was England's busiest port (as important as Liverpool would become in the 19th century).

This legacy is reflected in some glorious old buildings, a thriving town centre, and a number of visitor attractions. King's Lynn boasts many places to eat out, and seafood (especially inshore prawns, shrimps and cockles) are a local speciality.

Local history

King's Lynn was originally named Len Episcopi (Bishop's Lynn) while under jurisdiction of the Bishop of Norwich. In 1537, during the reign of Henry VIII, it was surrendered to the Crown and took the name of Lenne Regis or King's Lynn.

King's Lynn offers a range of high street shops.

Supermarkets include a town centre Sainsbury's and Morrisons, Lidl, a number of eastern European supermarkets and towards the edge of town, a Tesco superstore and Sainsbury's.

Central and riverside pubs serving food and restaurants include
The Eagle, 110 Norfolk Street
☎ 0333 320 2083
The Globe Hotel (Wetherspoon), Market Place
☎ 01553 668000,
The Gatehouse, Kellard Place
☎ 01553 766671
The Crown and Mitre, Ferry St,
☎ 01553 774669
The Rathskeller, S Quay ☎ 01553 773713
Marriott's Warehouse on the Quayside
Modern European food
☎ 01553 818500,
Riverside Restaurant, 27 King Street
☎ 01553 773134

Statue of George Vancouver in Purfleet Quay

Places to visit

Lynn Museum
www.museums.norfolk.gov.uk/lynn-museum,
Stories of Lynn
www.storiesoflynn.co.uk
True's Yard Fisherfolk Museum
www.truesyard.co.uk
17th century Custom House and dock,
Hanse House (Hanseatic warehouse),
15th century Trinity Guildhall,
12th-15th century Minster,
The Walks, historic 18th century park with trails.

Transport
Ferry across the estuary to West Lynn, three times/hour

Public Transport
Railway station connects to Littleport (Ely and Cambridge)

Tourist Information Centre
Stories of Lynn, Saturday Market Pl, King's Lynn PE30 5DQ
☎ 01553 76304.

Lynn Minster

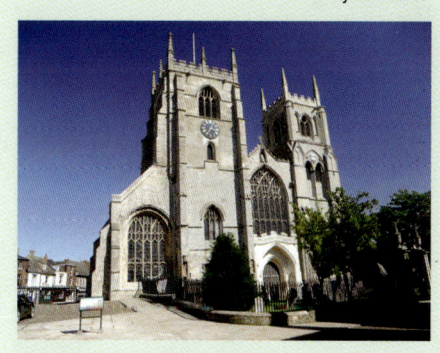

Tidal River Great Ouse

RIVER GREAT OUSE 177

Non navigable tributaries of the tidal River Great Ouse

Great Ouse Cut-off Channel

The cutting of an additional drainage channel had been first suggested by Cornelius Vermuyden in 1639, and again by John Rennie in 1810. Following serious flooding in 1937, 1939 and 1947 the Great Ouse Cut-off Channel was dug in three sections between 1954-64. The 28 mile channel required 35 new bridges. It diverts excess water from the head waters of the rivers Lark, Little Ouse and Wissey that could otherwise have caused the Ely Ouse to flood, to Denver, where they join the artificial Relief Channel. In summer months, flow is reversed and water diverted at Feltwell in Norfolk into a 12 mile tunnel, and then a 9 mile pipe, to supply drinking water to Essex. Up to 120 million litres/day can be transferred from the Ely Ouse to the Rivers Pant and Blackwater.

Sadly no provision was made for boat access during construction of the Cut-off Channel and navigation remains impossible. The A10 road crosses between Hilgay and Fordham and travellers frequently question why there are no boats on this wide piece of water that looks suitable for boating.

Walking

Similarly there is no provision for walking the Cut-off Channel, except where occasionally there are short sections, not connected to each other, where a path or drove briefly runs next to it, which is a great shame because it is an absolute haven for wildlife.

The Great Ouse Cut-off Channel

Impounding sluice at the bottom of the Cut-off Channel with the Relief Channel in the foreground

Middle Level Main Drain

The Middle Level Main Drain is a largely unnavigable drainage channel which joins the tidal Great Ouse approx 3 miles above Kings Lynn.

Walking

Most, but not all, of the Middle Level Main Drain is walkable. On the east side there is a path which starts at the confluence with the Tidal Great Ouse, you can follow this past the great pumping station for about 1½ miles. The path temporarily stops at Peter's Drove, but Common Road runs parallel for half a mile, where the path resumes at Magdalen Bridge. The path then continues until about a mile north of Outwell. One needs to leave the path at Morton's Bridge (the fourth bridge after Magdalen Bridge) and take Stow Road into Outwell.

On the west side the path begins about half a mile south of the confluence with the Tidal Great Ouse, at Wiggenhall St Germans. After 1 mile it temporarily finishes and you have to cross St Peter's Drove Bridge and briefly use Common Road, west of the Main Drain. At Magdalen Bridge you can cross back, and the path resumes. This path also then continues until about 1 mile north of Outwell. One needs to leave the path at Morton's Bridge (the fourth bridge after Magdalen Bridge) and take Stow Road into Outwell.

Local history

The **Middle Level Main Drain** was constructed in 1848 as an extension of the Sixteen Foot Drain running north east from Three Holes. It is navigable for 2 miles until **Mullincourt Aqueduct** where Navigation ceases. It runs a further 8 miles to **Wiggenhall St Germans**.

Originally the Middle Level mainly drained into the Great Ouse through Well Creek and Salter's Lode, and to a lesser extent though the Old Bedford River. When the height of the central part of the Level was dropped in 1848 and locks constructed at Marmont Priory, Welches Dam and Whittlesey, a new outlet, further north was required and Middle Level Main Drain was cut. Initially this relied on gravity and only discharged at low tide, However as the Middle Level lowered as a result of continued peat shrinkage, it became increasingly difficult to maintain gradient, and in 1934 a diesel pumping station was installed. Its capacity was extended in 1951 and again in 1970. In 2010 a new pumping station was built, the largest in Great Britain.

In August 2009 the BBC aired episode 5 of the television series *Rivers with Griff Rhys Jones* in which Griff and his dog Cadbury explored rivers in the east of England. Griff was given special permission to canoe the Middle Level Main Drain near St German pumping station. Allegedly one of the programme's producers inquired during

The Middle Level Main Drain

filming whether the pumps at the pumping station could possibly be turned on, to 'liven up the waters'. These six massive pumps can empty an Olympic sized swimming pool in 25 seconds, and a single pump would only take and a half minutes. If even one had been turned on, Griff, canoe and dog would all have been sucked through the massive pump, and a national treasure lost for ever!

The River Nar

The River Nar rises near Litcham in Norfolk and flows 15 miles west through Castle Acre and Narborough, joining the Ouse at King's Lynn.

Navigation on the River Nar was stopped by the construction of a pumping station and sluice across its confluence with the Tidal Great Ouse above King's Lynn and below the Relief Channel's Tail Sluice.

Today the Nar Valley Way walk runs 34 miles from King's Lynn to the Norfolk Rural Life Museum at Gressenhall.

The Nar was made navigable as a result of an Act of Parliament in 1751. It carried coal, timber, corn and malt. Trade fell off after the opening of the railway line between King's Lynn and Narborough in 1846 and it was closed in 1884.

The River Nar

Plans were promoted in 2001 to make the final part of the river navigable again (see p.164). Unfortunately, nothing ever came of these exciting and imaginative plans.

The Gaywood River

Also known as the River Gay, and in King's Lynn as the Fisher Fleet, the Gaywood rises near the village of Gayton in Derby Fen, west of King's Lynn. It winds its way for 7 miles to the Great Ouse. the river has never been navigable, and is not even suitable for self propelled craft because of its sensitive ecological status, with sightings of water voles, otters and trout.

Walking

The Gaywood River doesn't appear to be explorable by foot.

Kettlewell Lane in Lynn leads to a bend in the river where Kettle Watermill once stood. At the beginning of the 15th century horses supplied the power to lift water in 'kettles' from the river to supply the Town's wooden fresh water conduits. Evidence remains that later the mill was driven by the waters of the Gaywood.

The Rivers Purfleet and Millfleet

The River Purfleet outflows in King's Lynn through Bishop's Staithe to Purfleet Quay, next to the Custom House. It flows underground through King's Lynn. Similarly the Millfleet is another river now relegated to running below ground under King's Lynn.

The word 'fleet' is derived from an old Anglo-Saxon word meaning estuary, bay or inlet. The River Fleet, a subterranean river in London, gives its name to the world famous Fleet Street.

7

THE RIVER CAM
INCLUDING THE CAMBRIDGESHIRE LODES

Described travelling **upstream**

The River Cam rises near Debden in Essex and runs for 43 miles to its confluence with the Great Ouse at Pope's Corner. It is navigable for 14·5 miles to the Mill Pool above Silver Street Bridge in Cambridge, above which it is often called the Granta (its original name).

In the 17th century Cambridge merchants were keen to promote the river as a trading link with King's Lynn but felt that they were being blocked by the Bedford Level Corporation who prioritised the drainage of the Middle Level over navigation. An Act of Parliament in 1702 created 'The Conservators of the River Cam' for the express purpose of improving navigation of the River Cam from Byron's Pool, Grantchester, to Bottisham Lock, 13 miles downstream.

Midsummer Common, Cambridge

RIVER GREAT OUSE   181

Map 26

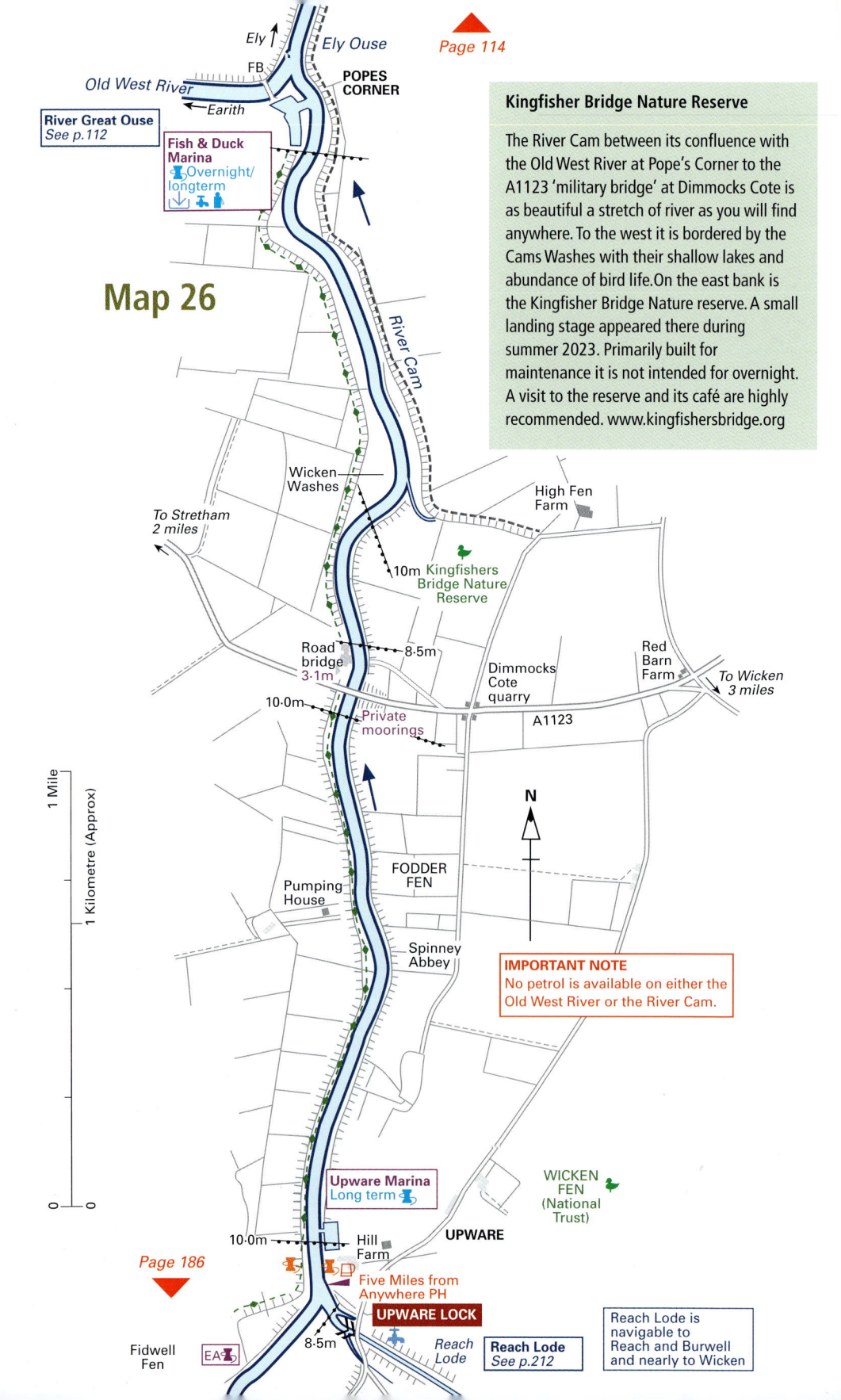

Ely ↑
Ely Ouse
FB
POPES CORNER
Page 114

Old West River
← Earith

River Great Ouse
See p.112

Fish & Duck Marina
Overnight/longterm

Kingfisher Bridge Nature Reserve

The River Cam between its confluence with the Old West River at Pope's Corner to the A1123 'military bridge' at Dimmocks Cote is as beautiful a stretch of river as you will find anywhere. To the west it is bordered by the Cams Washes with their shallow lakes and abundance of bird life. On the east bank is the Kingfisher Bridge Nature reserve. A small landing stage appeared there during summer 2023. Primarily built for maintenance it is not intended for overnight. A visit to the reserve and its café are highly recommended. www.kingfishersbridge.org

River Cam

Wicken Washes

High Fen Farm

To Stretham 2 miles

10m Kingfishers Bridge Nature Reserve

Road bridge 3.1m — 8.5m

Red Barn Farm

Dimmocks Cote quarry

To Wicken 3 miles

10.0m — Private moorings

A1123

N

1 Mile
1 Kilometre (Approx)

Pumping House

FODDER FEN

Spinney Abbey

IMPORTANT NOTE
No petrol is available on either the Old West River or the River Cam.

Upware Marina Long term

WICKEN FEN (National Trust)

Page 186

10.0m — Hill Farm

UPWARE

Five Miles from Anywhere PH

UPWARE LOCK

Fidwell Fen

EA

8.5m

Reach Lode
See p.212

Reach Lode is navigable to Reach and Burwell and nearly to Wicken

Map 26

River Cam Pope's Corner to Upware

Distance 7 miles

Time 2 hours

River Cam and Cambridgeshire Lodes

Map 26 Pope's Corner to Upware

Lowest bridge 3·1m Dimmocks Cote road bridge

Location	Moorings and facilities										Victualling	
	Short stay	48hr	72h	Long stay	Water point	CDP	Pumpout	Refuse	Diesel	Shops	Pub	Café/restaurant
Fish and Duck Marina		✓	✓	✓	✓	✓			✓			
Upware Marina					✓	Facilities for customers only						
Five Miles from Anywhere PH				✓	electric hook up						✓	✗
Moorings opposite PH				✓	Small vessel required to cross river							
Upware Lock					✓							
Fidwell Fen EA moorings		✓										

RIVER GREAT OUSE

Navigation notes

The confluence of the rivers Cam and Great Ouse is at **Pope's Corner**. Although the River Cam is a tributary of the River Great Ouse, you could easily assume that it is the Cam flowing on to Ely, as it is the much bigger river at this point.

From **Pope's Corner** you will be travelling **upstream** on the River Cam.

One of the Cambridge rowing clubs, Rob Roy, has relocated to the Fish and Duck, so caution is advised when navigating this stretch. Many of their rowers appear juniors. 'Robs' as they are known, bill themselves as 'Cambridge's leading non-university rowers'.

The river here is wide and open. **Wicken Washes flood meadow** is formed by side waters situated on the west side of the river. The washes are rich in birdlife, including shellduck, oystercatchers, swans, curlew, grebe, snipe, tufted duck and Canada geese. Geese often line the top of the flood bank, and as one passes, the whole flock can slowly turn to watch you pass, like spectators at a horse race. It is hard to image that in only 14 miles this comparatively wide open river, a haven for wildlife, will be the same confined and polite river that runs through the Cambridge Backs.

On the east bank, to your left travelling upstream, the land rises to what, in fen terms, could be described as a 'hill'. It's not clear whether this is natural or manmade, but there may be a clue in the name '**High Fen Farm**' on the map. It doesn't warrant a contour line and may be part of a quarry.

At **Dimmocks Cote the A1123 crosses the river** on an interesting **arched concrete bridge** which replaced a ferry in 1928. Its abutments include indistinct armorial shields, which appear to be those of the now defunct Isle of Ely County Council. Its appearance has lead to the local nickname the 'military bridge'. It's easy to imagine it in a scene from a Cold War spy exchange, or as one of the WWII bridges over the Rhine. A small community of boats is based here.

As the river bends gently to the left the ivy clad shape of an old boat house is just discernible, masked by trees. It is fun to speculate what is hidden there, and what its past was.

To your left is the slightly undulating Fodder Fen, on the right there is a pumping station and an ubiquitous **pill box**.

Further on, to your right, is an isolated collection of boats and water-sports equipment.

The rural idyll is briefly interrupted by **Upware Marina**, and the very appropriately named pub **Five Miles From Anywhere**. There are **72 hour moorings** with electric hook-ups outside this very popular pub. There are also pleasant **48 hour moorings** on the

Dimmocks Cote Bridge, known as the 'military bridge'

One of several pill boxes built along the Cam in WWII

opposite bank, but as the ferry no longer operates you need your own tender to cross. The post script to the pub's name is 'No Hurry', and it's a shame more boaters don't heed this sound advice. A sign advises us that we are still 9 miles from Cambridge.

Upstream of the pub, the Cam turns to the southwest. **Reach Lode** branches off to the southeast through **Upware Lock** (see p.212). Quarter of a mile up the Cam are the **EA moorings at Fidwell Fen**.

Walking

The Fens Rivers Way follows both sides of the River Cam along the top of the flood banks to **Upware**. On the east side of the river it briefly leaves the river before returning at **Dimmock's Cote Bridge**.

Local history

The **Upware pub 'Five Miles from Anywhere, No Hurry'** was the home in the 1850s to a Cambridge University club the **Upware Republic**. It had its own 'laws' and 'currency'. In the 1860s Richard Ramsay Fielder MA of Jesus College (and Member of Lincoln's Inn) declared himself 'King of Upware'. He boated about the Fens, easily identifiable

Moorings and facilities

Fish and Duck Marina
Pope's Corner, CB6 3HR
Overnight and long term moorings, sales, diesel, chandlery.
☎ 01353 648081

Upware Marina CB7 5ZR
Long term moorings, services, repairs, sales
☎ 01353 721930

72h moorings with electric hook ups **outside Five Miles from Anywhere PH**.
48h moorings opposite the pub (no access to PH without tender to cross river).
Popular **EA moorings** at **Fidwell Fen**.
Water through **Upware/Reach Lode Lock** (see p.212 for details).

Five Miles from Anywhere PH, Upware
☎ 01353 721654

in a red waistcoat and with corduroy breeches, drinking from a great jug of punch known as His Majesty's Pint, writing doggerel verses and fighting with bargees.

There is a certain irony that Fielder declared himself 'King' of the 'Republic of Upware' because republics don't have Kings. Similarly declaring yourself anykind of 'head of state' is absolutely contrary to every democratic tradition. However it appears that Fielder was such a pugnacious individual, perhaps no one dared point out to him these inconsistencies!

Upware was the site of a chain ferry.

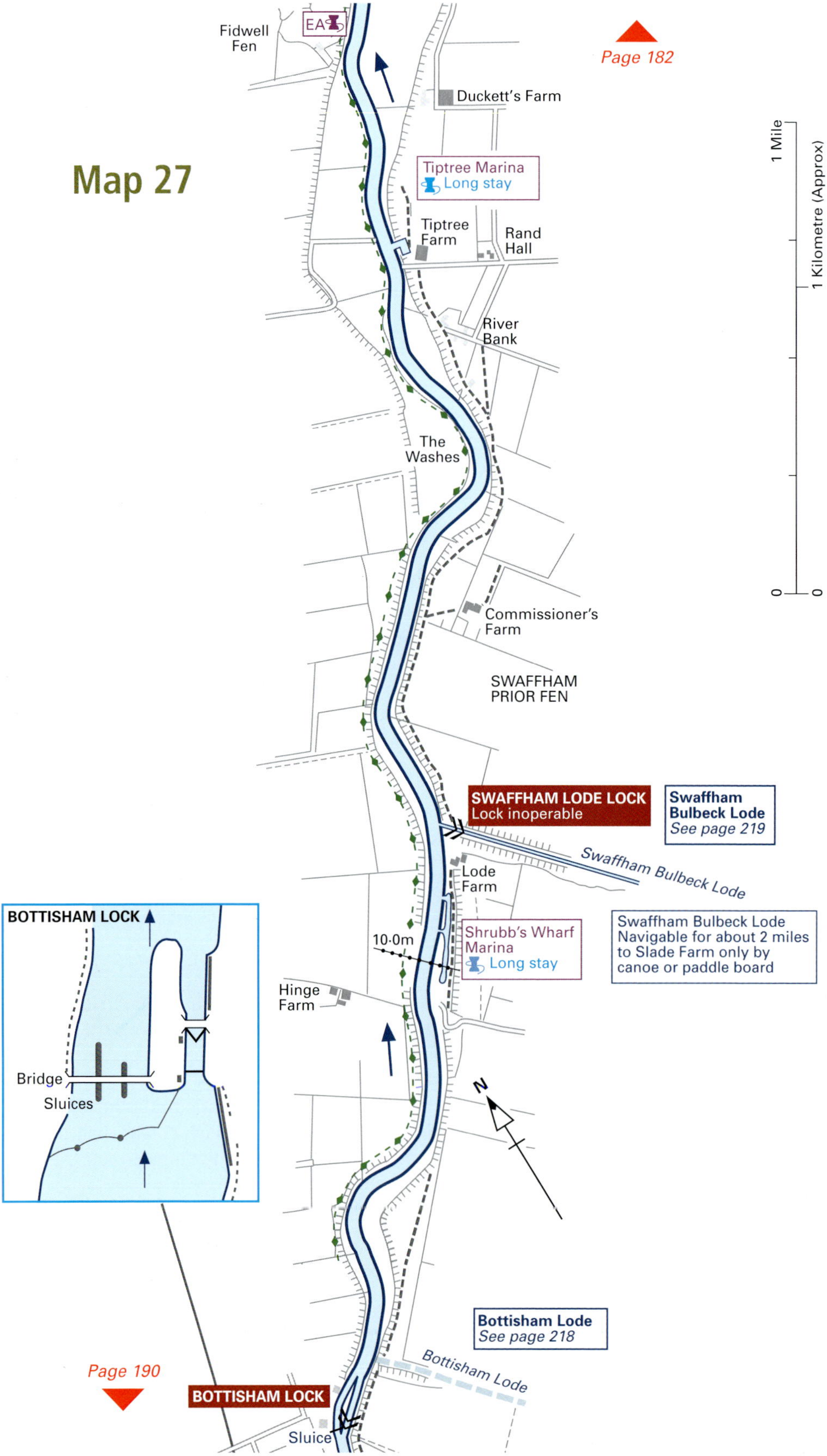

Map 27
Page 182
Page 190
Fidwell Fen
EA
Duckett's Farm
Tiptree Marina
Long stay
Tiptree Farm
Rand Hall
River Bank
The Washes
Commissioner's Farm
SWAFFHAM PRIOR FEN
SWAFFHAM LODE LOCK
Lock inoperable
Swaffham Bulbeck Lode
See page 219
Swaffham Bulbeck Lode
Lode Farm
Swaffham Bulbeck Lode Navigable for about 2 miles to Slade Farm only by canoe or paddle board
Shrubb's Wharf Marina
Long stay
10·0m
Hinge Farm
N
BOTTISHAM LOCK
Bridge
Sluices
Bottisham Lode
See page 218
Bottisham Lode
BOTTISHAM LOCK
Sluice
1 Mile
1 Kilometre (Approx)
0
0

Map 27

River Cam Upware to Bottisham Lock

Distance 7 miles
Time 2 hours

Map 27 Upware to Bottisham Lock

No bridges this reach
Bottisham Lock L 29·8m, W 4·5m (14'9"), D 1·5m, H 3·1m

Location	Lock width	Moorings and facilities							Victualling			
		Short stay	48hr	Long stay	Water point	CDP	Pumpout	Refuse	Fuel	Shops	Pub	Café/restaurant
Fidwell Fen EA moorings			⚓									
Tiptree Marina				⚓	Facilities for longstay customers only							
Shrubb's Wharf Marina				⚓	Facilities for longstay customers only							
Bottisham Lock	 〇〇											

RIVER GREAT OUSE

Leaving **Upware**, the flood meadows extends on the left, and behind them there are distant hills on the horizon.

About a mile beyond the Upware junction is **Tip Tree Marina** residential marina. Slow down for the boats moored on the river outside.

The river continues to lazily wind its way towards Cambridge. Judging from the profusion of 'private fishing' notices on the bank, the fishing rights here are fiercely guarded.

For a while the banks appear to close in on the river, with tall reeds and trees on either side. There is even the occasional non-willow. Odd chimneys appear on the left bank, heralding an imminent return to civilisation. To the left is Swaffham Bulbeck Lode (see p.219), and after that is **Shrubbs Wharf Marina**, which was the home mooring for the large Cambridge trip boat the *Georgina*, which carried over a hundred passengers. I fondly remember a lazy summer evening's cruise through Cambridge on her, complete with syncopated jazz band. Sadly the *Georgina* left the Cam in 2020 for a new life in Manchester.

Bottisham Lock

> ## Moorings and facilities
> **Tiptree Marina** CB7 5YJ
> Long term moorings.
> ☏ 01223 440065
>
> **Shrubbs Wharf Marina**
> CB25 9HF
> Long term moorings
> ☏ 01223 811812

After the marina the reeds and trees retreat from the water's edge and there is a return to more open vistas. The path on the right bank is popular with joggers, dog walkers and bird watchers.

A small community of residential boats, on both sides of the river, announces your imminent arrival at **Bottisham Lock**. On the left, shortly before the lock, is the entrance to the sadly no longer navigable **Bottisham Lode** (see p. 218). The gates to the lode stand resolutely closed. The Environment Agency often moor their weed cutting boats here.

Bottisham Lock has an upstream guillotine gate, and downstream V gates. Everything is electrically operated, so an Abloy key is a necessity, and your windlass temporarily redundant. This is definitely a gongoozler's lock, and at weekends, or on sunny days, expect an audience.

Walking

The Fens Rivers Way continues on both banks of the Cam between **Upware** and **Bottisham Lock**. These tracks are popular with both bird watchers and dog walkers.

Floating pennywort

The Cam was prone to spreading floating pennywort. Both the Environment Agency (below Bottisham) and the Cams Conservators (above Bottisham) regularly cut it, but it reproduced exponentially. It is fast spreading and chokes all the oxygen out of the water, killing fish and other plants. It can stop your boat dead in the water if you run into it !

Defra have licensed scientists to introduce a South American weevil which is a prolific eater of floating pennywort, but eats absolutely nothing else. There are always concerns about using one alien species to combat another. The weevil was set loose during summer 2021. During summer 2023 there was little evidence of the floating pennywort remaining.

Somewhat by chance it was discovered that water buffalo at nearby Chippenham Fen nature reserve absolutely love the stuff. However boaters can rest assured that there are no current plans to graze the floating pennywort of the River Cam with herds of roaming water buffalo!

Several other invasive species have colonised the river bank, including buddleia, which has been present for generations, and the more recent Himalayan balsam, much derided, but whose pretty little pink flowers are valuable to our dwindling bee population.

Floating pennyworth (*Hydrocotyle ranunculoides*)

Downstream lock moorings at Bottisham

RIVER GREAT OUSE

Map 28

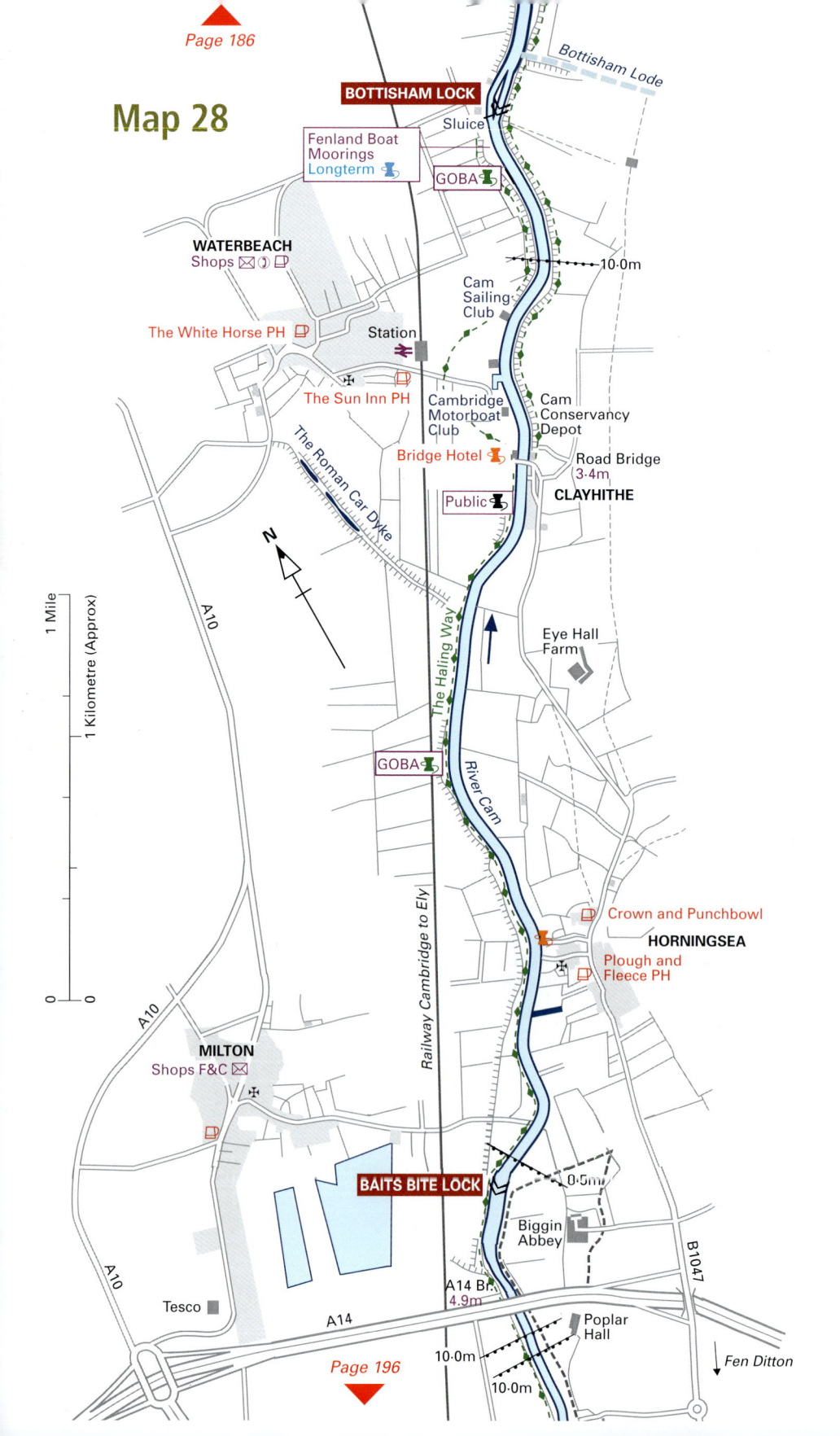

Page 186

Bottisham Lode

BOTTISHAM LOCK
Sluice
Fenland Boat Moorings Longterm
GOBA

WATERBEACH
Shops

10.0m

Cam Sailing Club

The White Horse PH
Station
The Sun Inn PH

Cambridge Motorboat Club
Cam Conservancy Depot

The Roman Car Dyke

Bridge Hotel
Road Bridge 3.4m
CLAYHITHE

Public

N

1 Mile
1 Kilometre (Approx)

A10

The Haling Way

Eye Hall Farm

GOBA

River Cam

Crown and Punchbowl
HORNINGSEA
Plough and Fleece PH

MILTON
Shops F&C

Railway Cambridge to Ely

BAITS BITE LOCK

0.5m

Biggin Abbey

A10
Tesco

A14 B. 4.9m

B1047

A14

Poplar Hall

↓ Fen Ditton

Page 196

10.0m
10.0m

Map 28

River Cam
Bottisham Lock
to Baits Bite Lock

Distance 4 miles
Time 1½ hours

Map 28 Bottisham Lock to Baits Bite Lock

Lowest bridge 3·4m Clayhithe Road Bridge
Navigation Authority Conservators of the River Cam
Bottisham Lock L 29·8m, W 4·5m (14'9") D 1·5m
Baites Bite Lock L 32m, W 4·3m (14'1") D 1·2m

Location	Lock	Moorings and facilities							Victualling		
		Short stay	48hr	Long stay	Water point	CDP	Pumpout	Refuse	Fuel	Shops	Pub	Café/restaurant
Fenland Boat moorings					⛲	Facilities for customers only						
Waterbeach GOBA moorings			⚓							🛒	🍺	🍴
The Bridge PH Clayhithe		⚓	Moorings for pub customers only								🍺	🍴
Clayhithe Bridge public moorings (short walk to Waterbeach Station)			⚓							🛒	🍺	🍴
GOBA moorings opposite Horningsea			⚓							🛒 Milton superstore 1½ miles		
Horningsea village council visitor moorings		⚓									🍺	
Baits Bite Lock	🔒											

River Cam and Cambridgeshire Lodes

Navigation notes

Above Bottisham Lock visitors need to display either a valid Anglian Pass (see p.11) or an annual Conservators of the River Cam licence, as you are moving from EA waters to Cam Conservancy waters. The lock is monitored by CCTV and licence evasion is actively pursued.

To your right, immediately above the lock, are some pleasant **permanent moorings**, managed by **Fenland Boat Moorings**. There are also some **GOBA moorings** here. These are only the second non-pub moorings since Pope's Corner, nearly 7 miles ago.

Above the lock you will find one or two large pink/orange buoys in the water. Red or green buoys are conventionally used to indicate the safe channel past hazards to navigation. The first time I encountered an orange buoy here I was mystified as to what navigational

Cam Sailing Club racing buoy and hut

GOBA moorings opposite Horningsea

information it was failing to convey to me. This reach is used by **Cam Sailing Club** to race dinghies and the buoys delineate the racing course. The only hazard they warn of is dinghy racing.

As you approach **Clayhithe Bridge**, the boater friendly **Bridge Hotel** is on your right. The hotel has constructed new **visitor moorings**. This is a popular pub for food and you are well advised to book a table in advance. On the left before the bridge the Cam Conservators keep their weed cutting boat. Peeping over the top of other buildings are the Dutch gables of the Victorian **Cam Conservators House** and former offices.

Upstream of the bridge, to your right, are **Clayhithe Bridge public moorings**. Just beyond the moorings the Car Dyke finishes its 85 mile journey from Lincoln to the River Cam, though it is not possible to discern the actual point of the former junction.

The Cambridge to Ely railway line then converges from the west. There is another **GOBA mooring on your right** here. This includes fixed cleats to tie to, removing the need to drive mooring pins in at the side of the towpath.

Moorings and facilities

Mooring against the tow path is expressly forbidden by the Conservators except in clearly designated locations:

Long term moorings above Bottisham Lock managed by **Fenland Boat Moorings.**
☎ 07939 003681

GOBA Waterbeach moorings, right bank when travelling upstream above Bottisham Lock

Visitor moorings outside The Bridge PH, Clayhithe

Clayhithe Moorings immediately after road bridge

GOBA moorings right bank opposite **Horningsea**

A long line of moored boats to your left heralds your arrival at **Horningsea**, where there is a Town Council provided short term mooring at the end of Dock Lane.

The Bridge PH at Clayhithe

Waterbeach
The White Horse, 12 Green Side, CB25 9HP
☎ 01223 505053
The Sun Inn, 7 Chapel St, CB25 9HR
☎ 01223 861254 (doesn't advertise food)
The Bridge, Clayhithe Rd, CB25 9HZ
☎ 01223 860622

In **Waterbeach** there are two convenience stores, a bakery, a pharmacy.

Takeaways include **The Beach Fryer** (fish and chips), 1 Denny End Rd, Waterbeach CB25 9PB
☎ 01223 440990

Supermarket
Large **Tesco** at **Milton**, 1½ miles from **GOBA Horningsea moorings**

Horningsea pubs
The Crown and Punchbowl, High St CB25 9JG
☎ 01223 860643
The Plough and Fleece, High St CB25 9JG
☎ 01223 860795

Places to visit

Anglesey Abbey National Trust house and gardens with Lode Mill is a 2½ - 3 mile walk from Bottisham Lock
www.nationaltrust.org.uk/anglesey-abbey-gardens-and-lode-mill

Denny Abbey and The Farmland Museum
3½ mile walk from GOBA Bottisham moorings.
www.dennyfarmlandmuseum.org.uk

River Cam and Cambridgeshire Lodes

RIVER GREAT OUSE

Beyond Horningsea, **Baits Bite Lock** is another lock with a guillotine top gate and bottom V gates. Once again it is entirely electrically operated, and another 'Mecca' for *gongoozlers*.

Above Baits Bite Lock you enter the world of Cambridge college rowing. The marshalling area for 'Head' races and 'Bumps' is just above the lock. During events this is the area of the river most congested with rowing boats. Having raced here myself, memories always flood back of sitting nervously on the water, generally in winter, waiting for the boom of the starting cannon, and trying to ignore that empty pre-race feeling in the pit of my stomach.

On the left, hidden behind trees is Biggin Abbey, a late 14th century summer residence of the Bishops of Ely. The **A14** then roars across the river on a **concrete bridge**.

Walking

The Fens Rivers Way continues briefly on the west bank, before diverting briefly into **Waterbeach**, before returning to the river opposite **Clayhithe**. The path on the east side of the river continues from **Bottisham Lock** until **Clayhithe**, where it crosses the river on the road bridge. The only path now runs next to the river on its west bank. It is also called the **Haling Way**, which means towpath. It continues to **Baits Bite Lock**.

Baits Bite Lock

Local history

Parts of the **Car Dyke** are Roman in origin. The exact age and function of Car Dyke remains a subject of debate in academic circles, but there is general consensus that in parts it acted as both a strategic boundary, a catch-water drain and as a canal. It ran for 85 miles between Lincoln and Cambridge, but can't have ever been navigable for that entire distance.

An archeological excavation in the 1990s found remains of a Roman era boat and a cargo of pottery in the Car Dyke near Horningsea. The site is a Scheduled Monument.

There was a Ferry at **Clayhithe** from the early 14th century until construction in 1872 of the bridge to Waterbeach railway station. A hithe was a loading quay on a river, and Clayhithe 'does what it says on the tin' - clay was moved here.

Below St Peter's Church in Horningsea, **Dock Lane** still leads down to the Cam where barges were unloaded. Coprolite (fossilised faeces) was loaded here during a boom in the 1870s. Upstream is a cut known as the 'Bricker' which was used by the local brickworks to bring fuel in, and finished bricks out. Horningsea was the southern extreme for sugar beet collection by the Ely beet factory barges.

I'm often asked about the origin of the lock name 'Baits Bite'. A 'bite' was an archaic term for the outside of a bend in a river. The lock is indeed built on a long bend in the river, and the lock keeper's cottage is on the 'bite' side. We are so far unable to shed any light on the identity of a Mr Baits.

Horningsea

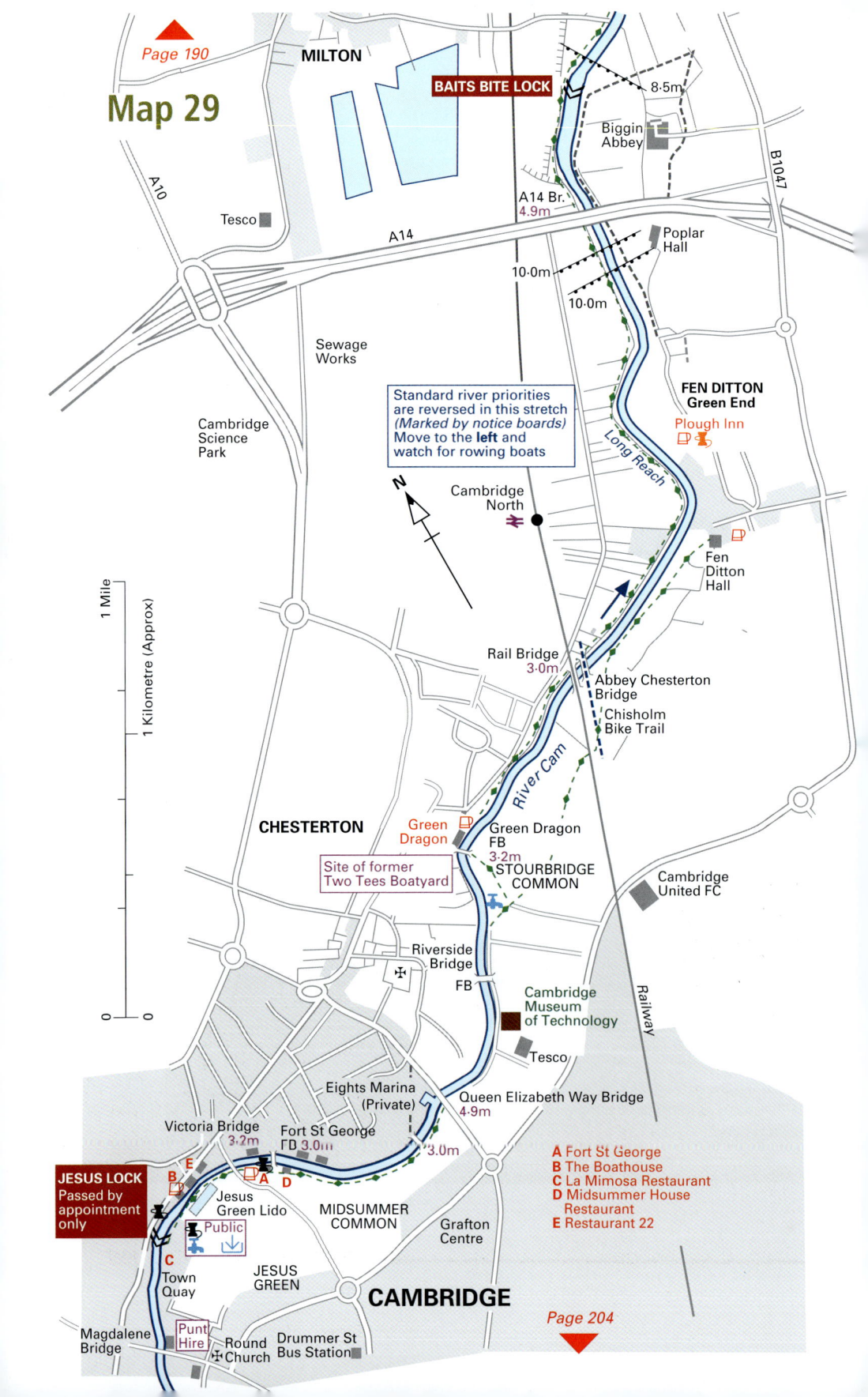

Map 29

Page 190

MILTON

BAITS BITE LOCK

8.5m

Biggin Abbey

B1047

A10

Tesco

A14 Br. 4.9m

A14

Poplar Hall

10.0m

10.0m

Sewage Works

FEN DITTON
Green End

Cambridge Science Park

Plough Inn

*Standard river priorities are reversed in this stretch (Marked by notice boards) Move to the **left** and watch for rowing boats*

N

Cambridge North

Long Reach

Fen Ditton Hall

1 Mile

1 Kilometre (Approx)

Rail Bridge 3.0m

Abbey Chesterton Bridge

Chisholm Bike Trail

River Cam

CHESTERTON

Green Dragon

Green Dragon FB 3.2m

STOURBRIDGE COMMON

Site of former Two Tees Boatyard

Cambridge United FC

Riverside Bridge FB

Cambridge Museum of Technology

Tesco

Railway

Eights Marina (Private)

Queen Elizabeth Way Bridge 4.9m

Victoria Bridge 3.2m

Fort St George FB 3.0m

3.0m

A Fort St George
B The Boathouse
C La Mimosa Restaurant
D Midsummer House Restaurant
E Restaurant 22

JESUS LOCK
Passed by appointment only

E
B A D
Jesus Green Lido

Public

MIDSUMMER COMMON

Grafton Centre

C Town Quay

JESUS GREEN

Magdalene Bridge

Punt Hire

Round Church

Drummer St Bus Station

CAMBRIDGE

Page 204

Map 29

River Cam
Baits Bite Lock to Jesus Lock

Distance 2½ miles
Time ¾ hour

Map 29 Baits Bite Lock to Jesus Lock Cambridge

Lowest bridge 3·0m Baits Bite Lock
Navigation Authority Conservators of the River Cam
Baites Bite Lock L 32m, W 4·3m (14'1") D 1·2m
Jesus Lock L 32m, W 4·3m (14') D 1·4m Head 4·0m

Location	Lock width	Moorings and facilities								Victualling		
		Short stay	48hr	Long stay	Water point	CDP	Pumpout	Refuse	Fuel	Shops	Pub	Café/restaurant
The Plough Fen Ditton		☕									🍺	🍴
Cambridge end of Stourbridge Common					🚰							
Town moorings adjacent to Fort St George PH			☕							🧺	🍺	🍴
Jesus Green moorings			☕		🚰	⬇	⛽			🧺	🍺	🍴
Jesus Lock (permission required)	◯◯											

River Cam and Cambridgeshire Lodes

RIVER GREAT OUSE 197

Navigation notes

Beyond the A14 bridge, **Fen Ditton** approaches on the left side and the towpath on the right bank is now an almost continuous stream of walkers, joggers and cyclists. After a line of moored boats is **The Plough PH** at **Fen Ditton**. This is a popular pub with large gardens which run down to the river, and which serves food. The pub has limited visitor moorings (two trip boats operate from here).

The narrow winding section of river near The Plough pub in Fen Ditton is known as the 'Gut'. Because of the difficulties in steering a 60ft rowing VIII through the Gut there are two crossover points where you move over to the opposite river bank (keep left, not the normal right), and later, back again. This applies to all boats, and both crossover points are signed, but the signs are sometimes part obscured by vegetation. Priority is also reversed for each of these sections and craft travelling downstream should give priority to vessels travelling upstream.

Crossover signs in the 'Gut' near The Plough, Fen Ditton

Fen Ditton church overlooking the river

Passing the pub, further signs tell you to swap back to the normal (right) side of the river. On your left is a little backwater alliteratively called **Fen Ditton Ditch**, which doesn't look navigable to powered craft.

A couple of bends further on you enter a straight with a 'Meccano' style wrought **iron railway bridge** at the far end. This brings me back memories of racing here and stealing a glance over my shoulder for a desperate first sight of this bridge which is close to the end of the rowing course.

The new **Abbey Chesterton Bridge** pedestrian and cycle bridge forms part of the Chisholm Trail, a new walking and cycling route linking north and south Cambridge. It is immediately downstream of the railway bridge. The contrast between the curvy, flowing lines of the new bridge and the rectilinear nature of the railway bridge is quite extreme.

There are five new town houses to your right, raised above ground level to minimise the potential effects of flooding. This had been the site of a pub

Moorings and facilities

Water at **Stourbridge Common** and at **Jesus Green** (outside the lido).

48h moorings outside the Fort St George PH.

Moorings on the right at **Jesus Green.**

Pump-out, **Elsan emptying** at **Jesus Green.**

Riverside pubs
The Plough, Fen Ditton,
CB5 8SX
Some mooring outside
☎ 01223 293264

The Green Dragon, Chesterton
CB4 1NZ
No moorings
☎ 01223-363506

The Fort St George, Midsummer Common
CB4 1HA
Visitor moorings outside
☎ 01223 354327

Supermarket shopping
Large **Tesco** off Newmarket Road short walk from the river, behind the Museum of Technology,

Places to visit
Cambridge Museum of Technology
www.museumoftechnology.com

Jesus Green Lido 90m outdoor pool

since 1850, first called the 'Pike and Eel' and latterly the 'Penny Ferry'. The pub was very popular with rowers, and served great food, and I mourn its loss every time I pass.

Further on the right are the wooden sheds of the former **Two Tees Boatyard**. On the left is **Stourbridge Common**, with residential boats moored along much of its length. Much of the growth of Cambridge between the thirteenth and sixteenth centuries can be attributed to the great fairs held here. These only finished in 1934, but their legacy continues in the current Strawberry Fair, held on Midsummer Common on the first Saturday in June.

As the great chimney of **Cambridge Museum of Technology** first appears ahead, Stourbridge Common finishes.

There is a **water point on the left**, which may be more convenient to use than the next water point at Jesus Green.

A road raised above the height of the river runs along to your left, with railings along its side. An eclectic mix of boats used to moor here, many with the appearance of being on the fringes of society. The City Council and Cam Conservators have cleared many of these, but a few cling on stubbornly.

Cambridge Museum of Technology

RIVER GREAT OUSE 199

The Riverside Bridge snaking its way to the Museum of Technology

A two-armed curving pedestrian bridge, slightly unimaginatively called **Riverside Bridge**, links to the Cambridge Museum of Technology. Next is the the concrete **Elizabeth Way Bridge** with traffic roaring across.

On the right is 'Eights Marina', a modern development of flats which is clustered around a small but mostly empty private marina.

More boats and college boathouses on the right herald the arrival of **Midsummer Common** on the left. Nestled among the boathouses are the headquarters of CUBC where their fleet of light green minibuses are kept.

Passing under the **Green Dragon wrought iron pedestrian bridge** leads to

Victoria Road Bridge looking upstream

the nearby **Green Dragon PH**. A popular pub, but sadly no moorings outside.

The eponymous **Fort St George Bridge** is a wrought iron pedestrian bridge connecting to the **Fort St George Pub**. There are **visitor moorings outside** the pub, and if one is available it is advisable to grab it. By now you are very close to the limit of regular navigation, and despite their proximity to a pub, these are probably more attractive than the nearby **Jesus Green moorings**.

The final bridge is the **Victoria Road Bridge**, a fine cast iron construction. On your left is **Jesus Green Lido**, with **services** in front of it. There are **48 hour visitor moorings**, though it appears some local residential boats moor there for longer periods. The area is also popular with fishermen. **Central Cambridge** is only a short walk away.

Walking

The Haling Way (still part of the Fens Rivers Way) continues on the east bank until the **Green Dragon footbridge** where it crosses to **Stourbridge Common**. At **Baits Bite Lock** the Fens Rivers Way continues on the east bank, briefly leaving the river at **Fen Ditton**. It is also

Fort St George visitor moorings

200 RIVER GREAT OUSE

University rowing and the 'Bumps'

The section of the river from the concrete A14 bridge, past Fen Ditton, under the 'Meccano' railway bridge, and almost to the Green Dragon pedestrian bridge is where racing takes place. The river is too narrow and winding to allow 'regatta style' side by side racing, so processional races are held, variously known as 'bumps' or 'head races' where a crew chases the crew in-front. During 'bumps' one boat physically hits (bumps) another, whereas during 'head races' crews compete against the clock.

'Bumps' are a spectacle well worth watching, but from the towpath, not your boat. If you try and travel this stretch of river on a race day, marshals will ask you to wait, before sending you on at the next opportunity. A notice on Baits Bite lock advises that it contravenes bye-laws to 'interfere with or obstruct' any event on the river.

Events largely take place in spring and autumn and fall outside the main leisure boating season. The Cambridge Rowing Association publish a full events calendar on their web site (www.crarowing.co.uk). University Lent Bumps are held in late February, University May Bumps in June, Town Bumps and the Cambridge Winter League on weekends in January, February and March.

Bumps Races started in 1827 as a result of a rivalry between rowing crews from Trinity and St John's colleges. In 1852 they were divided into divisions to accommodate an increasing number of colleges wanting to enter more than one boat. Names such as '1st & 3rd Trinity 2nd VIII' sound like an equation or chemical formula.

Each division of boats is started above Baits Bite Lock by a cannon. 18 boats set off with 90ft gaps between them (90ft is the length of 1½ VIIIs). The object is to touch ('bump') the boat in front. If contact is made the race is finished for both boats and they both pull to the side. The faster boat which has caught the boat in front assumes its position in the league table for the next race. In exceptional circumstances a chasing boat will row around the boat ahead without touching it, and chase down the next boat. This is called an 'over bump'. One of the rarest and greatest accolades in Cambridge rowing is a 'double over bump'. If two boats bump (so withdrawing from that race) in exceptional circumstances the boat following them catches and bumps the boat ahead of both of them.

Successful crews are often garlanded with branches and make on odd sight returning to their boat houses. The finishing order of each year's racing is the starting point for the next year. The ultimate goal is to reach the top of the table and achieve the much prized accolade of being 'Head of the River'.

Each Division starts in Ditch Reach, rounds First Post Corner into the Gut, around Grassy Corner into Plough Reach and finally around Ditton Corner, and down Long Reach to finish near the Green Dragon Bridge.

called **Harcamlow Way**. It is joined Stourbridge Common by the path from the west side of the river. It continues to the east (becoming south as the river bends) through **Midsummer Common**. A path continues as far as **Jesus Green** and the lock.

Local history

There used to be a number of **ferries** which plied their trade crossing the river. At the site of the former Pike & Eel there were two ferries, a large one which could accommodate a horse and cart, and a punt for foot passengers. Both were hauled across the river by chains. Travelling upstream from Bates Bite lock these represented the first of five ferries crossing the Cam.

In 1935 the Green Dragon Bridge was built and the Horse Grind and Pike & Eel ferries closed.

The **Two Tees Boatyard** specialised in building punts and working on wooden boats. There had been a boat building business here since the late Victorian period. In 1968 it was bought by Maurice Tyrell and Ernie Tile, who renamed it 'Two Tees' utilising the initial letters of their surnames. In 2023 the site was being redeveloped, and the two iconic riverside wooden boathouses are all that remain.

Stourbridge Fair was chartered by King John in 1211 and held on Stourbridge common. It was enormously popular, at one point the largest fair in Europe, with many merchants arriving by ship. Originally running for only two days, by 1589 the fair lasted from August 24 to September 29.

The fair fell into decline, and was last held in 1933. On this final occasion it was opened by the Mayor of Cambridge, Florence Ada Keynes, mother of John Maynard Keynes.

The fair was one of four important medieval fairs held in, or near, Cambridge, the others being Garlic Fair, Reach Fair, and Midsummer Fair.

The name of the pub and subsequently the bridge, **Fort St George**, refers to the first English fortress in India, founded in 1639 at the coastal city of Madras, the modern city of Chennai. The construction of the fort provided the impetus for further settlements and trading activity, in what was originally an uninhabited land and it is argued that the city grew up around the fort.

There was also a ferry at Fort St George until 1927 when the suspension bridge was built.

The existing iron bridge across the weir at **Jesus Lock** was built in 1829 to replace a wooden bridge.

Cambridge

The city of **Cambridge** takes its name from the bridge crossing the River Cam which is now called **Magdalene Bridge**. The present elegant cast-iron structure was erected in 1823, replacing a series of earlier wooden bridges generally called the Great Bridge. The earliest bridge was probably built by Offa in the 8th century.

In the 1970s there was a proposal to replace the historic iron bridge with a contemporary concrete structure. Fortunately this zealous excessive of misplaced modernism in one of the world's most traditional historic cities was defeated.

The author of what is probably the definitive history of navigation on the Great Ouse, Dorothy Summers, wrote in 1973
'…the watermen working on the Cam and Great Ouse traditionally were supposed to have a greater fund of bad language than those of any other river in England; or alternatively this was thrown into greater prominence by association with the rarified atmosphere of Cambridge. Navigation through Cambridge, where bridges and buildings constituted recurring obstacles, could hardly have been more effectively designed to elicit extremes of language. The towing horses had to be thrashed into the water near the 'Pike and Eel', and from this point on they waded through the river up to the public quay opposite Magdalen College…the rough appearance, conduct and language of the watermen, 'an unlettered, piratical crew …' came under perpetual fire from the University Authorities'.

Cambridge city centre supermarkets include Sainsbury's, Asda, Tesco Superstore (Newmarket Road), a small Waitrose, Co-op, and Budgens.

Less centrally located supermarkets include Waitrose (Trumpington Road), and two Tesco Superstores (Milton & Fulbourn).

Pubs close to the river serving food
The Fort St George, Midsummer Common, **The Pickerel Inn**, Magdalene St, **The Mill** and **The Anchor** (both at the Mill Pond), **The Maypole**, Portugal Place, **The Punter,** Pound Hill, **The Mitre**, Bridge Street, The Eagle, Bene't St, **The Bath House**, Bene't St.

Numerous other pubs and eateries are within a mile's walk of Jesus Green.

Markets
Cambridge General Market, Cambridge Market Square, Monday to Saturday all year
Sunday arts and crafts and local produce market, Cambridge Market Square, Sundays all year
All Saints Craft Fair, opposite Trinity College, Saturdays all year round, plus Fridays in June, July and August and Wednesday to Saturday in December.

Museums
The Fitzwilliam Museum, Trumpington St, **Scott Polar Research Institute**, Lensfield Rd, CB2 1ER
Museum of Archaeology and Anthropology, Downing St, CB2 3DZ

University Museum Of Zoology
Downing St, CB2 3EJ
Whipple Museum of the History of Science, Free School Lane, CB2 3RH
Museum of Cambridge, 2-3 Castle St,
Kettle's Yard art gallery and house
Castle St, CB3 0AQ
www.kettlesyard.co.uk

Culture and entertainment
Cambridge Arts Theatre, 6 St Edward's Passage, CB2 3PJ
Cambridge Corn Exchange (concert venue) 2 Wheeler St, CB2 3QB
Arts Picturehouse cinema, 38-39 St Andrew's St, CB2 3AR

Cambridge University Botanic Garden
1 Brookside, CB2 1JE
www.botanic.cam.ac.uk

Tourist Information Centre
The Guildhall, Peas Hill CB2 3AD
01223 791500

Public Transport
Main line railway stations - Cambridge and Cambridge North
Guided Bus to St Ives

Boat trips
Camboats run trips from Jesus Green to the Plough at Fen Ditton by narrowboat and solar catamaran.
www.camboats.co.uk

The world-renowned Fitzwilliam Museum

Peterhouse College

Map 30

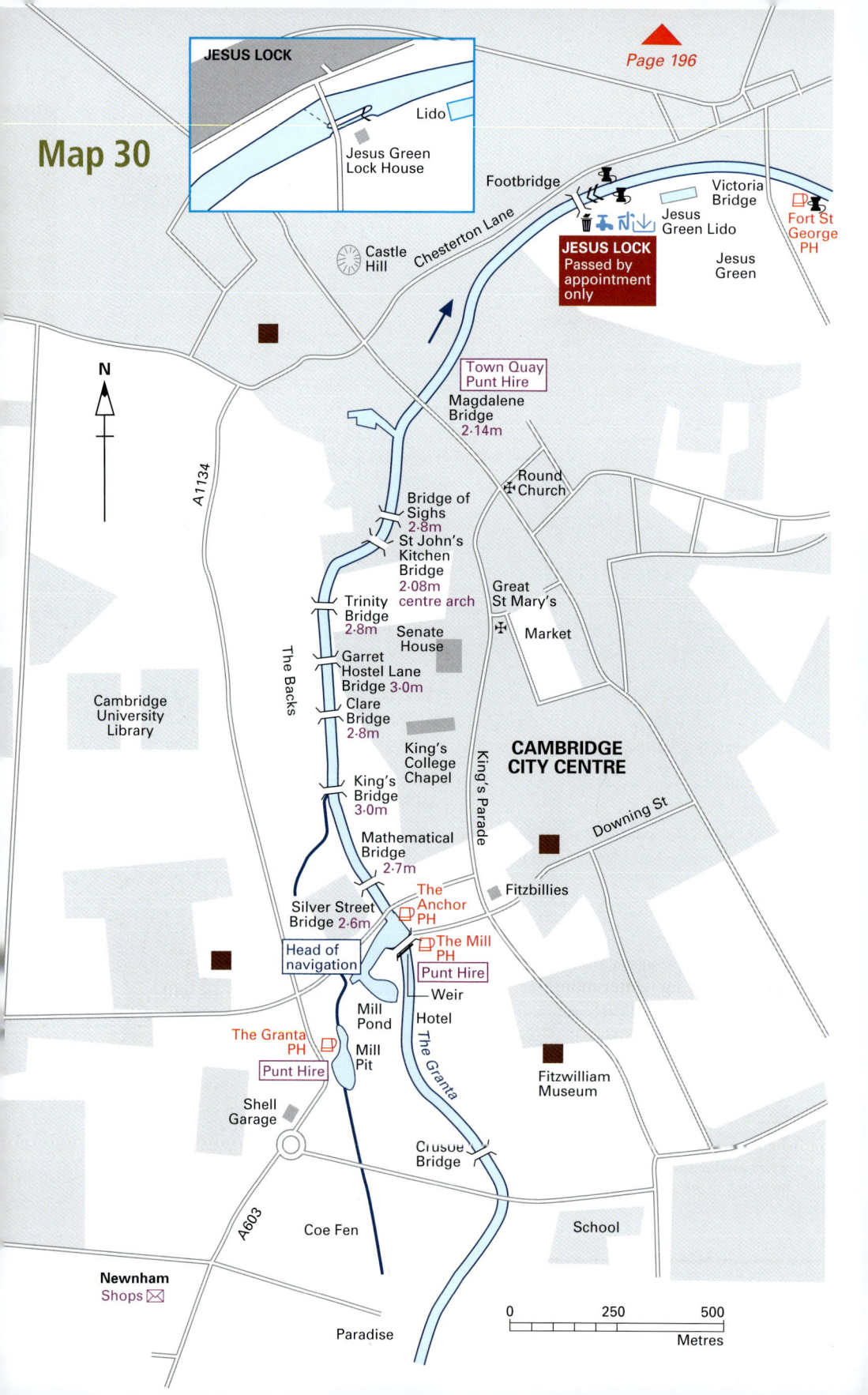

JESUS LOCK

Lido
Jesus Green Lock House

Footbridge
Victoria Bridge
Jesus Green Lido
Fort St George PH
Jesus Green

Castle Hill
Chesterton Lane

JESUS LOCK
Passed by appointment only

Town Quay Punt Hire
Magdalene Bridge 2·14m

Round Church

Bridge of Sighs 2·8m
St John's Kitchen Bridge 2·08m centre arch

Great St Mary's
Market

Trinity Bridge 2·8m
Senate House
Garret Hostel Lane Bridge 3·0m
Clare Bridge 2·8m

The Backs

Cambridge University Library

King's College Chapel

CAMBRIDGE CITY CENTRE

King's Bridge 3·0m
Mathematical Bridge 2·7m

King's Parade
Downing St

Fitzbillies

Silver Street Bridge 2·6m
The Anchor PH
The Mill PH
Punt Hire

Head of navigation
Weir
Hotel
Mill Pond

The Granta PH
Punt Hire
Mill Pit

The Granta

Fitzwilliam Museum

Shell Garage

Crusoe Bridge
School

A603

Coe Fen

Newnham Shops

Paradise

A1134

Page 196

N

0 250 500
Metres

Map 30

River Cam
Jesus Lock to Mill Pond
Return trip
(Cambridge Backs World Heritage Site)

Distance 1½ miles
Time 1 hour one way

Map 30 Jesus Lock Cambridge to Mill Pond (The Backs)

Lowest bridge
2·08m St John's Kitchen Bridge (at apex of middle arch)

Navigation Authority
Conservators of the River Cam

Jesus Lock
L 32m W 4·3m (14′) D 1·4m Head 4·0m

Access only allowed 1st October to 31st March
Permission from Cams Conservators required 48h in advance

No mooring
No stopping allowed

Turning
Mill Pool (not size restricted)

Navigating the Cambridge Backs downloadable guide from Conservators of the River Cam is essential reading for anyone considering making the trip.
www.camsconservancy.org

Navigation notes

Jesus Lock accesses **The Backs**. All powered boat traffic is completely forbidden between 1st April and 30th September. During winter months, permission for access must be obtained in advance. There are two considerations which the intrepid boater of Cambridge Backs ignores at their peril.

In high summer this part of the river becomes a confused mass of hundreds of punts, bobbing haphazardly across the river like a confused giant children's game of 'pick-up sticks'. The best way to enjoy the Backs in season is by punt. You can hire a punt and endeavour to propel it yourself. For those who have never tried before, punting is a unique skill in its own right, and your efforts will inevitably be a guaranteed source of hilarity to your passengers. The alternative is to hire a chauffeured punt and to lie back, relaxing as the breathtaking scenery glides past, while someone else, seemingly effortlessly, propels you along.

Jesus Lock

> **Moorings and facilities**
>
> **No mooring. No stopping allowed.**
>
> **Access only allowed between 1st October and 31st March. Permission required in advance.**
>
> **Turning** at the **Mill Pool** (not size restricted)

This is probably the most beautiful area of the River Cam, above Jesus Lock. It flows past some of Cambridge's finest buildings (including King's College Chapel) and provides those world famous views of Cambridge Backs.

Jesus Lock is one of those logic defying locks, with the only means of crossing from one side of the lock to the other via a swing bridge which spans the lock and has to be removed before you can fill the lock.

Above the lock, the short journey takes you under ten bridges. The height of the bridges requires careful attention. The third one you pass under, St John's Kitchen Bridge, is the lowest, with a published air clearance of six foot nine inches. However one is well advised to remember that:

- like any river, the water levels in the Cam rise after rain, and published clearances quickly reduce
- the published height is to the centre of the arch, and will be lower where the sides of your boat pass under
- the computation of air clearance assumes that your boat is passing under at right angles to the line of the bridge, and on a narrow and bendy river the effects of wind and other boaters can combine to make it harder to 'shoot the bridge' in a perpendicular line.

After the cast iron Victorian **Magdalene Bridge**, the next one is the Grade I Listed **Bridge of Sighs**. There are a number of similarly named bridges around the world, but the inspirational original was constructed in 1600 in Venice and given the nick-name (which stuck) by Lord Byron. Cambridge's was built in 1831, and bathed in strong, spring sunlight, is breathtaking.

The next bridge, **St John's Kitchen Bridge**, is a pleasant stone bridge. The Conservators *Guide to Navigating the Backs* here advises caution: 'This is the lowest and most challenging of all the bridges.

Magdalene Bridge

Headroom at the apex of the largest middle arch is 2·08m/6'9". The curvature of the arch constrains the width available. You must ensure that your vessel is aligned dead-centre before proceeding. On the return passage, the entrance to the bridge is blind.' Take especial care. **Trinity Bridge**, next, is another stone built bridge and is the second lowest bridge that you pass under. However, if you've just squeezed under St John's Kitchen Bridge, it shouldn't be a problem. After a nondescript modern pedestrian bridge (Garret Hostel Lane Bridge) you arrive at Cambridge's oldest, **Clare Bridge**. This is the only bridge to survive the English Civil War. Its considerable antiquity can be seen in its higgledy piggledy appearance. After **another stone bridge** (King's) you come to probably Cambridge's most famous, the **Mathematical Bridge**. There is a popular myth that this bridge was designed and built by Sir Isaac Newton without the use of nuts or bolts, and that in the past students dismantled it, but couldn't work out how to reassemble it

Bridge of Sighs

St John's Bridge Simon Judge

The famous Mathematical Bridge

RIVER GREAT OUSE 207

again without using bolts. In fact mechanical fixings were always part of the design, it's just that originally it employed spikes driven through the joints from outside (where they could not be seen from the inside of the parapets), whereas when it was rebuilt, big hand cut square bolts were used which are still highly visible. The bridge was originally constructed in 1749 to designs by a William Etheridge. Newton had already died in 1727 so his direct involvement in the bridge's construction appears unlikely.

The last bridge is **Silver Street**. It's a single span bridge, clad in Portland Stone, designed by Sr Edward Lutyens, and built in the late 1950s. In the middle it has a generous 2·6m (8'7") air draft, but immediately upstream (to the left as you are travelling) is **Mill Lane punting station** with rafts of moored punts. You have to turn 90 degrees right immediately as you emerge from under the bridge, a manoeuvre made harder by extremely slow speed and punts absolutely everywhere.

You will now have reached the **Head of Navigation**. There is a small weir, and the only boats that could access the river above the weir (here called the Granta, despite remaining the Cam) were either boats that could be lifted by hand, or punts which are dragged across rollers. You wind in the mill pond, known as the **Mill Pit**. The Conservator's navigation guide advises: 'allow the water coming over the weir to carry the bows around'.

Travelling up the Cam from Jesus Green Lock takes about an hour. It will take at least another hour to retrace your route back to Jesus Green Lock. It's quite likely that progress will be even slower on your return journey, as more punts take to the water. However, the slower you travel, the greater your opportunities to drink in the wonderful college views.

Walking

There is no footpath as most of the river bank is made up by private Cambridge Colleges.

Local history

There is no towpath along this section of the Cam. In the 18th and 19th centuries when deliveries were made to the Colleges it was by horse drawn barge. The Cam isn't deep, and old prints show the horses wading chest-deep through the water, pulling barges and lighters. To facilitate this a cobbled causeway was laid down the centre of the river.

Emerging from under Silver Street Bridge to enter the Mill Pool while avoiding a punt Simon Judge

19th-century print showing a horse using the cobbled causeway in the middle of the river to deliver to the colleges

Punting on the Cam

A punt is a flat-bottomed boat with a square-cut bow and stern, about 7·5m long and 1m wide, designed for use in small rivers and shallow water. The punter propels the punt by pushing against the river bed with a 4m long pole.

Pleasure punting developed on the River Thames in the 1860s and arrived in Cambridge in about 1902. The bows of a punt features a flat raised deck known as the 'trill' and the stern called the 'huff', which features cross planks (treads). The punter (propelling the boat) stands at one of the ends and pushes the boat away from him (or her). In Oxford the punter stands with a secure foot hold in the stern and proceeds bow first. However in Cambridge the punter stands on the flat raised bow or deck (with much less secure foot grip) and propels the boat stern first. This less stable Cambridge practice is said to have arisen in the Edwardian era when the lady undergraduates of Girton College felt it better showed off their ankles!

There are two kinds of punts in Cambridge, single width boats hired by the hour, generally to absolute novices, who laugh and splash and pose for selfies as they career haphazardly along the river, often crashing from side to side, sometimes assisted by the occasional alcoholic libation. There are also double width boats with 'professional' chauffeurs, propelling the boat, seemingly effortlessly, in a straight line (while dodging the beginners) straight up the middle of the river. These seasoned punters are following the hidden causeway along the centre of the river because it is far easier to propel their heavily laden boat by pushing off against solid cobbles than to allow the pole to sink into the clinging mud either side of this causeway.

The 'middle of the river' punt chauffeurs certainly aren't prepared to surrender the precious centre of the bridges to narrowboats, pinball punting novices, or even other chauffeur punts. On the Cam, everyone heads for the centre of the bridges, with little or no consideration for other boats eyeing up the same destination!

Nb Scholar Gypsy passing St John's College

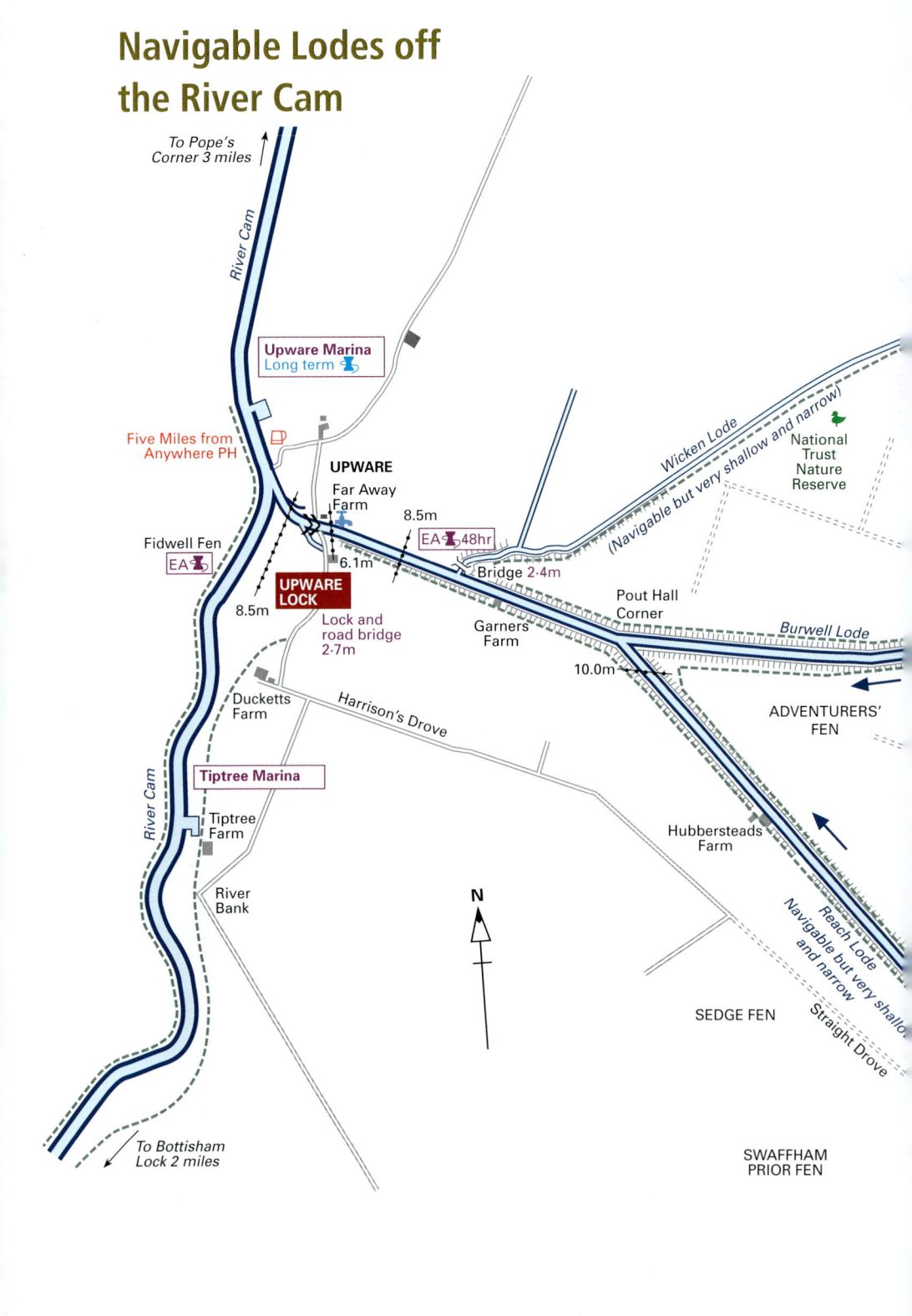

Navigable Lodes off the River Cam

To Pope's Corner 3 miles

River Cam

Upware Marina Long term

Five Miles from Anywhere PH

UPWARE

Far Away Farm

Fidwell Fen EA

8.5m

EA 8.5m

EA 48hr

6.1m

Bridge 2·4m

Wicken Lode
(Navigable but very shallow and narrow)

National Trust Nature Reserve

UPWARE LOCK

Lock and road bridge 2·7m

Garners Farm

Pout Hall Corner

Burwell Lode

Ducketts Farm

Harrison's Drove

10.0m

ADVENTURERS' FEN

Tiptree Marina

Tiptree Farm

River Bank

Hubbersteads Farm

Reach Lode
Navigable but very shallow and narrow

SEDGE FEN

Straight Drove

N

SWAFFHAM PRIOR FEN

To Bottisham Lock 2 miles

River Cam and Cambridgeshire Lodes

Wicken
Maids Head PH
A1123
WICKEN FEN Nature Reserve
National Trust Information Centre and cafe

New River
Monks Lode (Not navigable)
GOBA
Head of navigation

0 — 1 Mile
0 — 1 Kilometre (Approx)

Priory Farm
High Bridge Head 2.7m
Lifting bridge (generally left open)
6.1m
Burwell Lode
Lodeside Drove
Little Fen Drove
Old Fen Farm
Pits
Brick Works
10.0m
Turning point max 18m
BURWELL
6.1m
10.0m
EA
Shops
The Anchor
Anchor Lane Farm
Road Bridge 2.5m
BURWELL FEN
Newnham Drove
The Weirs
The Fox PH
B1103
Toft Farm
NEWNHAM
Hightown Drove
Caution: very shallow
Hurdle Hall
10.0m
REACH
Turning for boats up to 18m
The Dyke's End
GOBA

The Cambridgeshire Lodes
Navigable Lodes off the River Cam

Many of the Cambridgeshire Lodes were dug in Roman times for both drainage and trade. They were later used by monasteries and other religious orders. Their commercial use only declined after the railways took their trade away. Some of the Lodes, which weren't detailed in Section 1 of the 1977 Anglian Waterways Act, have been lost to powered navigation, but those that remain navigable and accessible offer a delightful alternative to the hustle and bustle of the modern world. They should be taken slowly and appreciated.

Approaching Upware Lock (sometimes called Upware boat lift) from the Lode

EA Upware visitor moorings near the junction with Wicken Lode

Reach Lode

Distance
Pout Hall Corner to Reach 2 miles
Time
½ to ¾ hour (depending on weed levels)
Turning at end
18m (60′) looks achievable

Navigation notes

Upware Lock at is a double guillotine lock. A road bridge crosses it, which makes it hard to operate the lock single handed. In summer months it appears that there is little difference in the relative heights of the water above and below the lock, but the presence of the neighbouring pumping station suggests this changes in winter. The lock often automatically resets itself. Red warning lights flash and a siren sounds, before the top gate closes, and the bottom opens. When the pumping station is active, the lock is disabled.

Immediately through the lock is a **water-point**. The speed limit here is 4mph, but as the next quarter of a mile is lined with boats on permanent moorings, you will travel slower. These moorings are followed by **EA 48 hour visitor moorings**, surely some of the most peaceful and picturesque moorings on these waters.

Immediately after the moorings, **Wicken Lode** joins under a 'cock-up' wooden pedestrian bridge. Reach Lode divides into two at **Pout Hall Corner**, shortly after its junction with Wicken Lode.

Moorings and facilities

Upware Lock
L 18.7m (61'4"), W 4.3m (14'1")
D 1.3m

Water and on Reach Lode **adjacent to the lock**.

EA 48 hour moorings before junction with Wicken Lode

GOBA 'Dyke's End' moorings at Reach

The Dyke's End PH, Fair Green, Reach
CB25 0JD
☎ 01638 743816

Straight on is **Burwell Lode**, and **Reach Lode** continues to the right.

From Pout Hall Junction, **Reach** is a further 2 miles in a straight lode. Reach Lode is extremely shallow and reeds brush the boat on most sides. Progress will be extremely slow, particularly for deep drafted boats. A solitary pedestrian and cycle bridge crosses Reach Lode and the sense of serene isolation is probably at its greatest anywhere on these waters.

At Reach the lode splits into two, providing plenty of room to turn. There are **GOBA moorings**, which are also available to non-GOBA members if they obtain prior permission from Reach Parish Council.

Walking

There is a footpath on the south west bank of Reach Lode the whole way from **Upware Lock to Reach**.

There is another footpath on the opposite, north east path, this finishes at the junction with **Burwell Lode**, as there isn't a footbridge here, you will need to head off east to **Burwell** before you can cross.

Local history

For what at first sight may appear a sleepy but attractive Cambridge commuter village, **Reach** has a truly remarkable history. It is the termination of the Anglo-Saxon defensive rampart and the ditch called the **Devil's Dyke** which ran for 7 miles to Woodditton in Suffolk. En-route the dyke skirts the edge of the July Course at **Newmarket Racecourse**.

Solitary bridge across Reach Lode

EA moorings at the junction with Wicken Lode

RIVER GREAT OUSE

Reach has been a trading port since Roman times. A fair has been held there since 1201, when it developed as a significant port. In Medieval times, while Cambridge was still a village, Reach was a city and boasted nine churches.

Sea going ships docked here until the construction of Denver Sluice in 1651, but the port continued to trade in agricultural produce, timber, peat, and clunch (a chalky building material). Trade spluttered to a halt after the advent of the railways.

The village surrounds a large village green which is the site of Reach annual fair, chartered by King John, now held on the early May bank holiday. It is opened by the mayor of Cambridge accompanied by the aldermen in full regalia and penny coins are thrown to visitors in the crowd **Upware Lock** (also known as Upware Boat Lift) was often left open, allowing gangs of eight 'turf float' boats to take it on the level. Turf was burnt on household fires. It was harvested and sold by the 'thousand' though there were only 600 turf in a 'thousand'. The domestic user bought in 'hands' of 60, or 'half hands' of 30.

Wicken Lode

Distance
Wicken Lode Junction Bridge to GOBA moorings (head of navigation): 1½ miles
Time
½ hour
Accessed from Reach Lode
Turning at end
18m (60′) comfortably if no other boats moored in the way

Navigation notes

Wicken Lode is off **Reach Lode**, just after the **EA 48hour moorings**. It is on the left, under a picturesque wooden pedestrian bridge. This leads about a mile to **Wicken Fen**, a nature reserve owned by the National Trust. The lode is narrow and winding, and can become heavily weeded.

There are good **GOBA moorings** at the junction with **Monk's Lode** and ample room to turn. This is a place to enjoy the sound of birdsong from the idyllic moorings at the end.

Walking

There is a footpath on the south side of Wicken Lode from the pedestrian bridge at the junction with Reach Lode. This

Reach turning point

Wicken Lode Bridge

Moorings

Wicken Fen 48h GOBA moorings at junction with Monk's Lode

The Maid's Head PH
12 High St, Wicken
CB7 5XR
☏ 01353 720727

Wicken Fen National Nature Reserve
with visitor centre and café
www.nationaltrust.org.uk/wicken-fen-nature-reserve

---

footpath crosses Monk's Lode and continues to **Wicken Fen visitor's centre** and on to the village of **Wicken**.

The Ordnance Survey map shows another footpath on the north side of Wicken Lode from the visitor centre to the junction of Wicken Lode and Monk's Lode but it appears to be part of the nature reserve.

Local history

Wicken Lode runs through **Wicken Sedge Fen** for nearly 1½ miles to the village of Wicken. The right of public navigation extends to its junction with Monk's Lode, but the stretch beyond that to Wicken is only navigable by local inhabitants. For much of the 19th century it was used to move peat from Burwell Fen and distributed to local farms. The trade only stopped in the 1940s with restrictions in peat cutting. Sedge continued to be transported from the fen for use in thatching.

In the early 1930s Norman's Mill drainage windmill was brought from nearby Adventurers Fen to Wicken Sedge Fen and is now the only surviving complete drainage windmill. There were once 750 windmills on the three Bedford Levels, of which 250 were on the Middle Level.

At the end of the nineteenth century Wicken Sedge Fen was given to the National Trust by Lord Rothschild, making it one of the oldest nature reserves in England and the first to be owned by the trust. The trust now manages 730 acres of wetland here. Technically it is not a true fen as it is higher than the surrounding land, but the wetland has been maintained by the drainage windmill. In effect this pumps water in, not out.

In 1936 Iris Wedgwood wrote in her book *Fenland Rivers*:

'Wicken Fen is a piece of land preserved in its virgin state, a piece of the past that is being saved for the present. As you enter it you see the fens as the Romans saw them, as the Normans saw them, as the impregnable morass they were. But also you see them as a wild and lovely place where beasts and birds of the marshes, insects and water flowers scramble for life in a merry confusion.'

Wicken moorings

Burwell Lode

Distance
Pout Hall Corner to Burwell 2½ miles
Time ¾ to 1 hour
Accessed from Reach Lode
Turning at end
18m (60') looks comfortable

Navigation notes

Reach Lode divides into two at **Pout Hall Corner**, shortly after its junction with **Wicken Lode**. From Pout Hall Junction, **Burwell** is a further 2½ miles on. The lode is almost dead straight, only turning once, after a **footbridge** with ample clearance, followed almost immediately by a **lift bridge** kept in an up position. At Burwell there are **EA moorings** and room to turn.

Walking

Burwell Lode has footpaths on both banks. The footpath on the north side of the lode leads from **Reach Lode Lock** to **Burwell**. Just as it appears to arrive in Burwell it is forced by private back gardens to deviate 0·5 mile to the north, before returning to Burwell on the road.

Burwell Lode

Moorings and facilities

EA moorings on south bank at end of navigation

The footpath on the south side of the lode runs between **Burwell** and the junction of **Burwell Lode** and **Reach Lode**. As there is no footbridge at this junction, you will need to either return to Burwell, or travel one mile in the opposite direction down Reach Lode before you can cross and continue to **Upware**.

Local history

Burwell means 'spring near the Fort', which suggests there may have been a Roman Fort here. The remains of an unfinished 12th-century castle remain. Burwell Lode was cut in the mid 17th century, probably on the route of a Roman canal.

At the head of the lode the **'Anchor Straights'** was to the south, and the **'Weirs'** to the north. Ships anchored at Anchor Straights whereas the Weirs were for lighters.

Burwell Lode EA moorings

Shops in Burwell include a butchers, a Co-op, a Londis, an optician, a chemist, a print shop and a phone shop.

The are several eateries in **Burwell** offering **takeaway food** including a chip shop, a coffee shop and a burger van.

The Anchor PH, 63 North St, Burwell
CB25 0BA
Pub serving food just round the corner from the EA moorings.
☎ 01638 743970

The Fox, 2 North St, Burwell CB25 0BA
Serves food.
☎ 01638741267

The Five Bells, 44 High St, Burwell CB25 0HD
Serves food.
☎ 01638 741404

The Bengal Fox Indian restaurant, 2 North St, Burwell, Cambridge CB25 0BA
☎ 01638 605559

Places to visit
Burwell Museum and Windmill
www.burwellmuseum.org.uk

In the 1870s there was a boom in digging coprolite (fossilised faeces) for fertiliser and a fertiliser factory with its own barge yard was built. The last barge was built in 1914, but barges were still repaired until 1938. Three steam tugs and a fleet of lighters moved goods, and it is reported that in 1898 a total of 8,600 tons of fertiliser and clunch were transported. Commercial traffic stopped in 1963.

The *Ipswich Journal* of 26 February 1774 reported that 'an old man who died recently near Newmarket, just before his death, confessed that he set fire to a barn at Burwell, Cambridgeshire on the 8th of September 1727 when no less than 80 persons lost their lives and that having an antipathy to the puppet showman was the cause of him committing the action'. This relates to a tragic incident when a visiting puppet show staged a performance in a wooden barn, nailing the doors shut to prevent any one sneaking in unpaid. Someone, unable to get in, knelt down and tried to spy through a hole, and his candle caught the barn alight.

The village church, **St Mary the Virgin,** is in a Perpendicular Gothic style and is Grade I Listed. **Burwell Museum** depicts life through the centuries on the edge of the Cambridgeshire fens. It includes **Stevens Mill,** a Grade II Listed windmill.

St Mary the Virgin, Burwell

The 'lost' lodes off the River Cam and River Great Ouse (no longer or only partially navigable)

Bottisham Lode

See Map 27 p.186
Distance ½ mile

Bottisham Lode flows into the River Cam just downstream of **Bottisham Lock**. The lode drains the higher ground to the south-east of the River Cam including **Lode** village and the grounds of **Anglesey Abbey**. At times of high water levels in the River Cam one pair of timber pointing gates close off the lode and drainage water is pumped into the river by the pumping station. It is believed that the lode may be Roman in origin.

Above and below: Bottisham Lode

Anglesey Abbey house and gardens and Lode Mill
www.nationaltrust.org.uk/anglesey-abbey-gardens-and-lode-mill

The potential navigable length of Bottisham Lode to small powered craft is about 600m, but the narrowness of the watercourse and absence of turning places is a constraint for all but the smallest boats. The gates are generally closed and a sign advises 'No unauthorised vessels'.

For self powered portable boats navigation as far as the village of **Lode** (and Anglesey Abbey) may be possible.

Walking

From the **pumping station** at the junction with the River Cam, there are footpaths along both banks of the lode. After half a mile these finish, but on the north east side **Lug Fen Drove** shadows the lode all the way to **Lode**.

Local history

Navigation on **Bottisham Lode** ceased around 1900. The lode was never wide enough to take fen lighters, but smaller boats used it for most of the 19th century.

The **mill at Lode** has been restored to working order by the National Trust.

Swaffham Bulbeck Lode

See Map 27 p.186

Distance ¾ mile

The lode flows northwest from **Swaffham Bulbeck** village to the **River Cam**, joining it about 1½ miles below Bottisham Lock. Entrance to the lode from the Cam was gained through **Swaffham Lock**, which consisted of a masonry chamber with two sets of timber pointing gates and an electrically-operated steel vertical lift gate. Prior to 2001 the guillotine gate was modified to stop it opening far enough to let boats through and the wooden 'V' gates removed. This has effectively closed the lode to navigation.

Had the EA not closed the lock, Swaffham Bulbeck Lode would still be navigable for small boats for its entire length to Swaffham Bulbeck.

Walking

There is a footpath along the south west bank of Swaffham Bulbeck Lode from the Cam all the way to **Swaffham Bulbeck**. On the north east bank there is a bridleway from the Cam to Cow Bridge shortly before Swaffham Bulbeck.

Local history

The wharf which served Swaffham Bulbeck Lode was at Commercial End. The mid-17th century **Merchants' House** and warehouse saw corn shipped to Newcastle and coal shipped back, as well as wine from Portugal.

Commercial End consists of a row of fine buildings, mainly dating from the late 17th and 18th century. The Commissioners of the Bedford Level were responsible for the Lode during this period, and they cleared the channel and straightened the banks on several occasions in response to complaints,

Like many of the other lodes it declined under competition from the railways.

The former Swaffham Lock, with missing gates

Soham Lode
Off the River Great Ouse

See Map 15 p.114
Distance 1 mile navigable by powered boat
Time Variable
(½ hour to 1½ hours one way)
No turning point

Unlike the other Cambridgeshire Lodes which are tributaries of the River Cam, **Soham Lode** flows into the River Great Ouse between Pope's Corner and Ely. It has a catchment area of about 11½ square miles - extending northwards as the River Snail from Snailwell (2½ miles north of Newmarket) to Fordham and Soham - it joins the River Great Ouse at **Soham Lode Land Drainage Pumping Station**. Access to the lode from the river is through a navigable sluice 4·6 m wide fitted with one set of steel pointing gates. The gates accumulate weed both above and below, and this gets worse as the summer progresses. These doors close automatically against high water levels in the river.

The navigable length of Soham Lode for most powered boats is at present 1 mile, up to the picturesque **Barway Bridge**, but the channel is very narrow and there is no winding point, so, unless good at steering in reverse, boats wishing to navigate the lode are advised to do so in pairs in a push-me-pull-you formation, stern to stern. There is potential for self powered portable boats to navigate further upstream, at least as far as **Soham**.

Walking

There is a footpath on the east side of the lode from its confluence with the river Great Ouse to **Barway Bridge**. This footpath continues all the way to **Soham**, until **Angle Common** where the railway finally crosses the lode. From Barway a footpath joins the other side (now north) and also continues until Angle Common.

Gates and pumping station where Soham Lode joins the River Great Ouse

Two boats travelling 'push-me, pull-you' on Soham Lode

Barway Bridge

Local history

Soham Lode was formed by diverting the **River Snail** at **Fordham** from its original course to the **River Lark** at **Prickwillow**. Differing sources give the date it was constructed as 1630 or 1790. **Soham** is midway down the Lode and was, until its draining in the late 18th century, close to **Soham Mere**.

It doesn't appear that the lode was ever navigable beyond Soham. **Lion Mills** at the effective head of Soham Lode was built in 1811. The arrival of the railway in 1879 led to a fall off in water traffic, and it had ceased by 1900. It was not listed as a navigation in the 1977 Anglian Water Authority Act, and the current authority, the Environment Agency do not consider there is a right of navigation.

The Soham rail disaster happened in 1944, when the driver of a train pulling 51 wagons of ammunition noticed that the first of the wagons was on fire. With the help of his fireman he uncoupled it and tried to pull it away into open country. When it was a few hundred yards away from the other carriages it exploded, injuring the driver and killing both the fireman and a signal man. The station was destroyed, 750 houses in the village damaged, and the explosion was heard 20 miles away. Both the driver and the fireman were awarded the George Cross for preventing the almost unimaginably greater damage which would have occurred if the rest of the train had exploded. The driver Benjamin Gimbert was very severely injured and fireman James Nightall was killed. In 2007 the Duke of Gloucester unveiled a permanent memorial in Soham Church and James Nightall is commemorated with a plaque outside the library in his home village of Littleport.

The railway station had opened in 1879. It was temporarily rebuilt following the 1944 rail disaster. Although the line remained open, the station was closed in 1965 and pulled down. A new station was opened in December 2021 at a cost of £18.6 million. It would be a real bonus if navigation to Soham could similarly be restored.

Around 1966 the bed of the channel of the Lode was lined with butyl rubber weighted down with gravel to prevent leakage into low lying farmland.

'Drunken' poles demonstrate the continous movement of the Fens

The quiet beauty of the River Lark

8

RIVER LARK

Described travelling **upstream**

The River Lark rises south of Bury St Edmunds and is about 23½ miles long. It flows north west and is joined by the River Linnet near Mildenhall, and the River Kennet east of Isleham. It enters the Fens north of Ely, and joins the Great Ouse Ouse near Prickwillow.

The river has a long history as a navigable waterway, with an Act of Parliament for the improvement of its navigation being passed in 1700. Until 1894 it was navigable to Bury St Edmunds.

At times of heavy rainfall excess water from the Lark is diverted into the head of the Cut Off Channel which it crosses south of Mildenhall at Barton Mills.

The River Lark is currently navigable for 10½ miles from the Ely Ouse to the current head of navigation at Jude's Ferry Bridge, West Row, near Isleham.

There is potential for extending navigation for powered craft from the present Head of Navigation as far upstream as the town of Mildenhall, 2½ miles further upstream. To enable this, however, a new lock and overflow weir would be needed in the vicinity of the existing King's Staunch and the Staunch demolished or modified to act as the weir. There is potential for self powered portable boats to navigate considerably further upstream.

In windy conditions care needs to be taken when leaving the River Lark and rejoining the Great Ouse. The Queen Adelaide straight (Sandy's Cut, see p.118) can sometimes be quite rough.

Map 31

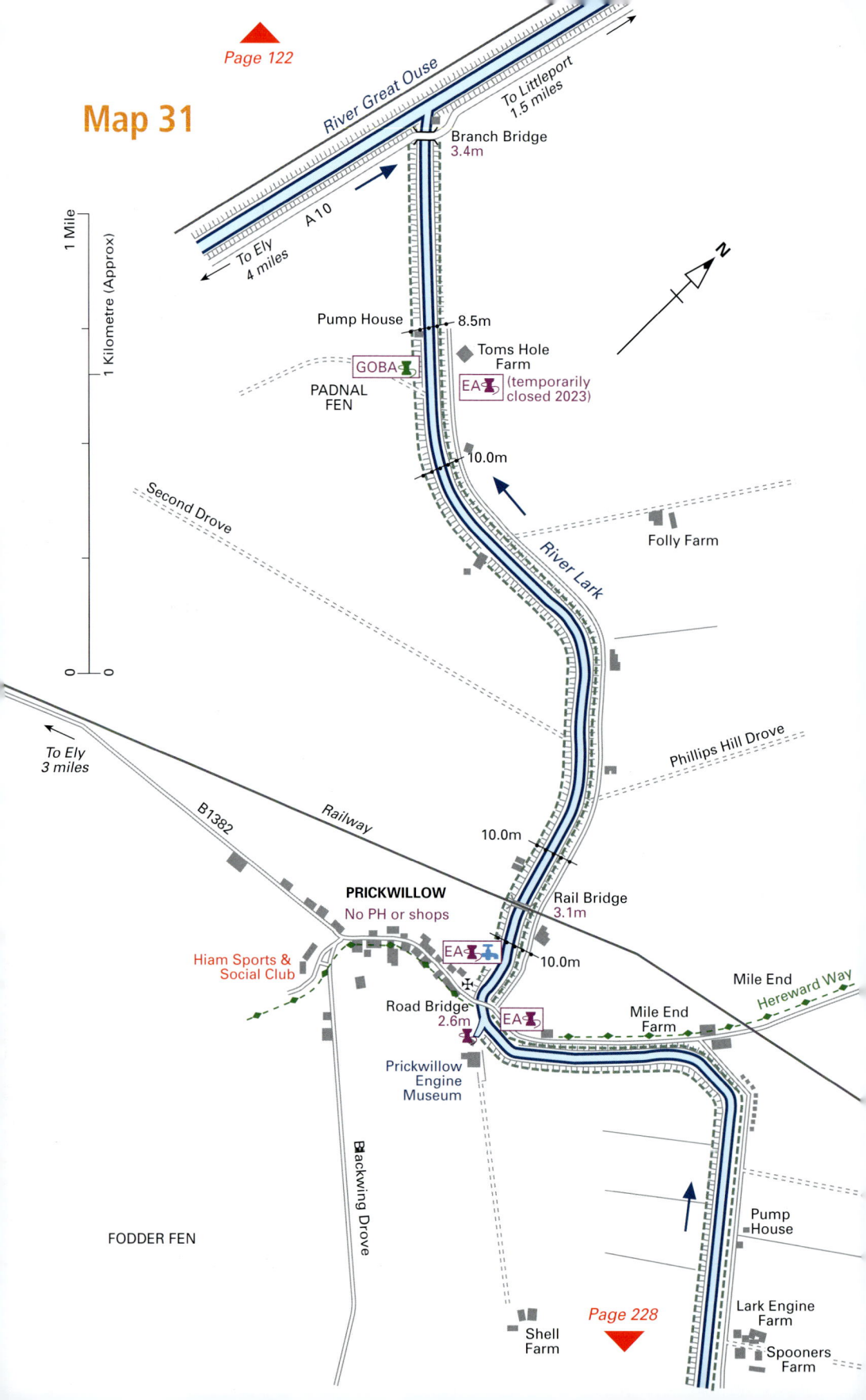

Page 122

River Great Ouse

To Littleport 1.5 miles

Branch Bridge 3.4m

A10

To Ely 4 miles

1 Mile / 1 Kilometre (Approx)

Pump House — 8.5m

GOBA

PADNAL FEN

Toms Hole Farm

EA (temporarily closed 2023)

10.0m

Second Drove

River Lark

Folly Farm

To Ely 3 miles

B1382

Railway

Phillips Hill Drove

10.0m

PRICKWILLOW
No PH or shops

Rail Bridge 3.1m

Hiam Sports & Social Club

EA

10.0m

Road Bridge 2.6m

EA

Mile End Farm

Mile End

Hereward Way

Prickwillow Engine Museum

Backwing Drove

FODDER FEN

Pump House

Shell Farm

Page 228

Lark Engine Farm

Spooners Farm

Maps 31/32/33

The River Lark

Distance 10 miles
Time 3 hours

Maps 31/32/33 River Lark Branch Bridge to Isleham

Lowest bridge 2·6m Prickwillow Road Bridge
Isleham Lock L 26·8m, W 4·55m (14'9"), D 1m
Turning at Head of Navigation max 20m (70') just below Jude's Ferry PH

Location	Lock	Moorings and facilities								Victualling		
		Short stay	48hr	Long stay	Water point	CDP	Pumpout	Refuse	Diesel	Shops	Pub	Café/restaurant
Map Lark 1												
Padnal Fen GOBA			🪝									
Tom's Hole 48h EA			🪝	Temporarily closed (2023)								
Prickwillow Bridge EA			🪝		🚰							
Prickwillow Mile End EA moorings			🪝									
Map Lark 2												
Fenland Boats moorings				🪝	Facilities for customers only							
Isleham Lock	🔒											
Riverside Island Marina				🪝	Facilities for customers only							
Map Lark 3												
Jude's Ferry PH		🪝									🍺	✕

RIVER GREAT OUSE   225

Map 31
Branch Bridge to Prickwillow

Distance 2 miles
Time ¾ hour

Navigation notes

You enter the **River Lark** under **Branch Bridge**. '**Toms Hole Farm moorings**' are short **EA moorings** on your left just over half a mile upstream from the Lark's junction with the Great Ouse. These were temporarily closed in 2023. Almost opposite on your right, are the **GOBA** '**Padnal Fen**' **moorings**. Both are popular, probably because there is less passing traffic creating a wash, than on the main river.

Although the section of the river does turn a few corners, the raised banks appear a constant, man made, distance apart. However as you pass under the **railway bridge** ¼ mile below Prickwillow, the character changes and suddenly it feels like river, not a channel.

Prickwillow boasts two **EA moorings**, both refurbished in 2020. To your right, immediately **before the B1382 road bridge, are extensive moorings which include a water point**. Under the bridge, to your left, are the **EA's 'Mile End Moorings'**. An improvised mooring of about 60ft is often made against the grass bank in front of Prickwillow Drainage Engine Museum - see photo opposite. The B1382 is not a busy road and all the Prickwillow moorings are normally fairly peaceful, although farm traffic can rumble through the night during harvest.

Prickwillow is popular with open water swimmers and kids jumping off the road bridge, so you are advised to keep a wary eye open both ahead of you and above!

The bridge at Prickwillow is the last bridge you will pass under before you reach the Head of Navigation at Jude's Ferry and there are no further visitor moorings upstream of the 'Mile End' moorings at Prickwillow.

What you may miss in bridges is made up for in pumping stations. I can't think of any other river described in these pages which more completely illustrates and educates on the evolution of pumping and drainage on the Fenland landscape. Along the entire length of the navigable river you will pass at least six current or disused former pumping stations.

Toms Hole moorings

Moorings and facilities

GOBA Padnal Fen moorings on right bank ½ mile above the Great Ouse junction.

EA 'Toms Hole Farm' moorings on **your left hand side**, shortly after GOBA moorings opposite (temporarily closed 2023).

EA moorings Prickwillow, right bank before B1382 road bridge, recently refurbished.
There is a **waterpoint** here.

EA 'Mile End Farm' moorings, left bank after road bridge, recently refurbished.

Walking

There are footpaths on both floodbanks between **Branch Bridge** and **Prickwillow**. The **Hereward Way** long distance footpath crosses the Lark at Prickwillow on the B1382.

Local history

It is said that no part of the course of the Ely Ouse is natural, but that over time every section has been recut or otherwise moved. This is best demonstrated by the **Queen Adelaide to Littleport** section of the Great Ouse which was cut in 1829-30, to assist flow. The river originally flowed through **Prickwillow**, where it met the **River Lark**, before it was moved west to its current course. The initial 1¾ miles of the Lark from Branch Bridge is the original course of the Great Ouse before the Queen Adelaide straight, originally know as 'Sandy's Cut', was dug.

Prickwillow Drainage Engine Museum.
Check opening times.
www.prickwillowmuseum.com
① 01353 688360

Prickwillow Drainage Engine Museum

Improvements to navigation on the River Lark were made in 1638 and early in the 18th century, when locks and staunches were constructed. Navigation was officially abandoned in 1888, but commercial use of the river continued until 1928. It came under the jurisdiction of the Great Ouse Catchment Board who rebuilt the locks at Barton Mills and Icklingham in the 1960s. Head of Navigation is now **Jude's Ferry**.

A **pumping station** was opened at Prickwillow in 1831, enlarged in 1880, and diesel replaced steam in 1923. In in 1958 it was replaced by a new electric pumping station.

The pumping station now houses **Prickwillow Drainage Engine Museum**, with a fascinating collection of diesel pumps and interesting information on many aspects of Fenland drainage. Check their website (above) for details of their 'steam days'.

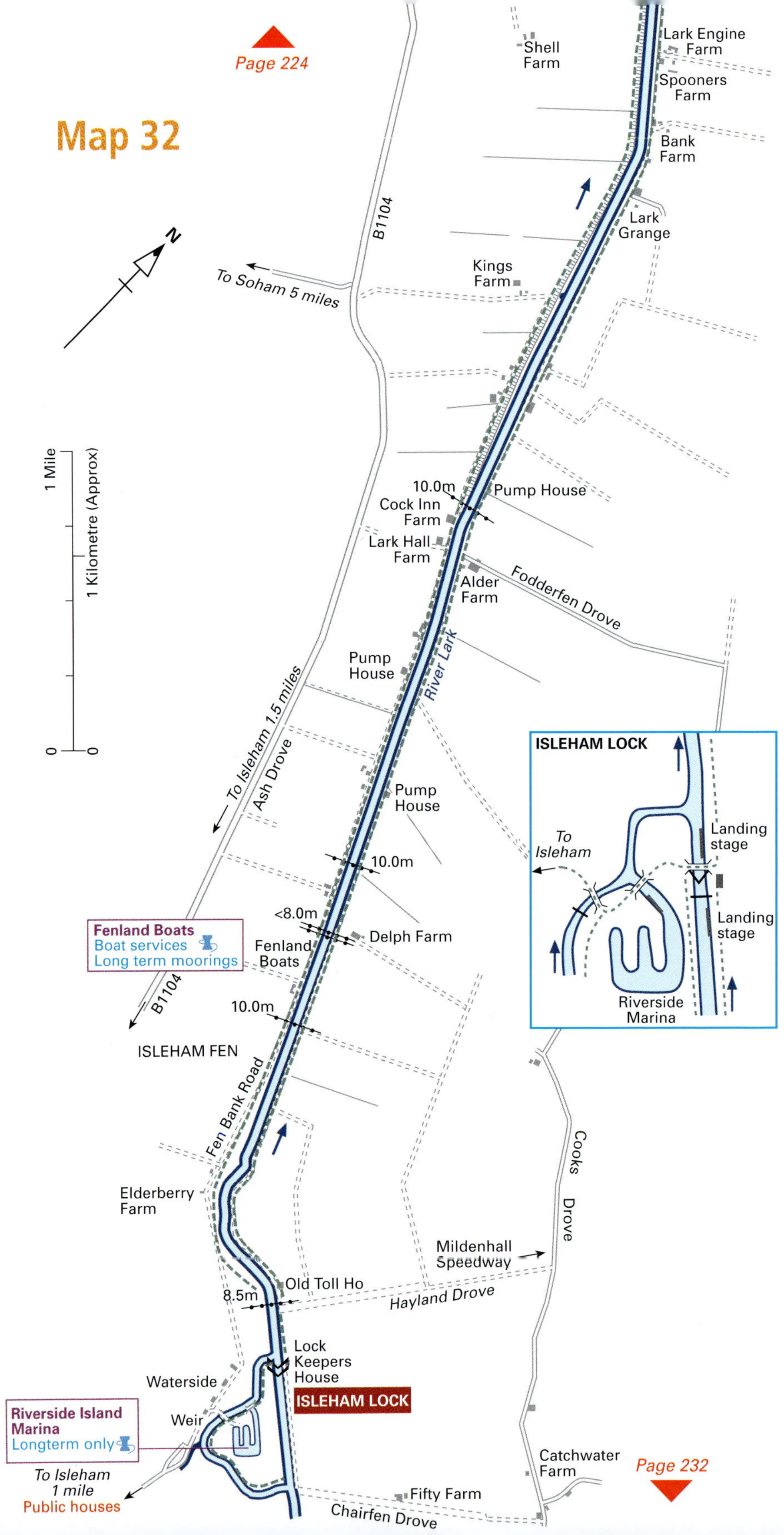

Page 224
Map 32
N
1 Mile
1 Kilometre (Approx)
0
0
Shell Farm
Lark Engine Farm
Spooners Farm
Bank Farm
Lark Grange
B1104
Kings Farm
To Soham 5 miles
10.0m
Pump House
Cock Inn Farm
Lark Hall Farm
Alder Farm
Fodderfen Drove
River Lark
Pump House
To Isleham 1.5 miles
Ash Drove
Pump House
10.0m
<8.0m
Delph Farm
Fenland Boats
Fenland Boats
Boat services
Long term moorings
B1104
10.0m
ISLEHAM FEN
Fen Bank Road
ISLEHAM LOCK
To Isleham
Landing stage
Landing stage
Riverside Marina
Cooks Drove
Elderberry Farm
Mildenhall Speedway
Old Toll Ho
8.5m
Hayland Drove
Lock Keepers House
Waterside
ISLEHAM LOCK
Weir
Riverside Island Marina
Longterm only
To Isleham 1 mile
Public houses
Catchwater Farm
Page 232
Fifty Farm
Chairfen Drove

Map 32

Lark Engine Farm to Isleham Lock

Distance 5¾ miles
Time 1½ hours

River Lark

Navigation notes

Leaving **Prickwillow,** reeds crowd the river and the flood banks are high and close. The river turns sharply to the the right (south) and the roofs of a row of cottages at **Lark Bank** peep over the top.

The river runs so straight that one can only conclude that its course was determined here by man, rather than nature.

Lark River Pumping Station with its two great tubular outlets sits on the bank to your left, and shortly after is **Lark Engine Farm House**.

The tranquility continues for around 2½ miles, with only the odd telegraph pole, leaning at a tipsy angle, to remind us of the outside world.

The next mile illustrates the changing nature of Fenland Pumping technology. First, on your left, you pass **Fodderfen Pumping Station**. This glorious, early Victorian building carries a date of 1844 on its gable end, and once housed a steam engine driving a scoop wheel (similar to the one surviving at Stretham).

Next, on your right, you pass the squat 20th century **Alder Fen pumping station**.

This was constructed in the late 1930s for a diesel pump, which has subsequently been replaced with electric pumps. The real rarity is next, on our left, a squat hexagonal building, affectionately know as the 'Pepperpot' is the bottom half of a wind pump, dating back to the late 18th century. Most of these were constructed from wood and no longer survive.

Fodderfen Pump

The 'Pepperpot'

RIVER GREAT OUSE

Together, these three encompass a large part of the history of pumped Fenland drainage.

The bank to your right will now be lined with moored boats for half a mile or so at **Fenland Boats, Isleham**. Beyond these moorings, the flood bank moves away and a rich area of natural habitat is created, with two lakes. The Ordnance Survey call this 'The Wash'. A telephone line crosses the second lake with a forlorn single pole in the middle of the lake. At first sight this can create the

A forlorn pole in the middle of 'The Wash'

Isleham Lock

> ### Moorings and facilities
> **Fenland Boats**, Isleham Fen
> Long term moorings and boat services.
> ☏ 07939 003681
>
> **Riverside Island Marina**, Isleham CB7 5SL
> Long term residential moorings.
> ☏ 01638 780663

illusion of the mast of a sunken sailing boat. The winding section of the river past 'The Wash' is the first time the river's course feels natural.

For much of this remote part of the river, you may be escorted by a patrol of herons. Each will accompany you to the edge of their territory, before another takes over, and so on, up the river.

Approaching **Isleham Lock**, the **Old Toll House**, recently restored and tiled with wooden 'shakes' (or shingles) stands guard over the river. **Isleham Lock** is entirely electrically operated with bottom timber gates and top guillotine gate. In normal conditions it only lifts you about 18 inches. **Riverside Island Marina** (residential) is accessed by a cut on the right below the lock. It is only as you leave the lock that you can look across a line of moored boats to the marina. There is another cut on the right, with moored boats. This stream leads to the weir.

Isleham is a small town which boasts a Co-op supermarket, two churches and three pubs. Although only one mile away from the lock, there aren't any convenient visitor moorings where you can leave your boat while you visit it.

Walking

There are footpaths on both floodbanks all the way to **Isleham Lock**.

Local history

North East of Lark Bank, where the river turns 90 degrees to the south, is **Burnt Fen** which acquired its name after Hereward the Wake set it on fire as a defensive measure against the Normans.

Isleham Lock, was constructed during the 1638 river improvements when the river above it was straightened. This created a water meadow island which was converted into Isleham Marina in 1988. Nineteenth century peat diggers used to take peat to Cambridge by lighter. Robert Simper relates:

> 'one man had his own barge and pulled it by hand the 30 miles to Cambridge. He managed to do this twice a week, including at one point, unloading the barge, hauling it across a road, a reloading it again.'

The region between Devil's Dyke and the railway line between Littleport and Shippea Hill has, over many years, produced a remarkable amount of archaeological finds of the Stone Age, the Bronze Age and the Iron Age. Finds in Isleham include the famous **Isleham Hoard** of more than 6,500 pieces of bronze, both manufactured articles and fragments of sheet bronze, all dating from the late Bronze Age, and discovered in 1959 by Bill Houghton and his brother, Arthur.

Beside the River Lark, near Isleham, is a memorial to the famous Baptist evangelist **Reverend Charles Haddon Spurgeon**, 'boy preacher of the Fens'. For many years total immersion baptisms took place in the river near the site of the Isleham Ferry, whilst the Minister preached from a barge in the river. Despite his later fame, Spurgeon occasionally returned to Isleham to preach. The memorial tablet records:

> The Rev Charles Haddon Spurgeon The Prince of Preachers was baptised here on May 3 1850.

Baptisms ceased in the 1970s due to the stagnant nature of the water and the consequent smell of those who had been baptised!

Isleham Lock moorings

Map 33

Page 228

- Elderberry Farm
- Old Toll Ho
- 8.5m
- Hayland Drove
- Mildenhall Speedway
- Cooks Drove
- **ISLEHAM LOCK**
- Lock Keepers House
- Waterside
- Weir
- Catchwater Farm
- Riverside Island Marina — Longterm only
- Fifty Farm
- Chairfen Drove
- Isleham
- Ferry Drove
- C.H. Spurgeon Memorial
- EAST FEN
- River Lark
- Lee Brook
- Gravel Banks
- Gravel Drove
- Manor Farm
- WEST ROW
- Shops
- Current Head of Navigation Turning for boats up to 20m
- Judes Ferry PH House Inn
- 10.0m
- Bargate Farm
- Danger Shoal, rocky bottom
- Judes Ferry Bridge
- Hm 3.2m

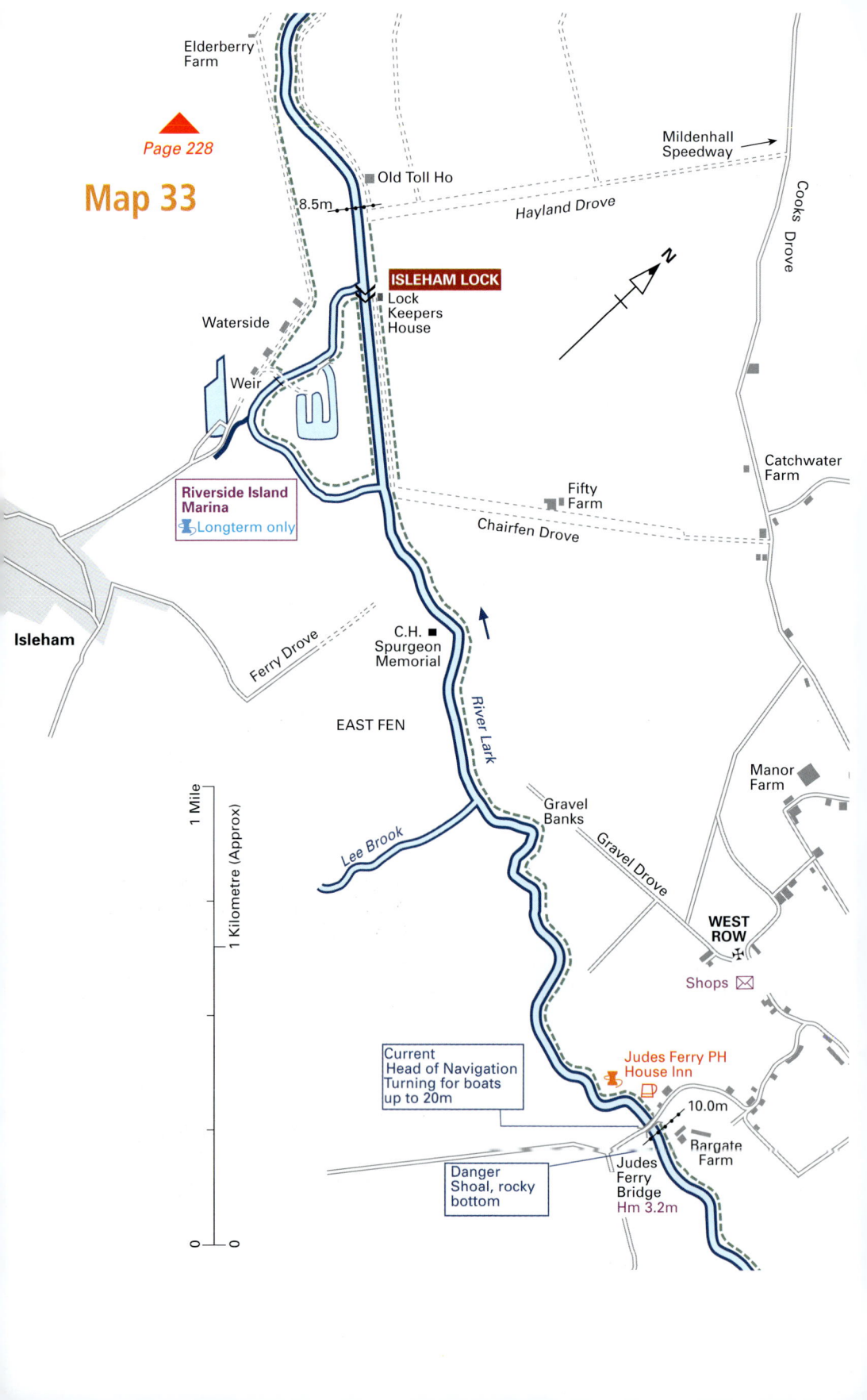

Scale: 1 Mile / 1 Kilometre (Approx)

Map 33

Isleham Lock to Jude's Ferry

Distance 2¼ miles
Time ¾ hour

Jude's Ferry PH customer moorings, looking upstream to the bridge

Navigation notes

As you leave the area of the lock and marina, the river narrows and becomes much more tortuous. Reeds crowd in, and the water becomes very clear. It feels that the river has returned to a completely natural course. The disappearance of the seemingly ever present flood banks provides views across a rural farming landscape.

The **Lee Brook** joins from the right. This is unnavigable (to powered craft) but its open water tempts the canoeist. As the river narrows again, and becomes more winding, we pass 'Gravel Banks'. This may be a description of the landscape, as well as the name of an idyllic remote cottage to your left.

The river briefly opens up again, and there is a short line of moored boats. However the trees close in as the river leads you to **Jude's Ferry Riverside Bar and Restaurant**. There are generous moorings outside, but it should be remembered that this is a popular destination in season. You need to use proper fenders on the moorings at the pub, as the landing stage has a protrusion at the wrong height.

The Environment Agency used to sign a turning point just below the road bridge. This has limited turning length, which could be reduced by the presence of boats on the moorings. There is a cut immediately downstream of the pub, which boats up to 20m (70') regularly turn in.

Moorings and facilities

Visitor moorings at **Jude's Ferry PH**

Turning at Head of Navigation max 20m (70') just below Jude's Ferry PH.

Jude's Ferry PH, Ferry Ln, West Row, Bury St Edmunds, IP28 8PT
☏ 01638 712277

Walking

From **Isleham Lock** a footpath continues on the north east floodbank (with a short detour around Gravel House) to **Jude's Ferry Bridge** (Head of Navigation), and on to **Mildenhall** (about 3 miles further upstream).

Local history

As the name suggests, there used to be a ferry at **Jude's Ferry** until the construction of the bridge in 1895. There was also a ford, until it was dredged out, which was used by the West Row Baptist Chapel for total immersion baptisms.

River Lark

RIVER GREAT OUSE

Poplars on the Lark and Little Ouse

Cruising both the River Lark and Little Ouse River, I've often looked across the flat fens and been struck by the great lines of Poplar trees lining the rivers and ditches. These dominate the landscape, and grow to a uniform height, appearing to me to 'guard' the Fens like soldiers on sentry duty.

In the 1940s Bryant & May, match manufacturers, were looking for a source of fast growing and straight wood. They decided Poplar trees were ideal and supplied local farmers with saplings and encouraged them to fill any spare bits of land with them. Rapid growing plants and trees need a good supply of water, which is why they were planted at the side of water courses.

However by the time these trees were ready to harvest, cigarette lighters had become increasingly popular and match sales dramatically reduced. Eventually the arrival of the cheap disposable lighter put an end to the popularity of growing Poplars for matches. It has, however, left us a legacy of great trees.

9

RIVER LITTLE OUSE

Described travelling **upstream**

The Little Ouse River rises east of Thetford close the source of the River Waverney. The Little Ouse flows west to join the Ely Ouse at Brandon Creek while the Waveney heads off to the east. The Little Ouse is about 37 miles in length. For much of its length it defines the boundary between Norfolk and Suffolk. The river has a long history as a navigable waterway with an Act of Parliament for the improvement of its navigation being passed in 1670. It was navigable to Thetford until 1890s and to below Thetford until 1933.

At times of heavy rainfall floodwater is diverted into the Cut Off Channel which the Little Ouse crosses west of Brandon.

The Little Ouse is currently navigable from the Ely Ouse for 13 miles to Brandon, the present Head of Navigation for powered craft. If you can fit through Brandon Lock, the potential for extending navigation upstream would appear to be only about 2½ miles to Santon Downham due to shallowing water.

The Little Ouse has two tributaries: the River Thet that joins at Thetford and the Black Bourn that joins just upstream of Thetford, both of which are un-navigable to powered craft.

There is potential for self powered portable boats to navigate to Thetford.

Looking towards RSPB Lakenheath nature reserve from Hockwold Fen

Map 34

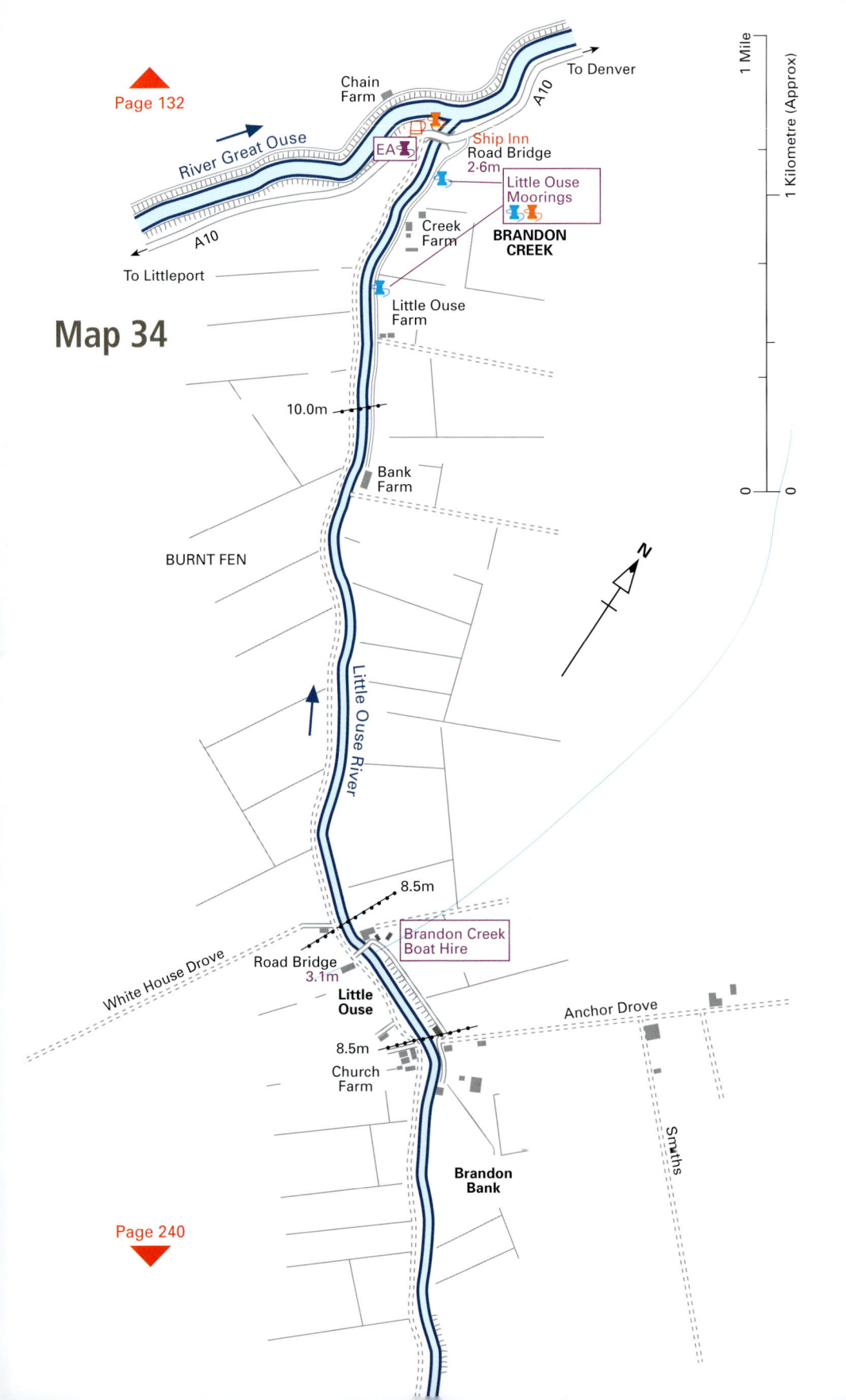

Maps 34/35/36/37

River Little Ouse

Distance 10¾ miles

Time 4 hours

Maps 34/35/36/37 Great Ouse Junction to Brandon

Lowest bridge 2·6m A10 Road Bridge
Brandon Lock L 12·0m W 4·0m D 1·2m H 2·7m Max length 12m (40')
Turning at Head of Navigation max 20m (70') just below Brandon Lock and Brandon Staunch

Location	Lock width	Moorings and facilities								Victualling		
		Visitor	48hr	Long stay	Water point	CDP	Pumpout	Refuse	Fuel	Shops	Pub	Café/restaurant
Map 34												
The Ship PH		🛟									🍺	🍴
EA Great Ouse moorings			🛟								🍺	🍴
Little Ouse moorings		🛟		🛟								
Map 36												
Hockwold Fen GOBA			🛟									
Map 37												
Brandon EA moorings below lock		🛟								🛒	🍺	🍴
Brandon Lock (12m max)	⏐											
Brandon EA moorings above town bridge		🛟	Only accessible to boats under 12m (40')							🛒	🍺	🍴

RIVER GREAT OUSE   237

Map 34
The Ship Inn at Brandon Creek to Little Ouse Bridge

Distance 1½ miles

Time ¾ hour

Navigation notes

The confluence of the **Little Ouse River** and the **River Great Ouse** is at the small hamlet of **Brandon Creek**. The River Little Ouse is sometimes mistakenly called 'Brandon Creek', but this is just the name of the hamlet, not the river.

There are **pub visitor moorings outside The Ship Inn PH** on the Little Ouse. These moorings are next to the A10 road bridge and suffer from the noise of road traffic. A good alternative are the **EA moorings on River Great Ouse** (almost outside The Ship PH) which are ideal over night moorings for anyone planning to head up the Little Ouse.

Passing under the concrete A10 bridge there are residential moorings on both sides of the river. On your left are **Little**

Moorings and facilities

The Ship PH moorings on Little Ouse (noisy because of nearby A10 road).

EA moorings on **River Great Ouse** (almost outside The Ship PH).

Little Ouse Moorings, Little Ouse Farm, Brandon Creek PE38 0PP
Long term and chargeable visitor moorings
☏ 07713 465791

Brandon Creek Boat Hire, Ironbridge Farmhouse, Anchor Drove, Brandon Bank PE38 0UP
Day boat hire.
☏ 07944 965978

The Ship at Brandon Creek
Popular pub serving food ☏ 1353 676228

The Ship Inn at Brandon Creek

Little Ouse 'cock up' Bridge

Ouse Moorings. This part of the river is generally raised above the surrounding countryside and offers occasional views between trees across the fields. Eventually the lines of moored boats peter out and you find yourself alone in the countryside. Less than 1½ miles upstream from the Little Ouse moorings is the village of **Little Ouse** with a steeply inclined 'cock-up' bridge. Little Ouse is a pretty little village with residential boats moored through it. Many of the moored boats boast that ultimate boater's accessory - a shed on the river bank!

Brandon Creek Boat Hire just past Little Ouse road bridge provide day boat hire on *Matilda*, a steel narrowboat. Day boat hirers often have less experience than those boaters who hire by the week. It is advisable to keep an eye out for *Matilda* as those in charge of her may be less aware of speed limits, rules of the river, and boating etiquette.

Local history

During Vermuyden's second attempt in the mid-17th century to drain the Fens, at the end of the English Civil War, Irish and Dutch prisoners were forced to dig the New Bedford River. One prisoner escaped, and with an associate went on the run. One night, hungry and desperate, they reached **The Ship at Brandon Creek**. At the time the pub was run by a Dutch couple, and the escapees murdered the landlord and lady, taking money and food.

When they were caught, punishment was swift. Anyone found guilty of murdering someone from another country was executed in the manner of the victim's home country. They were taken back to the inn and executed in the Dutch manner. Prior to the construction of Denver Sluice, the river was still tidal at this point. A beam was placed across the river, the prisoners stood in a barge at high tide, and nooses hung from the beam around the offenders' necks. As the tide went out, they were hanged.

It is said that the beam was thrown into the river, and remained an obstacle to navigation, until it was eventually pulled out and used when the pub was extended. It may still be there.

Map 35

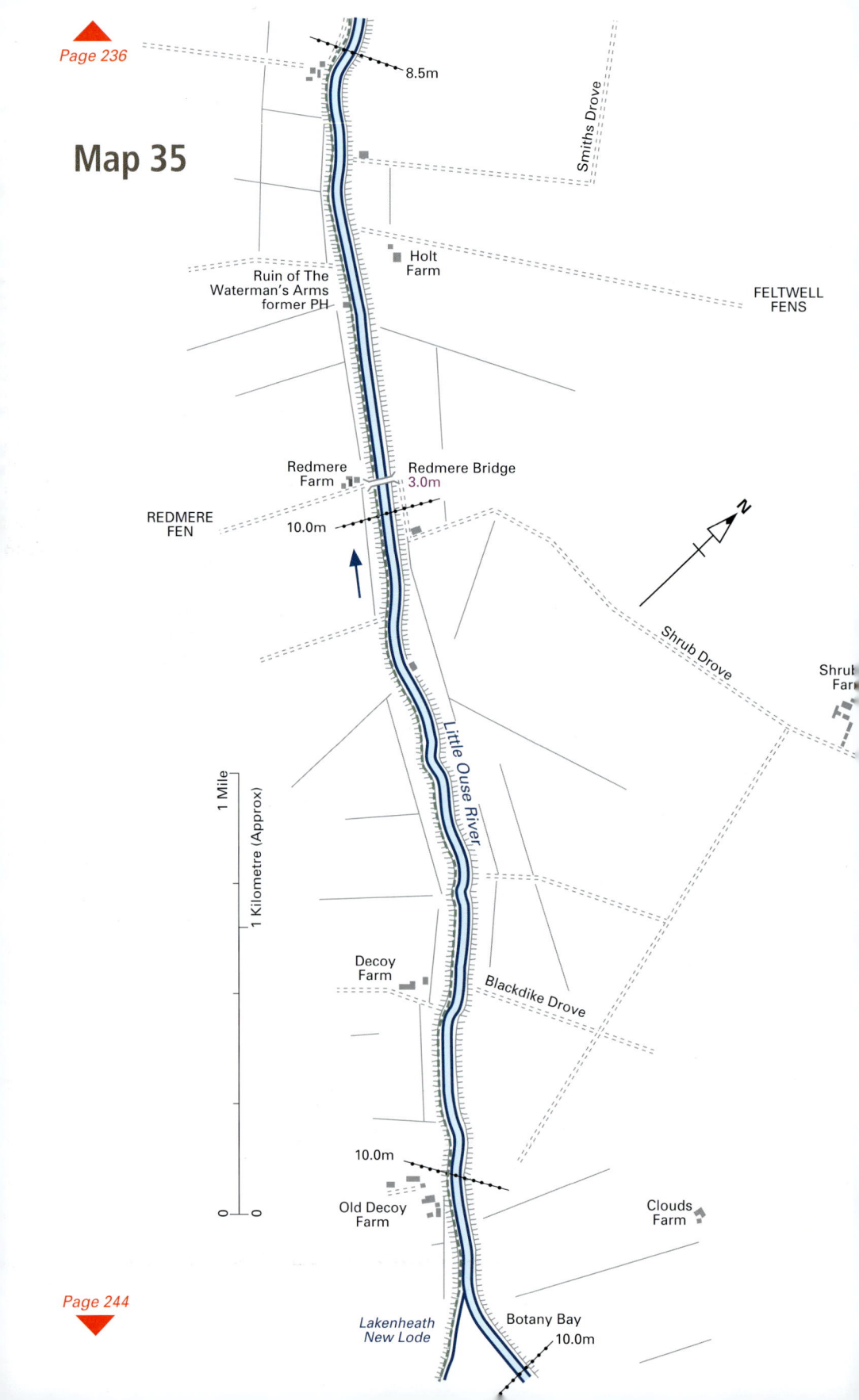

Page 236

8.5m

Smiths Drove

Holt Farm

Ruin of The Waterman's Arms former PH

FELTWELL FENS

Redmere Farm

Redmere Bridge
3.0m

REDMERE FEN

10.0m

Little Ouse River

Shrub Drove

Shrub Farm

1 Mile
1 Kilometre (Approx)

Decoy Farm

Blackdike Drove

10.0m

Old Decoy Farm

Clouds Farm

Lakenheath New Lode

Botany Bay

10.0m

Page 244

Map 35
Little Ouse Bridge to Lakenheath Lode

Distance 3 miles
Time 1¼ hours

Navigation notes

Above the village of **Little Ouse** you will discover just how beautiful, and peaceful, this river is. You can often travel for an hour or more without ever seeing another person. Your companions are a rich assortment of brightly coloured damselflies and dragonflies, and a wide variety of different birds.

To your right are the dramatic ruins of a pub, **The Waterman's Arms** at **Redmere**. This closed in 1956 and would appear to have been gently collapsing ever since. The gable ends are built from brick, and it boasts a central brick chimney, but its front is timber weatherboard which appears to resolutely survive the very strongest of winds.

The navigable section of the Little Ouse is only crossed by five bridges. The next of these is **Redmere Bridge**, a gated farm access bridge, massively engineered.

A mile or so further on, the river turns to the east around a long bend called 'Botany Bay'. This name can be found in more than one place in the Cambridgeshire Fens. It's not clear whether it was the Australian Botany Bay (site of Capt. Cook's first landing in Australia) which popularised the name here, or whether our locations inspired the naming of the Australian bay.

The long abandoned Waterman's Arms

Redmere farm bridge

RIVER GREAT OUSE   241

Map 36
Lakenheath Lode to Brandon Fen

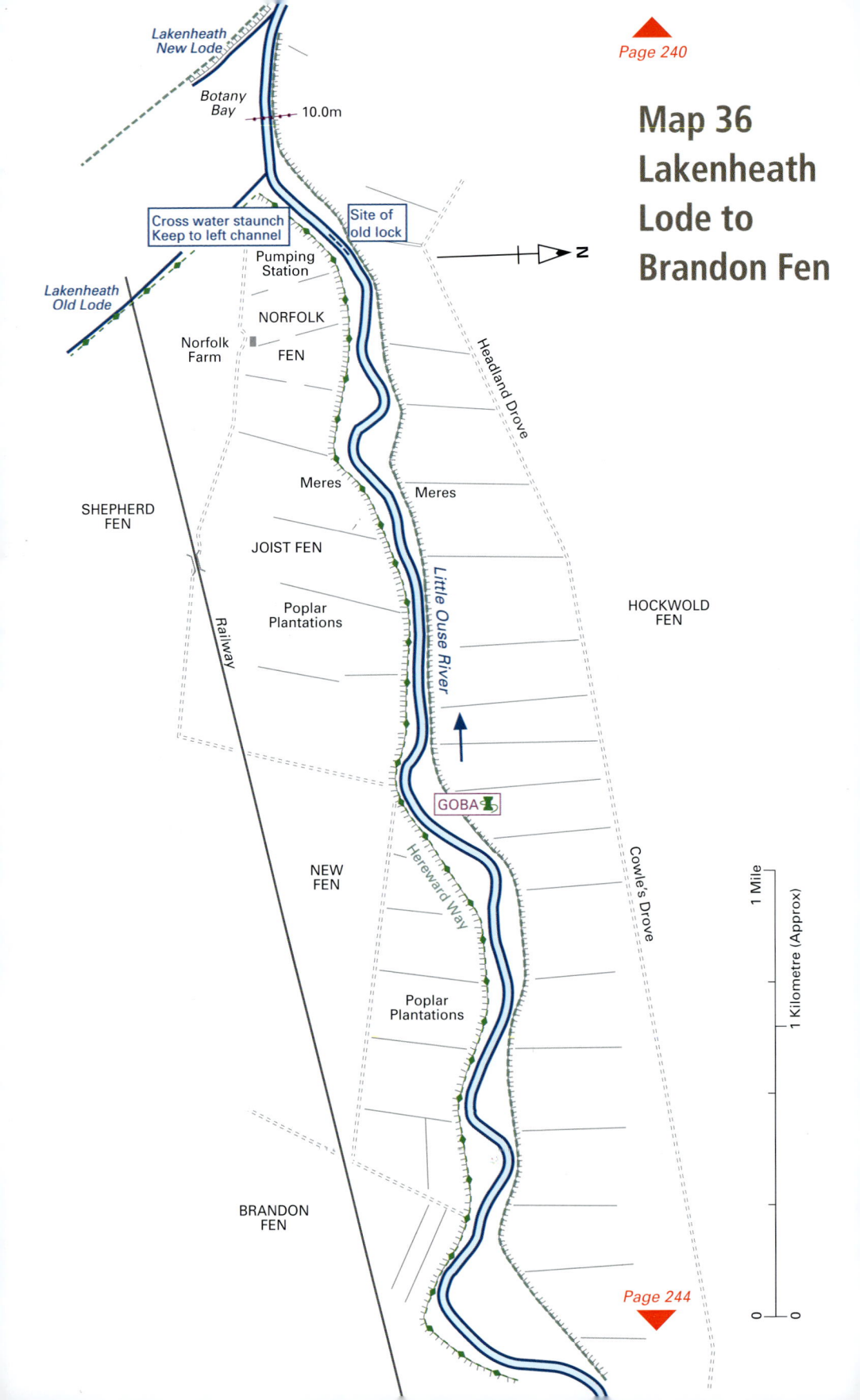

Lakenheath New Lode

Botany Bay

10.0m

Cross water staunch
Keep to left channel

Site of old lock

Pumping Station

Lakenheath Old Lode

NORFOLK FEN

Norfolk Farm

N

Headland Drove

Meres

Meres

SHEPHERD FEN

JOIST FEN

Poplar Plantations

Little Ouse River

HOCKWOLD FEN

Railway

GOBA

Hereward Way

NEW FEN

Cowle's Drove

Poplar Plantations

1 Mile

1 Kilometre (Approx)

BRANDON FEN

Page 240

Page 244

Distance 3 miles
Time 1½ hours

Navigation notes

Two lodes join on the right, **Lakenheath Old Lode** (or Cross Water) and **Lakenheath New Lode** (or Stallode) but in summer there is little to indicate their presence other than a line of reeds and it is unnavigable in winter because of weed. On your left are the collapsing landing stages of the **former Xanadu Boat Hire**. How long ago this business ceased trading is hard to establish, but it is difficult to go past without quoting Samuel Taylor Coleridge:

> 'In Xanadu did Kubla Khan
> A stately pleasure-dome decree:
> Where Alph, the sacred river, ran…'

Even the greatest admirers of the Little Ouse River may not be tempted to elevate it to the status of 'sacred'!

Around the next bend, on the right hand side, are the remains of an old staunch. This is sometimes known as Green Dragon Corner after a former inn on the south bank which operated between 1844 and 1937.

You should now catch your first glimpse of the **three incongruous radomes** (radar devices for tracking satellites) at **RAF Feltwell** which look like giant golf-balls.

You are now entering one of the most beautiful areas of remote cruising in the

Hockwold Fen GOBA Moorings

Moorings and facilities

GOBA Hockwold Fen Gloriously remote moorings on left bank.

The New Inn, 50 Station Rd,
Hockwold cum Wilton, Thetford IP26 4JA
☏ 01842 828668
Short walk from river, no official moorings.

The Red Lion, 114 Main St,
Hockwold cum Wilton, Thetford IP26 4NB.
☏ 01842 829728
Short walk from river, no official moorings.

Transport
Lakenheath Station, request stop on the Breckland Line between Cambridge and Norwich.

entire country. For the next hour you will have **Hockwold Fen** on your left. There are **GOBA 48h moorings** here where I have heard nightingales sing, and beyond that, splendid isolation.

Lakenheath Railway Station is ¾ mile south along the road. There are no moorings here, but you could improvise a pick up/set down point under at the road bridge. If you go north along the same road, the New Inn PH Hockwold is close by, and the Red Lion PH a bit further on.

Walking

There is a footpath along the south flood bank from **Brandon Creek** to **Lakenheath Station**. It briefly leaves the riverside at Botany bay where Lakenheath Old & New Lodes both outflow. Hereward Way joins the footpath here and continues as far as Wilton Bridge where it heads of south along the B112. This section of the Hereward Way is very popular with walkers, almost all carrying binoculars.

RIVER GREAT OUSE

Map 37

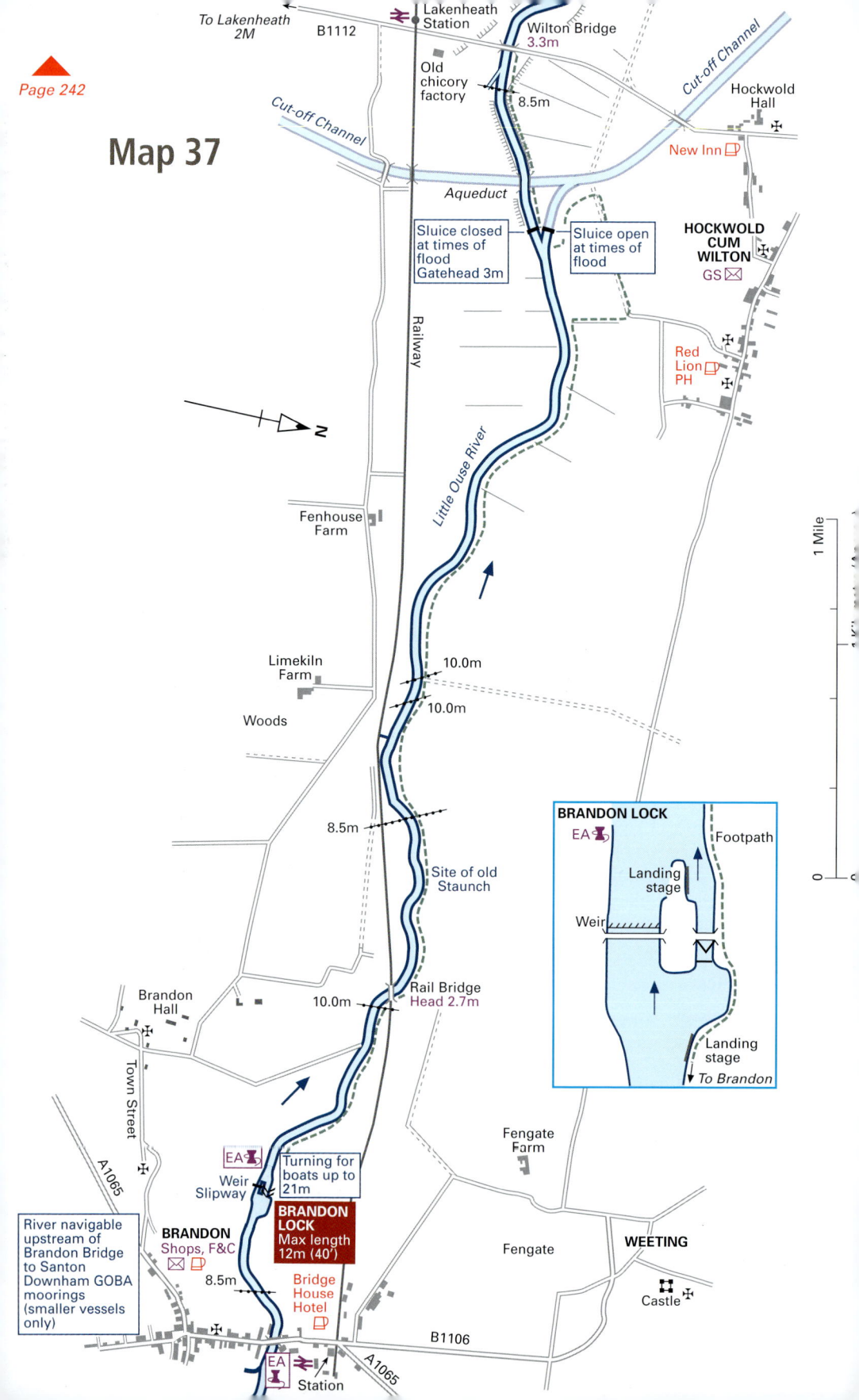

Page 242

To Lakenheath 2M — B1112 — Lakenheath Station — Wilton Bridge 3.3m — Cut-off Channel — Hockwold Hall

Old chicory factory — 8.5m — New Inn

Cut-off Channel — Aqueduct

Sluice closed at times of flood Gatehead 3m — Sluice open at times of flood — HOCKWOLD CUM WILTON GS

Red Lion PH

Railway — Little Ouse River

Fenhouse Farm

Limekiln Farm — 10.0m — 10.0m

Woods

8.5m

Site of old Staunch

Brandon Hall — 10.0m — Rail Bridge Head 2.7m

BRANDON LOCK
EA — Footpath
Landing stage
Weir
Landing stage
To Brandon

Fengate Farm

Town Street

EA — Turning for boats up to 21m
Weir Slipway

BRANDON LOCK Max length 12m (40′)

River navigable upstream of Brandon Bridge to Santon Downham GOBA moorings (smaller vessels only)

BRANDON Shops, F&C — 8.5m

Fengate — WEETING — Castle

Bridge House Hotel

B1106 — A1065

EA — Station

Map 37
Hockwold cum Wilton to Brandon Lock

Distance 2½ miles
Time ½ hour

River Little Ouse

Navigation notes

A third of a mile beyond **Wilton Bridge**, high concrete walls indicate that you are crossing the **'Cut-off Channel'** on an **aqueduct**. You then come to a set of **sluices across the River Little Ouse**. The sluice to the left is for diverting excess water from the river into the 'Cut-off Channel' below. In normal conditions the sluices across the river will be open, permitting passage upstream, and the diversion sluices to the Cut-off Channel closed. In strong stream conditions the river sluices close and the diversion sluices open, directing the water into the Cut-off Channel and shutting down navigation.

There are no official moorings posted here, but immediately down-stream of the river sluices, on your left as you

Little Ouse aqueduct carrying the River Little Ouse over the Cut-Off channel

Moorings and facilities

EA moorings just below Brandon Lock.

EA moorings above **Town Bridge, Brandon** (smaller vessels only).

Turning at Head of Navigation
Max 21m (70') just below Brandon Lock and Brandon Staunch

approach, there appears to be an **'unofficial' mooring**, including tying points. In summer it is weedy and the water not moving.

Shortly after the Cut-off Channel, on your left, is a spot used by the villagers of **Hockwold cum Wilton** to sunbathe, swim and generally enjoy the river. This was the site of the former ferry before the B1112 Station Road Bridge was built.

The countryside now becomes less wild and more farmed but the wooded banks are popular with kingfishers. The railway approaches on the right bank, following the river, before eventually crossing it. The constriction of the river underneath the bridge causes it to temporarily increase in flow. For some years the advice was to use the north opening under the bridge, but new signs indicate that both openings can be used.

RIVER GREAT OUSE

You are now quite near Brandon. Because of the comparative narrowness of the river, longer boats may start to wonder if they are actually going to be able to turn further on. These fears are unnecessary.

There are good, albeit limited, **moorings at Brandon**. The lock is restricted to boats no more than 12m (40') long. There is a weir next to the lock. There is ample turning room, but because of the flow from the weir, turning on your back rope is advisable : Attach your stern rope - with slack - to the mooring and allow the current to turn your bows. There are further moorings at Brandon Bridge above the lock for smaller vessels able to fit through the lock.

Rail bridge

Brandon Lock (max length 40')

Brandon is a pretty Suffolk Market Town, with several pubs, and take-aways including fish and chips, Indian and Chinese.
There is a Tesco Metro, not in the town centre.

Grimes Graves Neolithic flint mine with visitor centre 5 miles north east of Brandon
Lynford, Weeting, Thetford
IP26 5DE
☎ 0370 333 1181
www.english-heritage.org.uk/visit/places/grimes-graves-prehistoric-flint-mine/

Weeting Castle, Castle Cl, Weeting, Brandon
IP27 0RQ
Ruins of a substantial early medieval moated manor house, built in local flint, 2 miles north of Brandon

Transport
Brandon Railway Station

Walking

A footpath follows the north bank, taking a short detour at the sluices.

Local history

The construction of many of Brandon's buildings are a strong clue to the presence of flint locally. One of the town centre pubs is called the Flintknappers Arms. Five miles north east of Brandon lies the remarkable **Grimes Graves**, the site of a Neolithic flint mine, which includes a visitor centre.

10

RIVER WISSEY

Described travelling **upstream**

The River Wissey flows west from its source east of Swaffham, entering the Fens near Stoke Ferry and joining the Ely Ouse just upstream of Denver Sluice. It is about 25 miles in length in total and navigable for 11 miles from the Ely Ouse to about ½ mile east of Stoke Ferry. The upper river passes through the parkland of the Arts and Crafts Pickenham Hall, and through the Army's Stanford Training Area (STANTA), which was created in 1942 by evacuating six villages.

The river was already navigable in 1068 at the time of the Domesday survey.

The original course of the river Wissey has hugely altered over the centuries, originally flowing into the sea at Wisbech. It has been argued that Wisbech derives its name from Wissey, however the River Great Ouse also once met the sea at Wisbech and an alternative argument suggests that Wisbech is in fact 'Ouse beach'. When the Great Ouse was diverted to the sea at King's Lynn, the river Wissey joined it above Denver, no longer flowing to Wisbech.

During heavy rain its floodwaters are diverted into the Cut-Off Channel south of Stoke Ferry. This is 11 miles from its confluence with the Ely Ouse.

The potential for extending navigation upstream of the present Head of Navigation would appear to be only about 1¾ miles due to shallow water.

Navigation further by self powered portable boats requires getting round the weir and sluices at Watermill Farm some 3 miles further on.

River Wissey at Hilgay

RIVER GREAT OUSE   247

Map 38

Page 139

White House Farm

To Denver 1 mile

SILT FEN

Railway Ely - King's Lynn

Ouse Bridge 4.0m

Wissey Bridge 2.7m

Khartoum Wood

River Great Ouse

GOBA

River Wissey

Ten Mile Bank

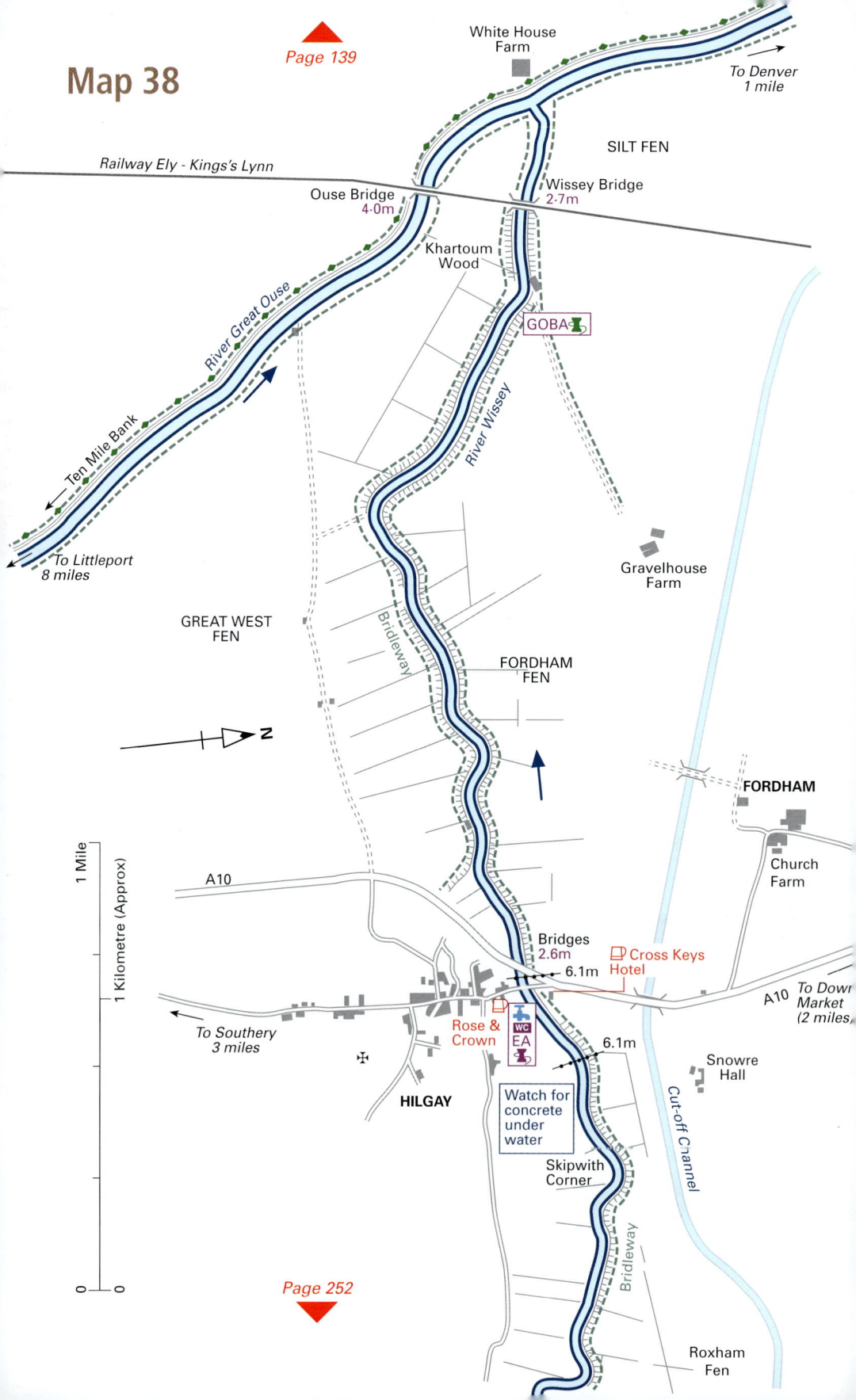

To Littleport 8 miles

GREAT WEST FEN

Gravelhouse Farm

Bridleway

FORDHAM FEN

FORDHAM

N

Church Farm

1 Mile
1 Kilometre (Approx)

A10

Bridges 2.6m
6.1m

Cross Keys Hotel

A10 To Downham Market (2 miles)

To Southery 3 miles

Rose & Crown
WC
EA

6.1m

Snowre Hall

HILGAY

Watch for concrete under water

Skipwith Corner

Cut-off Channel

Bridleway

Page 252

Roxham Fen

Maps 38/39/40

River Wissey

Distance 13 miles

Time 4 hours

Maps 38/39/40 River Great Ouse to Whittington

Lowest bridge
Map 38 2·6m Hilgay A10 bridge
Map 39 2·4m Wissington pipe bridge
Map 40 2·3m Whittington road bridge

Turning at Head of Navigation
Max 21m (70') using Stringside Drain junction at Whittington

Location	Moorings and facilities								Victualling		
	Short stay	48hr	Long stay	Water point	CDP	Pumpout	Refuse	Fuel	Shops	Pub	Café/restaurant
Map 38											
GOBA moorings opposite Khartoum Wood		🛟									
Hilgay EA moorings		🛟		🚰						🍺	
Map 40											
GOBA Stoke Ferry Bridge		🛟									

RIVER GREAT OUSE 249

Map 38
Great Ouse to Hilgay

Distance 1¾ miles
Time ¾ hour

Navigation notes

The mouth of the Wissey is slightly narrow and unprepossessing, but don't be put off by this - it only disguises the glories to come! There is a 4mph speed limit sign. It is not clear whether this applies just to the entrance, or the whole river. However, much of the river is narrow and shallow, and faster speeds would be difficult to achieve and inappropriate.

Almost immediately you pass under a **railway bridge** which carries the same railway line which crosses the Great Ouse on an attractive green wrought iron Ouse Bridge. The bridge across the Wissey is rather less attractive. Although the two bridges are near each other, the air clearance underneath them dramatically varies: By the Environment Agency's own figures, the normal clearance over the Great Ouse is 4m (13'1") whereas over the Wissey it is 1·3m (4'3") lower at 2·7m (8'10"). This may appear surprising as neither river nor railway line have significantly changed height over this short distance, however the bridges were constructed in different styles. Don't assume that just because you've easily passed under the railway bridge on the Great Ouse, you will similarly 'sail' under its sister on the River Wissey.

The trees on your right form **Khartoum Wood**. On your left are shaded **GOBA moorings**. The bank comprises uncapped steel piles which finish proud of the ground, so these moorings are better suited to the more agile.

A line of moored boats heralds a temporary return to less exotic surroundings. You will first pass under the **modern bridge** which carries the A10 past Hilgay and then another **newish bridge**, on the line of the old village bridge. A large colony of doves, many of them pure white, live under these bridges. These bridges are called respectively Hilgay Bypass Bridge and

Hilgay, travelling upstream

Hilgay

Moorings and facilities

GOBA 'Railway Bridge' moorings shortly after you enter the Wissey

EA Hilgay moorings with **waterpoint** on the right just past the second bridge.

The Rose and Crown, Bridge St, Hilgay, Downham Market PE38 0LJ.
☎ 01366 384507

Hilgay Bridge. However another bridge crossing the River Great Ouse 1½ miles away is occasionally called Hilgay Bridge (or alternatively Modney Bridge) and confusion can arise.

Hilgay is a pleasant village with **EA moorings** just above the second bridge on your right with a water point, public slipway and toilet. To the north the cut-off channel passes close by. It is home to a fun raft race, generally held in the middle of July.

Hilgay GOBA moorings

Walking

The River Wissey has a bridleway on its south bank from its confluence with the Great Ouse to **Hilgay**.

Footpath along the Wissey

Local history

George William Manby, school friend of Nelson's, lived for much of his life in Hilgay. He was brought up with a military and naval background. After hopelessly witnessing ships in distress he invented a rocket-like apparatus to throw a line to a ship and it is said that he experimented from the roof of Hilgay church tower. Use of this mortar resulted in over a thousand lives being saved. He died in Yarmouth but is buried in Hilgay where his memorial tablet commemorates his invention.

RIVER GREAT OUSE

Map 39

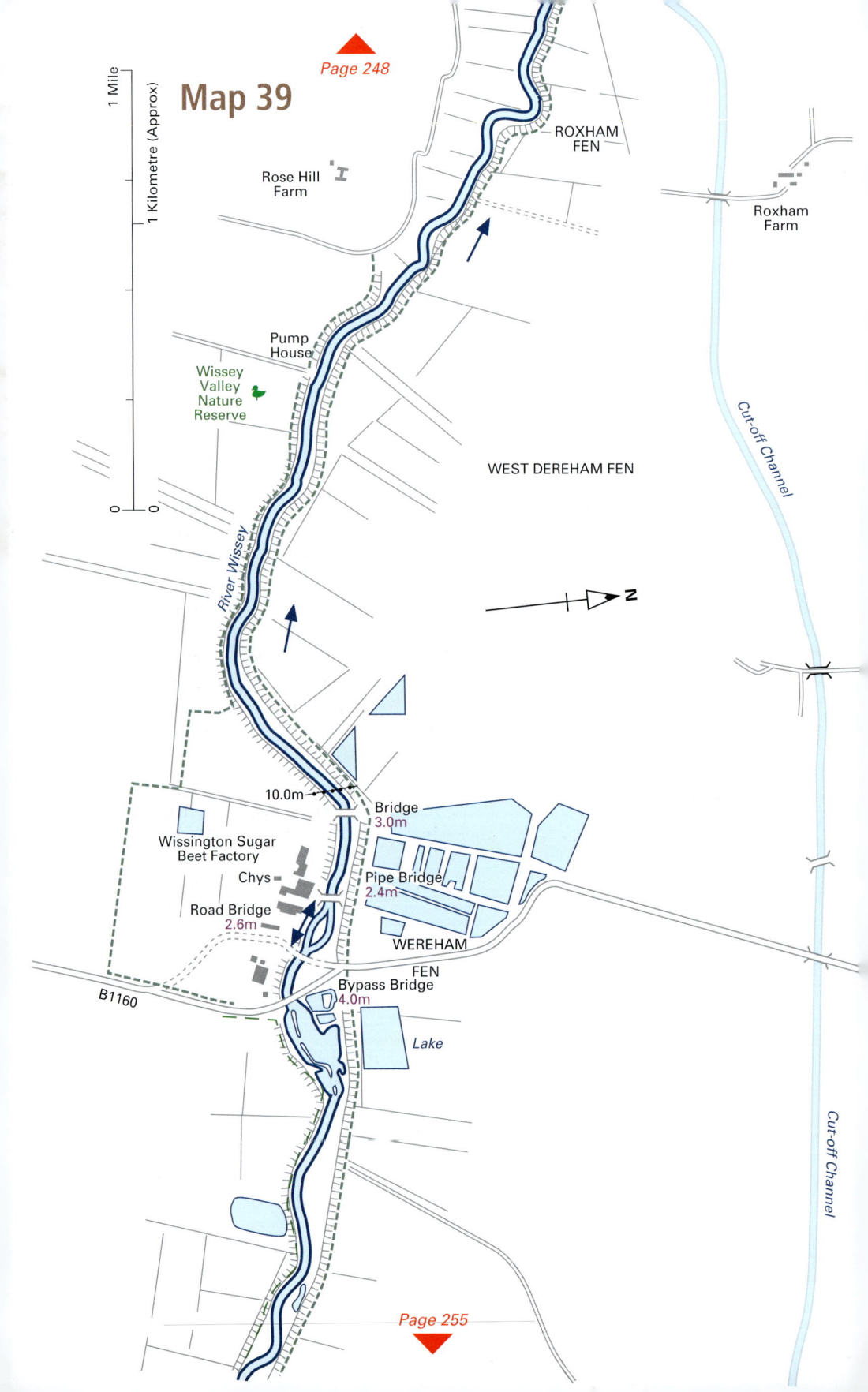

Page 248

ROXHAM FEN

Rose Hill Farm

Roxham Farm

Pump House

Wissey Valley Nature Reserve

WEST DEREHAM FEN

River Wissey

Cut-off Channel

10.0m

Bridge 3.0m

Wissington Sugar Beet Factory

Chys

Pipe Bridge 2.4m

Road Bridge 2.6m

WEREHAM FEN

Bypass Bridge 4.0m

B1160

Lake

Cut-off Channel

Page 255

Map 39 Hilgay to Wissington

Distance 2¾ miles
Time ¾ hour
No moorings

River Wissey

Navigation notes

Above **Hilgay** the river snakes on through about 2 miles of remote countryside. When a **former pumping station** converted into holiday accommoation appears on the right you should be rewarded with commanding views over Norfolk Wildlife Trust's Wissey Valley Living Landscape reserve.

Trees start to crowd down to the river. Between the trees you get your first glimpse of **Wissington Beet Factory** and its glasshouses which might more appropriately be better described as 'grass houses' (see photo p.254).

Although still one mile away, giant silos start to dominate the landscape. Sugar beet harvesting takes place from early autumn through to spring and Wissington is the site of British Sugar's largest UK refinery. The river passes next to the factory.

In 2007, Wissington became the site of the UK's first bioethanol power plant, from which spare heat was used to heat on-site greenhouses which produced 70 million tomatoes per year. In 2017, the greenhouses switched to producing cannabis plants for medicine production. Around harvest time that year a mysterious sweet smell spread over part of East Anglia, nick-named the 'great stink', which was suspiciously like the

Wissey Valley Living Landscape reserve
www.norfolkwildlifetrust.org.uk/wildlife-in-norfolk/a-living-landscape/wissey

smell of cannabis. The mystery was finally solved when the smell was eventually traced back to Wissington's glass houses.

Passing past the beet factory when it is fired up and operating is an unforgettable experience; steam belches everywhere, machinery grinds and whirrs, and great conveyor belts all create an image suggestive of Dante's Inferno!

You will pass first underneath a **green wrought iron bridge**, which carried a railway until 1957, then another **bridge**, and then a giant tube. There is an island which you keep to your left, heading straight on. The abutments of a concrete bridge stand on opposite banks, with the bridge itself removed. There is then one final **modern bridge** which carries the fleets of lorries serving the factory which have replaced both water and rail.

As you leave the industrial mayhem of the factory a surprise awaits, you enter a great lake. There is an island immediately ahead, and navigation is signposted to the left. The lake appears to be used only by a few fishermen, but it is possible to anchor here.

Walking

From **Hilgay** a bridleway runs along the north bank to **Wissington**. About two miles upstream of Hilgay another bridleway joins the south bank but then detours around Wissington Beet factory before rejoining the river at the lake.

Wissington glass/grass houses

Local history

At **Skipworth** corner, just after Hilgay the river passes very close to the **Cut-Off Channel**. On the opposite side of the Cut-Off Channel is **Snore Hall**, a Grade-II Listed manor house where it is believed that in 1646 Charles I held a Civil War council (possibly his last). The building is privately owned and not open to the public.

The sugar-beet factory was opened in **Wissington** in 1925. This brought commercial traffic back onto Fenland waters. Three tugs pulled a total of 24 iron barges, bringing coal up from King's Lynn, and sugar beet to the factory from farms. In 1943 a bomb sank one of the barges, the fleet was transferred to the factory at Queen Adelaide (Ely) (see p.124) and water transport to Wissington finished.

Wissington Lake

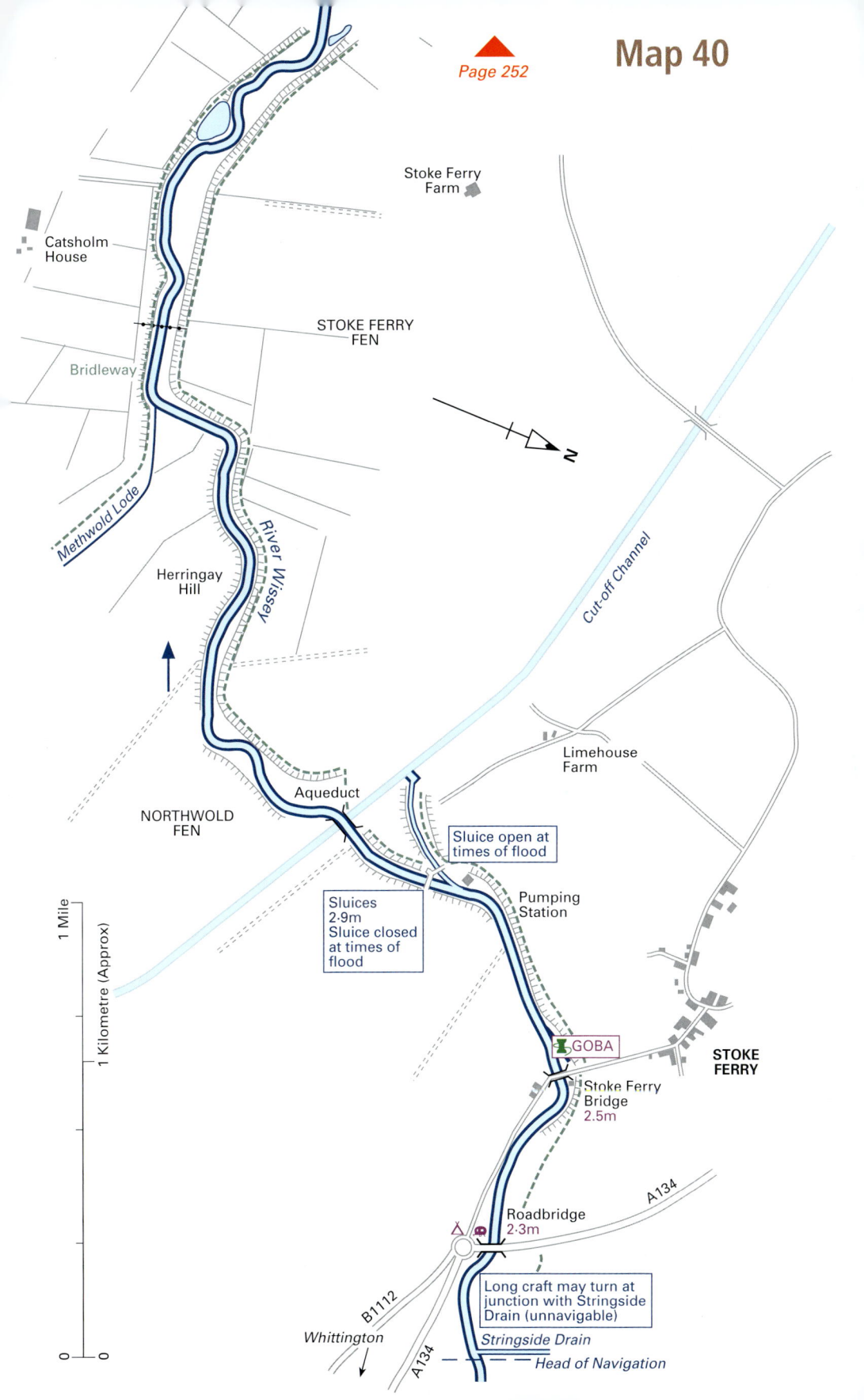

Map 40

Page 252

- Catsholm House
- Stoke Ferry Farm
- Bridleway
- Methwold Lode
- STOKE FERRY FEN
- Herringay Hill
- River Wissey
- NORTHWOLD FEN
- Aqueduct
- Cut-off Channel
- Limehouse Farm
- Sluice open at times of flood
- Sluices 2·9m Sluice closed at times of flood
- Pumping Station
- GOBA
- Stoke Ferry Bridge 2.5m
- STOKE FERRY
- Roadbridge 2.3m
- A134
- B1112
- Whittington
- Long craft may turn at junction with Stringside Drain (unnavigable)
- Stringside Drain
- Head of Navigation

Scale: 1 Mile / 1 Kilometre (Approx)

N

Map 40

Wissington to Whittington

Distance 4 miles
Time 1½ hours

Navigation notes

Soon after the lake the river returns to a normal size, and you are left pinching yourself and wondering if the alien intrusion of the factory really happened. The wooded banks and clear waters make this prime kingfisher territory. The river meanders on for another mile where **Methwold Lode** joins it. Methwold Lode is not navigable to powered craft. The River Wissey turns sharp left (north) at this point. As you approach it can be confusing which is the actual navigation.

1¼ miles after Methworld Lode you cross the **Cut-off Channel** in a concrete trough aqueduct. This is followed by a diversion sluice, with a second sluice off to the left. These only come into play during winter flood conditions, when excess water is diverted into the Cut-off Channel. Both sluices are wide, single gate, sluices unlike the River Little Ouse which uses narrower double gate sluices. Immediately after the sluices is a pumping station. No mooring is possible.

Stoke Ferry soon appears on your right. After you pass under a wrought iron trough road bridge, there is a community of long-term moored boats. On a sunny summer Sunday afternoon this looked a truly idyllic mooring, with families relaxing in the shade by their boats.

GOBA moorings on left bank (heading upstream) just before the Stoke Ferry Bridge. The GOBA mooring is the first one in the line of boats moored there

Cut-off sluice

There are relocated **GOBA mornings** on the straight section downstream of the old bridge, near Stoke Ferry Bridge. The **A134 road bridge** marks the end of your journey, but longer boats may have to travel slightly further upstream to Stringside Drain to turn. Turning is available slightly further upstream. It is unfortunate that no other mooring is provided between Hilgay and Whittington as this represents a cruising time of 3¼ hours and the opportunity to stop and enjoy the scenery would be welcome.

Walking

The bridleway on the south bank continues from **Wissington** until the junction with **Methwold Lode**, where it departs the Wissey and follows Methwold Lode. The bridleway on the north bank continues to **Whittington**.

Appendix
Further reading

The Water and Steam Mills of Huntingdonshire's Great Ouse,
Hugh Howes, 2020, The Mills Archive

The Story of Ely
Michael Rouse, 2016, Phillimore & Co. Ltd.

Exploring Historical Cambridgeshire
Robert Leader, 2014, The History Press

The Cambridgeshire Fens
Trevor Bevis and Malcolm Allen, 2010, Cottage Publications,

Cambridge: Treasure Island in the Fens
Nicholas Chrimes, 2009, Hobs Aerie Publications

Along the River Cam
Andrew Hunter Blair, 2007, Sutton Publishing

The River Great Ouse and the River Cam
Josephine Jeremiah, 2006, Phillimore

Hereward, The Last Englishman
Peter Rex, 2004, Amberley Publishing

Vanishing Cambridgeshire
Mike Petty, 2003, Breedon Books Publishing Ltd.

From Punt to Plough
Rex Sly, 2003, History Press Co.

Great Ouse Country
Andrew Hunter Blair, 2002 John Nickalls Publishing

Memory Lane Ely and the Fens
Mike Petty, 2001, Breedon Books Publishing Ltd.

Rivers to the Fens
Robert Simper, 2000, Creekside Publishing

Navigating the Future, extending navigation within the Great Ouse system, 1999, GOBA

Times of Flood
Anthony Day, 1997, S B Publications,

The Jewel in the Town
Myra Chowins, 1997, Fingerprint Productions

No Tall Story, Just a Giant's Tale
Carol Moon, 1997, Fingerprint Productions

St Neots Past
Rosa Young, 1996, Phillimore & Co. Ltd.

Etheldreda
Moyra Caldecott, 1987, Mushroom Publishing Ltd.

The Great Ouse
Wilson Stephens, 1985, Muller, Blond & White

St Neots, C.F. Tebbutt, 1978, Phillimore & Co. Ltd.

The Canals of Eastern England John Boyes and Ronald Russel, 1977, David & Charles Ltd

The Great Level
Dorothy Summers, 1976, David & Charles Ltd.

The Lark Navigation
DE Weston, Circa 1976 Denny Bros.

Fenland Rivers
Alan & Michael Roulstone, 1974, Balfour

The Great Ouse
Dorothy Summers, 1973, David & Charles Ltd.

God's Englishman: Oliver Cromwell and the English Revolution
Christopher Hill, 1972, Penguin Books

Tom's Midnight Garden
Philippa Pearce, 1958, Oxford University Press

The Black Fens
A K Astbury, 1957, County History Reprints

The Buildings of England, Cambridgeshire,
N Pevsner, 1954, Yale University Press (2002 ed)

Cambridgeshire: Huntingdonshire and the Isle of Ely, E A R Ennion, 1951, Robert Hale Ltd

Inland Waterways of Great Britain
L. A. Edwards, 1950, Imray, Laurie, Norie & Wilson

The County Book of Cambridgeshire
EAR Ennion, 1950, Robert Hale Ltd.

The County Book of Bedfordshire
Laurence Meynell, 1950, Robert Hale Ltd.

Fenland Rivers
Iris Wedgwood, 1936, Rich & Cowan Ltd.

Ouses's Silent Tide, Rev. C.F. Farrar, 1921, County History Reprints (reprinted 1969)

Highways and Byways of Cambridge and Ely, Rev. E Conybeare, 1910, Macmillan and Co

Bradshaw's Canals and Navigable Rivers
Henry de Salis, 1904, David and Charles reprint (1969)

The Cambridge, Ely and King's Lynn Road, The Great Fenland Highway, Charles Harper, 1902, Forgotten Books 2018 reprint

Cheap Jack Zita
S. Baring-Gould, 1896, Amazon reprint

Hereward The Wake
Charles Kingsley, 1865, Nelson Classics.

The Ouse, A.J. Foster, (c.1895)
Society for Promoting Christian Knowledge

Navigable connections with the Great Ouse proposed over the years

The Industrial Revolution is generally regarded as starting around 1760. It required improved transport links to move goods, and early canals, such as the Bridgewater (1761) highlighted the many benefits of moving goods by water over horse and cart. The period between the 1770s and 1830s that is often called the Golden Age of Canals, and financial speculators, across the Country were soon busy devising schemes to either make existing rivers navigable, or to dig new canals. This 'Canal Mania' continued until the invention of the railway. Smart money moved to 'Railway Mania' and the 'get rich quick' canal schemes were generally forgotten about.

It is interesting to consider some of the many schemes once proposed for extending a navigable transport system linking to the river Great Ouse. It's a shame that the railways didn't arrive a generation or two later, and that, for example, the London & Cambridge Canal was never built.

1758 - linking Bishop's Stortford (river Stort) to Thetford (river Little Ouse)

1788 - linking Cambridge with the proposed Bishop's Stortford to Thetford navigation, with a branch to Burwell Lode

1787/1790 - linking Bury St Edmunds (river Lark) to Mistley (river Stour)

1790 - linking Bury St Edmunds (river Lark) to Stowmarket (river Gipping)

1811 - 1824 Linking Bedford (river Great Ouse) with Fenny Stratford (Grand Junction Canal)

1812 - linking Bishop's Stortford (river Stort) to Clayhithe (river Cam)

1817 - Linking Bedford (river Great Ouse) with the Newport Pagnell Canal

1817 - linking Kimbolton (river Kym) with St Neots (river Great Ouse)

1817 - Linking St Neots (river Great Ouse) via a new cut to Bedford (river Great Ouse) with the Newport Pagnell Canal

1824 - linking Fenny Stratford (Grand Junction Canal) with Shefford (river Ivel)

1824 - linking Shefford (river Ivel) with Hitchin (river Hitz - tributary of river Ivel) and Hertford (river Lea)

1892 - resurrection of the proposed Bedford to the Grand Junction Canal via 20 miles of canal and 25 locks

The two of the proposed routes which linked with the upper reaches of what is now the Lee & Stort Navigation, had they been built, would represent significant savings on current routes:

A. The journey by road from Fenny Stratford, via Shefford and Hitchin, to Hertford is about 70 miles, but by boat is currently 94 miles, 96 locks and takes 8 days. A direct navigation could have cut 6 days from this.

B. Travelling between Bishop's Stortford and Clayhythe (near Cambridge) although only 30 miles by road, without the proposed Bedford to Milton Keynes link, requires the intrepid boater to travel by Northampton, the River Nene and the Middle Level. This is 250 mile, 176 lock 17 day trip by boat. Had it been built, the London & Cambridge Canal would have cut 16 days off this journey.

More recent proposed links:

Bedford and Milton Keynes Waterway Trust

The Boston to Peterborough Wetland Corridor has taken over the aspirations of the former Fens Waterways Link. The announcement that two new East of England reservoirs are to be built, one in Fenland, the other in south Lincolnshire have added significant momentum to this project.

Glossary of Terms

Ague — A former of malaria which was once common in the marshy fens

Bandy — An early form of ice hockey which originated in the fens

Becket — A metal flanged spade for digging peat

The Black Shug — A canine ghost, whose sighting is an omen of bad news

Bog oak — A tree buried in peat for centuries, known for its exceptionally hard wood, not necessarily oak

Bow hauling — Using men, rather than horses, to pull boats along

Butty boat — A boat towed by a motor boat

Cockup bridge — A bridge where the central section is higher to allow boats to pass underneath, sometimes this section could be raised to allow masted boats through

Coprolite — Fossilised dung, when ground up a rich source of fertiliser which lead to a mining boom in the fens in the 1850s and 1860s.

Cutters — Navvies who cut the drains

Clunch — Chalk

Cut — A section of canal between locks, so called because it has been cut rather than the natural channels of a river, also an artificially rerouted course of a river as in 'new cut'

Day boat — A working boat without a cabin, used on distances short enough to allow the bargee to return home at night

Docky — A Fen term for a lunch break, so named because tight fisted employers docked a man's wages when he stopped to eat

Doors — A Fen term for lock gates

Draw — To open a sluice to let water through

Drove — A rough track in the Fens

Dydle (Norfolk) — To dredge or clean out

Fen blow — When dry fen soil blows up like a sand storm

Fen camels — Short stilts strapped to the legs for crossing marshy fens

Fen runners — Fen ice skates

Ferry glide (v) — To move a boat sideways in a controlled manner, generally when coming alongside a pontoon or pier

Flash — A sudden release of accumulated water to carry a vessel over an obstruction

Fly boat — Originally a fast moving boat towed by teams of horses, it now applies to any boat travelling non stop - 'working fly'

Gang — A number of Fen lighters (generally five) chained together and towed by the lead boat

Gauging — Measuring how deep a boat sits in the water to establish the weight of its cargo, enabling the charging of tolls

Gault — Clay

Gongoozler — An idle spectator watching activity on a river or canal, often at a lock

Hane (Norfolk) — High - e.g. 'the water is hane today' means 'the water is high today'

Haling Way — The riverside path on which a lighterman's horse walked with the horseknocker boy. On the Great Ouse boundary fences generally ran all the way down to the water, and horses had to learn to jump the fences, sometimes up to 2½ foot high, while pulling a string of lighters

Hard water — Water that is frozen, but not yet hard enough to walk on

Horse boat — A small open boat, generally towed on the end of a string of lighters, used to ferry the tow horse to the other side of the river when there was no bridge. For example, boats leaving Salter's Lode couldn't bring their horse up the west bank (because there was no bridge across the New Bedford River), and the alternative, land based route, involved a two mile detour through Denver

House lighter — A lighter with a cabin on it, used for sleeping in

Hythe — A quay (Old English)

Invert — An inverted brick arch forming the bottom of a lock or tunnel. The bottom of Stanground Lock is an invert, and if your boat is deep drafted the lock keeper will instruct you to keep to the middle of the lock when locking down

Key — A windlass used to operate lock sluices

Land water — Water in a river originating from rainfall - the opposite being water brought in from the sea on a flood-tide

Leaping poles — Wooden poles used to vault across fen drains and ditches

Level	A length (or reach) of water, on one side of a lock. If one side of the lock is tidal, twice a day a 'level is made' when both sets of gates can be opened at the same time. For example, Salters Lode Lock can only accommodate 70' boats 'on the level'
Lighter	A flat bottomed barge used for transporting goods, generally 42' x 10'
Lock, to	To work a vessel through a lock
Lode	A fen river, usually artificial and straight, possibly dug by the Romans or local monasteries for drainage or trading
Loodel	A vertical extension to a tiller arm to enable better vision from a higher position when transporting high loads such as straw or hay
Narrow-boat	A craft measuring a maximum of 70' x 7', extensively used in the Midland canal system. Also known as a 'monkey boat' or 'long boat'
Navvies	Short for navigators, men who cut and dug out water courses
Osier	Willow harvested in the fens for basket making
Packet boat	Regular fast moving boats, in the 18th and 19th century, which carried passengers and mail between towns and cities
Paddle	A sluice valve which empties or fills a lock or a reach. Also called a 'slacker' or a 'clough'. 'Ground paddles' let water into a lock by built-in culverts, whereas 'fly paddles', 'ranters' or 'flashers' are fitted to the gates
Pen	A lock chamber
Penstock	A ground paddle
Piece	An open space (e.g. Parker's Piece, Cambridge)
Pill box	A concrete WWII defensive structure, often at the side of a river
Poling	To propel a boat by pushing a pole (or sprit) against the bottom of a river or canal
Poppy head tea	Made from opium poppies and drunk to cure the fen ague
Pound	A stretch of water on a canal between two locks
Pudlers	Men who worked the clay into banks to make them watertight
Quant (Norfolk)	A pole or shaft used for propelling a vessel
Reach	A stretch of water on a river between two locks
Roddon	A dried up river bed, the lighter soil can sometimes only be discerned when the land is bare of crops
Slacker	Gate daddler, a paddle or a sluice- device wound up or down to let water into, or out of, a lock
Sluice	A pound lock
Staunch	Originally a single gate lock
Staith	A wharf
Stem	The stem is the front (or bows) of a boat, the opposite of the stern
to stem a vessel (verb)	To turn it against the tide or flow of a river
Stemmed	Run aground on a mud-flat or sand-bank
Sprit	Steering pole on a Fen lighter
Stop lock	A low-rise lock built at the junction of two pieces of water to prevent water from passing between them
Swim, to	A boat light in draft and which handles well, 'a good swimmer'
Tail	The area immediately below the bottom (of a lock) gates of a lock. similarly the area immediately above the top gates of a lock is called the 'head'
Toll	Charge payable for use of part of a canal or river
Turf	Peat
Turns/ waiting turns/ working in turns	A water saving system employed during periods of low water levels when any boat wishing to pass through a lock must wait until another boat comes through the opposite direction, so ensuring the maximum of traffic passes for the quantity of water used
Wash lands/ washes	Land next to a river prone to flooding
Wind	To turn a boat around
Winding (verb)	To turn a boat, pronounced as in 'north wind', not as in 'winding a clock'
Windlass	A handle, or key, used for opening and closing lock paddles

Wildlife on the Great Ouse and its Tributaries

Christine Colbert

Wildlife is abundant. Below are some examples of what can be seen across the seasons.

Birds

In addition to the usual field or garden birds, you may see a range of birds of prey. Red kites, buzzard, kestrel, harrier and, at twilight, barn owls flapping silently over the reeds or fields.

On the water or waterside you may see mute swans, coots and moorhens, a range of ducks, greylag and Canada geese, great crested grebe, kingfishers, herons and egrets, gulls and terns. Occasionally oyster catchers towards the tidal Great Ouse.

In spring and summer skylarks hover high over fields, singing. Swifts (with their screeching cry) fly high catching insects, while swallows and martins will feed flying low over the water.

The area benefits from a number of nature reserves, which attract both resident and migratory birds. The most significant are:

Ouse Washes , **Welney Wetland Centre** (WWT) **Wicken Fen** (notable visitors are cuckoos and bitterns) and **Gt Paxton Nature Reserve** which benefits from the presence of nightingales, woodpeckers and a large colony of shags. Shags appear elsewhere and are particularly partial to sitting at the tops of dead trees.

Autumn migrant visitors to the nature reserves include hen harrier, widgeon, redwing, fieldfare, murmerations of starlings, whooper swans and Bewick swans.

Other notable avian residents are:
Little grebe or 'dabchick' on the Cam, Egyptian geese at Earith, Muscovy ducks at Ely, whilst in 2020 peregrine falcons nested on Ely Cathedral. For a number of years purple gallinule (waterfowl fondly called 'blue chickens') were seen in the Holywell/St Ives area but the writer is not aware of sightings since 2015.

Mammals

In spring and summer you will find hares and bats (tiny pipistrelles and Daubenton's bats, and the larger (but still small!) noctule.)

Grey seals are regularly seen on the tidal Great Ouse and Old West and frequently at Holywell and sometimes beyond.

Porpoise have been known to swim as far upstream as Stowbridge, on the tidal Great Ouse. In 2023 a dolphin and her calf tragically swam upstream to Earith.

Otters have been sighted on the Lark and Little Ouse, also upstream near Danish Camp at Willington.

Beaver have been seen in the Buckden / Godmanchester area.

Water voles are present, though possibly in smaller numbers than on the Middle Level.

Muntjac deer are the most likely deer to be seen but possibly roe, fallow, or Chinese water deer, with their curious 'tusks'.

Grey squirrels are common whilst black squirrels are occasionally sighted in the area between Hermitage Lock and Buckden.

Non-native mink which are predators that originally escaped from or were freed from fur farms are occasionally seen, though they have now largely been eradicated, to preserve the native wildlife.

(Coypu were similarly introduced and at one time were common - the last are believed to have been captured in St Neots in 1987).

Insects

There is a range of damsel and dragon flies, mayfly, bees and beetles. Also a wide range of moths and butterflies. Occasionally the rare hummingbird hawk moth has been sighted. Grasshoppers, ladybirds, water boatmen.

Fish

The Environment Agency carefully monitors fish stock and a wide range of fish are present in the waters. Interesting examples are the rudd, with its red fins, the pike, a predatory fish that can grow to several feet in length and eels, after which Ely was named. Eels travel to the Sargasso Sea to spawn so to help them Eel ladders are present at some locks to assist the young eels (elvers) on their way upstream. An eel ladder can be seen at Salters Lode.

Miscellaneous

During the warmer months you may see a grass snake swimming across the river.

There are a number of escaped or released terrapins; they have been sighted at many spots on the Great Ouse and Cam.

White clawed crayfish are the native and protected species and are under threat from North American signal crayfish that have been found in the Great Ouse.

The rather bizarre looking Chinese mitten crabs may also be present in the Great Ouse. These creatures pose a threat not only to native wildlife but to the waterway itself as they burrow and cause damage to the banks.

Index

Page numbers in **bold** refer to maps

access for wider boats, 20
addresses, contacts & links, 11–12, 24–9
aeronautical history, 29, **42**, 45
A.G. Wright Sluice & Lock, 137, 140, **142**, 156, 161
 moorings & facilities, 19, 27, 28, 133, 136
Aickman, Robert, 21
Akeman Street, 107
Alconbury Brook, 10, **68**
Alder Fen Pumping Station, **224**, 225
Aldreth, **100**, 101, 103, **104**, 106
Aldreth River (West Water), 107
Alfred Jewel, 62
Anchor PH (Great Barford), **46**, 47, 48, 49
Angle Common, 216
Anglesey Abbey, 189, 214
Anglian Pass, 11
Anglian Water, 11, 12, 14, **64**, 66, 188

Babingley, River, 10
Baits Bite Lock, **186**, 187, 190, **192**, 193, 195, 197
Barnes Hotel (Bedford), **32**, 33, 37, 38–9
Barway Bridge, **112**, 216
Battle of St Neots, 62
Battock's Island, **80**, 82
beavers, 257
Bedford, **2**, 14–15, 30, 31–41, **32**, 254
 Borough Council & Borough Hall, **32**, 33, 34, 36
 moorings & facilities, 20, 27, 28, 33, 36, 37
 River Festival, 14, 40, 41
 Bedford & Milton Keynes Waterways Trust, 30, 36
 Bedford Level Corporation & Barrier Bank, 91, 96, 177
Bedford Lock, 17, **32**, 33, 36, 40
Bedford Ouse, **2**, 10, 31–91
 contacts & links, 24–9
 distances, 2
 locks & changing river conditions, 14–17
 moorings & facilities, 18–20
birds, 24, 97, 151, 180, 184, 241, 247, 252, 257

Black Bourn, River, 231
Black Horse Farm EA moorings, **126**, 127, **128**
Black Horse PH (Littleport) see *Swan on the River*
Blunham, 51
Bluntisham, **92**
boat engineers (list), 24
boat licensing & registration, 11–12
Boat Race history, 125
boat trips, 30, 36, 37, 45, 85, 117, 199
Boat Yard (Ely), 26, **112**, 115
Boater's Handbook, 19
boatyards & marinas (list), 25–6
books, 19, 253
Boston, Lucy (Green Knowe books), 83
Botany Bay, **236**, 237, **238**
Bottisham Lock, 11, 177, **182**, 183, 184, **186**, 187, 189, 190
Bottisham Lode, **182**, 184, 214
Boudicca, 116
Brackley, 30
Brampton, **68**, 70, 71, 73
Brampton Lock, 15, 17, **68**, 69, 70
Brampton Mill & moorings, **68**, 69, 70
Branch Bridge, **220**, 222, 223
Brandon, 27, 231, 233, **240**, 241–2
Brandon Creek, **128**, 130, 131, 231, **232**, 233, 234, 235
Brandon Lock, 27, 231, 233, **240**, 241–2
brickmaking, 39, 191
Bridge Boatyard (Ely), 26, 28, **112**, 113, 115
bridge heights, 20, 162
Bridge PH (Clayhithe), **186**, 187, 188, 189
Brogborough, 30
Brown, Potto, 87
Brownshill Staunch & Lock, 10, 17, **88**, 89, 90, 91, **92**, 93, 94, 96
Buckden, 66, 67, **68**
Buckden Marine, 25, 28, **68**, 69, 70
Bunyan, John, 40, 50
Burnt Fen, 227
Burwell, **207**, 209, **212**–13
Burwell Lode, 2, 27, **206**–7, 209, 212–13, 254

262 RIVER GREAT OUSE

Bury Fen, **92**, 96
Cam, River, **3**, 10, 11, 12, 177–205, **178**, **182**, **186**, **192**, **200**
Conservators of the River Cam, 11, 24, 177, **186**, 188, 189, 201
  contacts & links, 24–9
  distances, 2
  history, 107, 160, 177, 181, 190, 197–8, 254
  moorings & facilities, 18–20, 179, 181, 183, 184, 187, 189, 193, 195
Cam SC, **186**, 188
Cambridge, **3**, **192**, 193–205, 254
  Backs World Heritage Site return trip, **200**, 201–5
  bridges, 194, 195, 196, 198, 202–4
  history, 197–8, 201–5, 254
  moorings & facilities, 20, 28, 195, 199
  rowing & the 'Bumps', 197
  University Boat Club, 54, 87, 117, **118**, 120, 122
Cambridgeshire Lodes, **3**, 18, 20, 206–217, **206–7**
Canal & River Trust (CRT), 11, 12, 19
canals & other navigable scheme proposals, 30, 254
canoeing & paddleboarding, 23, **32**, 36, 59, 162, 175–6
Canute, King, 124
Car Dyke, 188, 191
Cardington Lock, 14, 17, 20, **42**, 43, 44, 45
Castle Mill Lock, **42**, 43
Cathedral Marina/Ely Marine, 26, 28, **112**, 113, 115
Cawdle Fen, **112**, 113, 114, 115, 116
Chesterton, **192**, 194
Clapham, 40
Clayhithe & moorings, **186**, 187, 188, 189, 190, 191, 254
Colmworth Business Park, 55
contacts, addresses & links, 11–12, 24–9
Cook's Stream/Backwater, **68**, 72, 73, **74**
Cosgrove, 30
Cottenham Lode, 10
Counter Wash Drain, **150**
Covid-19 pandemic, 19, 23, 29, 125
Crane's Fen, 94
Cromwell & Civil War, 63, 77, 78, 152, 235
Crosshall Marine, 25, **56**, 57, 59, 60
Crown & Anchor PH (Wiggenhall St Germans), 157, **158**, 171
Cut-Off Channel, 10, 16, 137, 156, 174, 231, 240, 241, 250, 252
  history, 138–40, 159–60, 161, 174
cycling, 39, 90, 194

Danes & Vikings, 45, 78, 124
Danish Camp, **42**, 43, 45
Daylock Marine Services, 25, 28, **74**, 75, 77
Delph/Delf, River, 16, 97, **150**
Denny Abbey & Farmland Museum, 189
Denver, **3**, 16, 133–40, 149, 160
  crossing to & from Salter's Lode (tidal), 141–7, **142**
  Denver to King's Lynn (tidal Great Ouse), 2, **3**, 16, 18, **158**, 161–73
  New Bedford River (tidal), 149–52, **150**
  moorings & facilities, see under Denver Complex
Denver CC, **128**, 130, **132**
Denver Complex, 24, **135**, 136, 137, 139–40, **142**, 143
  Interpretation Centre, 139
  moorings & facilities, 18, 19, 26–8, 133, 136, 143, 147, 168, 169
  see also A.G. Wright Sluice; Denver Sluice & Lock; Relief Channel Lock
Denver Moorings, 26
Denver SC, **135**, 137, **142**
Denver Sluice & Lock, 14, 16, **135**, 137, 147, 167, 168, 170
  history, 138–40
  tides & timings, 162
  moorings & facilities, see under Denver Complex
Devil's Dyke, 209, 227
Diamond 44 moorings, **118**, 119, 121
Dimmock's Cote Bridge, **178**, 180, 181
distances, 2
Diversion Sluice, 137
Dolphin Hotel (St Ives), **80**, 81, 84, 85
Downham Market, 97, 136, **154**, 155, 156, 163, 171
dragon boats, 59, 61
drainage history, 107, 111, 214, 216, 217, 222, 223, 225–6
Duck Mill Weir, 35
Duxford, 29
Dyke's End PH (Reach), **207**, 209

Earith, **2**, 16, 17, **92**, 93, 94, 96, 149, 152
  moorings & facilities, 10, 19, 27, 28, 95
Eaton Socon, **52**, 53, 55, **56**, 58
  Lock, 14, 15, 17, **52**, 53, 55, **56**, 57
'Eights Marina', **192**, 196
Ely, **3**, 19, 26–8, **112**, 113, 115–17, **118**, 120, 124
Ely Marine/Cathedral Marina, 26, 28, **112**, 113, 115

Ely Ouse, **3**, 10, 16, 113–40
  contacts & links, 24–9
  distances, 2
  history, 107, 111, 153, 159–60, 216, 231, 243
  moorings & facilities, 18–20
  self-timing speed checking, 12
  weather & wind, 17
emergency contacts, 24
Environment Agency (EA), 11–12, 24
  boat licensing & registration, 11–12, 24
  flood line & incident hotline, 24
  moorings & facilities, 14, 18–20
  Strong Stream Advice (SSA), 16
  Waterway Users Information leaflet, 19
estuary crossings (general advice), 144, see also tidal & estuary waters
Etheldreda (Saint), 116
etiquette, 12–13, 18–19
Eynesbury, **52**, 55, 62

facilities, 18–20, 24–9
fairs, medieval, 195, 198, 210
family-friendly pubs with moorings, 29
Feltwell (RAF), 239
Fen Ditton, **192**, 193, 194, 195, 197
Fen Drayton Lakes, **88**
Fenlake Meadows, **32**, 33, 36
Fenland Boat Moorings, 26, **186**, 188, 189
Fenland Boats (Isleham), 221, **224**, 226
Fens Waterway Link, 254
Fidwell Fen, **178**, 179, 181, **182**, 183
fish, 176, 249, 257
Fish & Duck Marina, 25, 28, **108**, 109, 110, 111, **178**, 179, 181
Five Miles from Anywhere PH, 27, **178**, 179, 181, **206**
Flatbridge, 107
Floating pennywort, 185
flood line (EA), 24
flooding, 16, 73, 138–40, 160, 161, 174, 194–5, 231, 251, 252
Fodderfen Pumping Station, **224**, 225
Fordham, 216, 217
Fort St George PH & moorings, **192**, 193, 195, 196, 198
fuel sales (list), 28

gas & diesel sales (list), 28
Gaywood River, 10, 176
geocoding system, 26
Gill's Houseboat Corner, 62–3
glossary of terms, 255–6
Godmanchester, 27, **68**, 69, 71–3, 73, **74**
  Lock, 15, 17, **68**, 69, 71

Goldie, John, 87
Goldington, **42**, 43
Goldsmere moorings, **108**, 109, 110
Grange Farm Touring Park, 245, **251**, 252
Granta, River, 177, 204
Grantchester, 177
Great Barford, **46**, 47, 48–9, 50
  Lock, **46**, 47, 48, 49
Great Ouse, River, **2–3**, 9, 31–140
  licensing & registration, 11–12
  marinas & boatyards (list), 25–6
  moorings & facilities (general/lists), 18, 27, 29
  tributaries, 10, 174–6
  see also Cut-Off Channel; Relief Channel; tidal & estuary waters
Great Ouse Boating Association (GOBA), 18, 20
Great Ouse Moorings (Brandon Creek), **232**, 233, 234
Great Ouse Valley Trust, 22
Great Paxton, 60, **64**, 65, 66, 67
Green Dragon Corner, 239
Green Dragon PH, **192**, 195, 197
Greenwich Meridian, 90
Grimes Graves, 242
guided bus way, **88**, 90
guillotine gates, 14, 15

Hanratty, James, 40
Harley, William, 124
Harpur, Sir William, 40
Hartford, **74**, 76, 77, 78–9
Hartford Marina, 25, 28, **74**, 75, 76, 77
Hemingford Abbots, **74**, 80, 82
Hemingford Grey, **80**, 81, 82–3, 85, 86
Hemingford Lock, 15, 17, **80**, 81, 86
Hemingford Meadow, **74**, **80**, 81, 82
Hen Brook, **56**, 58, 62
Hereward the Wake, 103, 115, 116, 227
Hermitage Lock, **2**, 14, 24, **92**, 93, 94–6, **100**, 101–3, **150**, 152
  moorings & facilities, 93, 95, 101, 103
Hermitage Marina, 25, **92**, 93, 95, **100**, 101–3, **150**
Heron PH, **154**, 157, 171
Hilgay (village), **244**, 245, 247, 250
Hill, Darryl, 24
Hinchingbrooke Arm & Country Park, **68**, 72
Hinchingbrooke House, 77
hoards, 79, 227
Hockwold cum Wilton, 239, **240**, 241
Hockwold Fen moorings, 233, **238**, 239
Holme Lock, 51
Holt Island nature reserve, **80**, 83
Holywell, **88**, 90–91

Horningsea, **186**, 187, 189, 191
hotlines, 24
Houghton, **74**, 75, 76, 77, 79, **80**
   Lock, 14, 15, **74**, 75, 76, 77, **80**, 81, 85
Howard, John, 40
Hundred Acre moorings, **108**, 109, 110
Hundred Foot River *see* New Bedford River
Huntingdon, **2**, 27, **68**, 75, 76–9
Huntingdon Boat Haven, 25, **68**, 72, 73

Imperial War Museum (Duxford), 29
Impounding Sluice, 137, 140
Imray Laurie Norie & Wilson HQ, 87
Inland Waterways Association (IWA), 21, 24
insurance, 11, 144, 164
Iron Trunk Aqueduct, 30
Isle of Ely Rowing Club, **118**, 120, 125
Isleham, 26, 27, **224**, 226, 227, 228
   Lock, 20, 221, **224**, 226, 227, **228**
Ivel, River, 10, **46**, 50, 51, 254

Jesus Green, **192**, 193, 195, 196, 199
   Lock, 20, **192**, 193, 197, 198, 199, **200**, 201, 202, 204
Jesus Green Lido, 27, 28, 195, 196
Jewson & Sons, 96
John Bunyan (trip boat), 30, 36, 37
Jones, Griff Rhys, 175–6
Jones Boatyard & Marina, 25, 28, **80**, 81, 85
Jude's Ferry PH, 221, 223, **228**, 229

Kelpie Marine, 25, **46**, 47, 50, **52**
Kempston, **32**, 34
keys & pump-out tokens, 14, 19
Khartoum Wood (Railway Bridge) moorings, **244**, 245, 246, 247
King's Lynn, 11, 24, 156, **158**, 159, 161, **166**, 167, 171, 172–3
   history, 107, 159–60, 243
   moorings & facilities, 165, **166**, 169, 173
   tides & timings, 153, 157, 161, 162–5, 167, 170
Kym, River, 10, 254

Lakenheath Lodes, **238**, 239
Lammas Meadows *see* St Neots Common
Lark, River, 2, 3, 10, 11, 16, 18, 20, 121, 219–30, **220**, **224**, **228**
   history, 160, 174, 217, 219
   moorings & facilities, 18, 20, 26, 27, 29, 221, 223, 226, 229
Lark River Pumping Station, **224**, 225
Lazy Days Boat Hire, 25, 72, 73
Lazy Otter PH & Meadows Marina, **104**, 105, 106, **108**

Leck, River, 10
Lee Brook, **228**, 229
licensing & legislation, 11–12
Little Barford, **52**, 54–5
Little Ouse (village), **232**, 235, 237
Little Ouse, River, 2, **3**, 9, 10, 11, 16, **128**, 231–42, **232**, **236**, **238**, **240**
   history, 107, 160, 174, 230, 231, 235, 242, 254
   moorings & facilities, 18, 20, 26–8, 130–31, 233–5, 239, 241–2
Little Ouse Moorings (Brandon Creek), 26, 28, **126**, 127, **128**, 130, 131, **232**, 233, 234, 235
Little Paxton, 56, 63
Little Thetford moorings, **112**, 113, 114
Littleport, **3**, 27, **118**, 119, 122–3, 124, **126**
Littleport Boat Haven, 26, **118**, 119, 122
location system (what3words), 26
locks, 2, 14–15, 16–17
   and canoes, 23
   windlass & keys, 14, 19
Lode (village), 214
lodes, navigable *see* Cambridgeshire Lodes
Lovat/Ouzel, River, 10

Mailer's Meadow moorings, **68**, 69, 70
Major, John, 78
Manby, George William, 247
Manea, 97
map symbols, 8
maps (Ordnance Survey), 10
marinas & boatyards (list), 25–6
marine services (contacts & links), 24
markets, 37, 59, 77, 85, 117, 199
Marmont Priory, 175
match manufacture, 230
Mepal, 148, **150**, 152
Methwold Lode, **251**, 252
Middle Level, 11, 12, 136, 177, 254
   tidal crossing (Denver Sluice/Salter's Lode), 141–7, **142**
Middle Level Commissioners, 11, 12, 24
Middle Level Main Drain, 10, **158**, 169, 175–6
Midsummer Common, **192**, 195, 196, 197
Mildenhall, 229
Mile End Farm moorings, **220**, 221, 222, 223
Mill Pond/Pool (Cambridge), 177, **200**, 201, 202, 204
Miller, Glenn, 40
Millfleet, River, 10, 176
Milton, **186**, 189, 190
Milton Keynes, 30, 254
Modney/Hilgay bridge, 27, **132**, 133, 134, **135**
Monkey Island, 40
Monk's Lode, **207**, 210, 211

moorings (general), 18–20, 29

Nar, River, 10, **158**, 160, 176, 254
nature reserves see Holt Island; Ouse Washes; Paxton Pits; Roswell Pits; Welney Wetland Centre; Wissey Valley
navigation, 9–15
navigation authorities, 11, 24, 28
navigations, connection proposals, 30, 254
Needingworth, 88, 90
Nene, River, 14, 15, 254
New Bedford (Hundred Foot) River, **2–3**, 10, 11, 94, 96, 140, 149–52, **150**, 161, 170
Noble's Field (St Ives), **80**, 81, 82, 83
Northamptonshire river system, 9, 254

Oasis Centre (Bedford), **32**, 36, 37, 38
Offord Cluny, **64**, 67, 68
Offord D'Arcy, **64**, 66, 67
Offord Lock & moorings, 17, **64**, 65, 66, 67, **68**, 69, 73
Old Bedford River, 3, 10, 11, 16, **92**, 94, 140, **150**, 175
Old Croft River (Well Stream/Creek), 107, 122, **142**, **150**, 175
Old Ferry Boat Inn & moorings (Holywell), **88**, 89, 90, 91
Old River Nene, 107
Old Warden, 29
Old West River, **2–3**, 10, 16, 94, 99–111, **100**, **104**, **108**, 160
   contacts & links, 24–9
   history, 102, 103, 106, 107, 111, 160
   moorings & facilities, 18, 101, 105, 106, 109
   self-timing speed checking, 12, 102
One Pound moorings, 88, 89, 90, 91
Ordnance Survey maps, 10
Ouse river names in England, 9
Ouse Valley River Club, **52**, **56**, 60
Ouse Valley Way, 22
Ouse Washes nature reserve, 16, 94, 97, **150**, 161, 257
Ouzel (or Lovat), River, 10
Over, **88**, 91
Overcote Ferry moorings, 88, 89, 91
overtaking, 13

Padnal Fen, **220**, 221, 222, 223
Paper Mills Lock *see* St Neots Lock
paths & trails (general), 22
Paxton Pits nature reserve, **56**, 60, 61, **64**, 66, 67, 257
peat (turf), 210, 211, 227
Pepys, Samuel, 73
Perceval, Spencer, 63

Pike & Eel PH, **88**, 89, 90, 91
pill boxes, 180
Plough PH (Fen Ditton), **192**, 193, 194, 195
Pope's Corner, **3**, 16, 17, **108**, 110, 111, **112**, 114, 177, **178**, 180, 181
Popham's Eau, **150**
poplar trees, 230
Portholme Meadow, **68**, 71, 72, 73
Pout Hall Corner, **206**, 208–9, 212
Prickwillow, 27, 217, **220**, 221, 222–3
Prickwillow Engine Museum, 111, 134, **220**, 222, 223
Prime Meridian, 90
Priory Centre (St Neots), **56**, 57, 58–60
Priory Marina (Bedford), 25, 28, **32**, 33, 36, 37, 38
public moorings (general), 18, 19
public slipways (list), 27
pubs with moorings (list), 29
pump-out services (list), 28
pump-out tokens, 14, 19
punting, 201, 204, 205
Purfleet, River, 10, 176
Purvis Marine, 25, **74**, 76, 77

Queen Adelaide, **118**, 119, 120–21, 124, 125, 223
Quiet Waters Marina, **92**

rail travel, 20, 124, 217, 254
Reach (village), **207**, 209–210
Reach Lode & Lock, 2, 27, **178**, 181, **206–7**, 208–210, 212
Redmere, **236**, 237
regattas, 41, 61, 77, 78, 82, 83, 117, 138, 197
registration & licensing, 11–12
Relief Channel, 2, **3**, 10, 11, 16, 163
   return trip, 153–60, **154**
   history, 138–40, 159–60, 161, 254
   moorings & facilities, 18, 27, 133, 155, 157, 171
Relief Channel Lock, 133, 136, 137, **142**, 153, **154**, 155, 156
Relief Channel Tail Sluice, 153, **158**, 159, 160, **166**, 170, 176
Rennie, John, 30, 139, 174
Residual Flow Sluice, 137, 140
reversed locks, 16–17
river & canal emergencies, 24
river levels, 16–17
Rivermill Marina (Eaton Socon), 25, **52**, 53, 55, 56
Riverside Island/Marina (Isleham), 26, 221, **224**, 226, 227, 228
Riverside Marine (Needingworth), 25, 28, **90**, 91, 92, 93

Riverside Park (Bedford), **32**, 33, 36
Riverside Park (Huntingdon), **76**, 77, 78, 79
Rolt, Tom, 21
Romans, 75, 109, 118, 193, 210, 211, 214, 216
Roswell Pits nature reserve, **122**, 124, 127–8
Roxton Lock, **46**, 47, 49–52
RSPB, 24, **90**, 99
RSPCA, 24
rules of the river, 12–13

safety, 11, 14, 19, 20, 24
St Ives, **82**, 85, 86–9, **90**, 99
   Bridge, **82**, 88
   Lock, 14, 15, 17, **82**, 83, 86–7
   moorings & facilities, 27, **82**, 83, 87
St Neots, **2**, 27, 57, **58**, 59, 60–65, 258
   Common (Lammas Meadows), **58**, 59, 61, 62, 63
   Lock (Paper Mills Lock), **58**, 59, 62
St Neots Marina, 25, **58**, 59, 60, 61
Salter's Lode Lock, 3, 24, 99, 145–51, **146**, **154**, 155, 172, 261
sandbanks, 148, 149, 151, 164, 165, 167, 168, 169, 174
Sandy's Cut, 125, 227
Santon Downham, 235, **244**
seals, 96, 261
services (lists), 24–9
Ship PH (Brandon Creek), **132**, 133, 134, 135, 142, **236**, 237, 238, 239
Shrubbs Wharf Marina, 26, **186**, 187, 188
Shuttleworth Collection, 29
Silt Fen Farm moorings, 137, **139**, 140
Sinclair, Sir Clive, 89
skating, 98, 128
slipways (list), 27
Snail, River, 220, 221
Soham, 220, 221
Soham Lode, 10, **114**, 116, 220–21
Southery, **132**, 134, 135, **136**, 142
Sovereign Quay, **32**, 33, 34, 36
speed limits, 12–13, 104
Spurgeon, C. H., **229**, **230**
Stewartby, 30
Stoke Ferry, 247, **255**, 256
Stourbridge Common, 27, **196**, 197, 199, 201, 202
Stowbridge, 11, **158**, 159, 161, 171, 162, 174, 175
Stretham Ferry Marina, 25, **106**, 107, 108, **110**
Stretham Old Engine & moorings, **110**, 111, 112, 113
Stringside Drain, **255**
Strong Stream Advice (SSA), 16

sugar beet, 195, 251, 253, 254
Sussex Ouse, 9
Sutton Gault, **154**, 156
Swaffham Bulbeck, 219
   Lode, **186**, 188, 219
Swaffham Lock, **186**, 219
Swan on the River PH & moorings, **122**, 123, 126, 127
swimmers in open water, 14

Tail Sluice *see* Relief Channel Tail Sluice
telephone contacts & links, 11–12, 24–9
Tempsford, **46**, 47, 49–53, **54**
Ten Mile Bank/River, 10, 27, **130**, 131–35, **132**, **136**
Thetford, 235, 258
tidal & estuary waters
   general advice, 148
   Great Ouse (Brownshill Staunch to Hermitage Lock), **2**, **3**, 10, **94**, 95–9
   Great Ouse (Denver to King's Lynn), 2, 3, 16, 18, **162**, 165–77
   see also Middle Level; New Bedford River
Tiptree Marina, 26, **186**, 187, 188, **210**
Toller, James (Eynesbury Giant), 64
Tom's Hole Farm moorings, **224**, 225, 226, 227
tourist information centres, 37, 61, 87, 161, 177, 203
Tove, River, 10
transport connections, 20
Trout Stream, **82**
turf (peat), 214, 215, 231
Turner, J.M.W., 35
Twenty Pence Marina, 25, 28, **106**, 107, 108
Two Tees Boatyard, 26, **196**, 199, 202

Upware, 27, **182**, 185, 188, **210**, 212, 216
   Lock, 20, **182**, 185
Upware Marina, 26, **182**, 183, 185, **210**
Upwell, 109

Vermuyden, Cornelius, 109, 143, 163, 178, 239
Vikings & Danes, 43, 45, 80, 128

The Waits (St Ives), **82**, 83, 86, 87
walking (general), 22
Wappenham, 9
The Wash, 9
Wash Pilot, 24
Washes *see* Ouse Washes
water points (list), 27
Waterbeach & moorings, **186**, 187, 189
Waterman's Arms PH (Redmire), 237
Waterway Recovery Group (IWA), 21

Watlington Station, **154**, 157, 159
weather, 16, 17, 144
websites, 11
weed, 102–3, 144, 184, 185, 188, 216
Weeting Castle, **240**, 242
Welches Dam, 175
Well Stream/Creek (Old Croft River), 107, 122, **142**, **150**, 175
Welmore Lake Sluice, 97, **150**, 151, 161
Welney, 149, **150**
Welney Wetland Centre, 97, **150**, 151, 257
West Water (Aldreth River), 107
Westview Marina, 25, 28, **92**, 93, 94, 95
what3words digital geolocation, 26
Whittington mooring, **251**, 252
Whittlesey, 175
Wicken (village), **207**, 211
Wicken Fens, **178**, **206–7**, 210–211, 257
Wicken Lode, 2, **206–7**, 208, 210–211
Wicken Washes, **178**, 180
Wiggenhall St Germans, 157, **158**, **166**, 169, 170, 171, 175
Wiggenhall St Mary, **154**, 155, 157, **158**, 159, 171
wildlife, 22-3, 73, 176, 180, 185, 257, *see also birds*; *nature reserves*
Wildlife Trust for Beds, Cambs, Northants, 23, 67
Willington & Lock, **42**, 43, 45
Willow Walk (Ely), **112**, 113, 115
Wilton Bridge, **240**, 241
wind speed & direction, 17, 144, 162
windlass, 14
Windmill moorings (Hilgay Bridge), **132**, 133, 134, **135**
Wisbech, 243
Wisbech Ouse & Wisbech Canal, 107
Wissey, River, 2, **3**, 10, 11, 16, 243–52, **244**, **248**, **251**
  history, 160, 174, 249, 250
  moorings & facilities, 18, 20, 27, 245, 252, 276–7
Wissey Valley Living Landscape reserve, **248**, 249
Wissington, 247, **248**, 249–50
Wyboston, **52**, 54
Wyton, 77

Yorkshire Ouse, 9